C000243849

Sicily,
It's Not Quite
Tuscany

Sicily,
It's Not Quite
Tuscany

SHAMUS SILLAR

ARENA
ALLEN&UNWIN

Arena Books, an imprint of
Allen & Unwin
Sydney, Melbourne, Auckland, London

83 Alexander Street
Crows Nest NSW 2065
Australia
Phone: (61 2) 8425 0100
Fax: (61 2) 9906 2218
Email: info@allenandunwin.com
Web: www.allenandunwin.com

Cataloguing-in-Publication details are available
from the National Library of Australia
www.trove.nla.gov.au

ISBN 978 1 74237 679 0

Map by Guy Holt
Set in 11/15 pt Adobe Garamond Pro by Post Pre-press Group, Australia
Printed and bound in Australia by the SOS Print + Media Group.

10 9 8 7 6

To Gill

Contents

1. Arriving

Si cacci lu sceccu, tardu arrivi; si camina tardu, prestu arrivi.

If you urge the donkey on, you'll arrive late; if you let the donkey amble, you'll arrive early.

— Sicilian proverb

I'm sipping *arancia rossa* (blood orange juice) and gazing down on the Mediterranean, its surface puckered in a westerly wind. Gill has given me the window seat; she always does — it's why I married her.

An hour out of Rome, seven tiny islands appear, like the backs of swimming turtles. These are the famous Aeolians. In my best Italian accent, I recite their vowelly, singsong names from my map: 'Alicudi, Filicudi, Lipari, Vulcano, Panarea, Stromboli, Salina!' (My best Italian accent, it turns out, is part Joe Dolce's 'Shaddup You Face' and part Gary Oldman in *Dracula*.) Then our plane is over the Sicilian mainland. I see parched rivers and russet hills; a landscape sucked dry by the sun.

Finally, Mount Etna. She's dark and indistinct, swathed in cloud, keeping her cards up her sleeve. At the bottom of the volcano's slope, sprawling blackly against the stained sea, a city: Catania.

'Big and grim': that's how Paul Theroux described Catania (in *The Pillars of Hercules*). Awash with drugs and pollution. A place only a *mafioso* could love. It's a place Gill and I will call 'home' for the coming year. I haven't told Gill about Theroux's sketch. I feel a twinge of guilt about this. Then again, she knows about the Mafia in general, of course, and about the risk of Etna's eruptions. Neither of those things has dampened her enthusiasm.

The pilot mustn't like the place either. He seems almost reluctant to land. We pass directly over the city and its port full of oxidised ships and swing out to sea again. Minutes tick by. We're heading in the direction of Libya. Hijacked?

Finally the plane circles back towards land. Gill grabs my hand for the descent. Outside I see a yellow smear of beach on Catania's southern edge. That's where we head now, dropping steadily. A circle of choppy sea fills my window. I can make out individual waves, a man on a bobbing boat. The beach flits by within jumping distance. Then, the thud of asphalt.

A few days later, standing on the sand myself, I marvel at how low the planes fly before they land. The Catanese around me hardly glance up. September is here, so they're desperately wringing the last good times out of a fading summer, focusing not on the 747s above but on the even noisier circus of the beach and its clutter of deckchairs, umbrellas, cabins and volleyball nets; the men in those tight, skimpy swimming shorts so mysteriously favoured in Europe, and the women in bikinis dancing to novelty remixes of 'La Macarena'.

Gill has accepted a job in Catania with a private language college called Giga. The word is a combination of the first two letters of Giorgio and Gaia, the names of two Sicilian children whose mother, Palmina, is the founder and director of the college – Gill's boss. She's waiting to pick us up at the airport.

Palmina drives a red Smart car – smart, indeed, when it comes to manoeuvring through the dangerous, stony narrows of an Italian city; highly stupid, however, if you need to fit three people and several heavy suitcases. We somehow houdini ourselves inside and set off.

Gill and Palmina make small talk – Palmina in thickly accented English, Gill trying to convert her respectable French into passable Italian. But I'm muzzled by a faceful of luggage. I can't even turn my head to look out the window. I do *hear* the city, though – a constant salvo of car horns, Italian ambulances with their distinctive warbling sirens, and the shrill, two-stroke buzz of Vespas.

'We're here,' says Palmina after twenty minutes. 'Your apartment.'

The women shovel bags aside in the manner of rescue workers, freeing me from my seat. I fidget my way out of the car's micro-door onto the herringbone cobbles of a grimy backstreet. This is Via Gesuiti – 'Street of the Jesuits' – our new address.

'So,' I ask Gill, 'how was your first glimpse of Catania?'

'Nice,' she says politely, with an anxious sideways glance at Palmina. Somewhere in the distance, a polygraph machine scribbles furiously on a page.

Palmina doesn't notice: she's fiddling around with our front-door keys. Once we and our luggage are inside, she speeds off down the road in a red blur. It seems a mildly hasty departure, almost as though she's hoping to evade our scrutiny of the accommodation that Giga has found for us.

The apartment occupies one corner of the ground floor of a *palazzo*. What an exciting word, '*palazzo*'. For me it evokes ornate, Versailles-style buildings full of frescoed corridors and manicured lawns, with estate owners in Mozart wigs drinking fortified wines on the lawn and calling from time to time on the services of a piss boy.

That, however, would be to misinterpret the word. *Palazzo* is a 'false friend' – its meaning is different to what you might expect. Another false friend in Italian is *dottore* (doctor). In Italy, a doctor isn't necessarily a highly educated medical practitioner; rather, it's anyone who's done a three-year university degree at undergraduate level. And it doesn't have to be a medical degree – even doing a Bachelor of Arts is enough to earn you the title *dottore*. How very different from Australia, where we refer to BA graduates not as 'doctors' but as 'drug dealers' or 'the unemployed'.

Similarly, a *palazzo* is not a palace at all. Well, it *can* be. But it can also be something far less impressive – a shabby multistorey apartment block with peeling stucco and rusted balconies, for instance. And that's exactly where Gill and I find ourselves now.

Further disappointment awaits. The apartment's large living area and master bedroom are both padlocked shut. All

4

that's left is an L-shaped corridor with a tiny table and two chairs, and a couple of cramped side rooms. We're effectively renting one third of an apartment. And it's costing a considerable chunk of Gill's modest salary.

Later, when I ask Palmina about the extra rooms, she tells us they're being used as storage and aren't part of the rental deal.

'Land*lady*,' she corrects me, after I make disparaging remarks about the landlord. 'She's a nun.'

I'm surprised a nun needs storage space, let alone owns a *palazzo*. I thought they abandoned all their worldly possessions. Or is that prison inmates?

Miffed about these two out-of-bounds rooms, I'll spend hours over the next months trying to pick both locks. I'll also hear sporadic shuffling from behind the two doors in the night; even a low, ghostly moan. It turns out I'm just hallucinating from sleep deprivation – more about that later.

The nun hasn't locked everything away. A liberal assortment of religious trinkets remains: crucifixes, church calendars, saintly ornaments – more Jesuses than a Spanish phonebook. On the wall above the rusty stove in the kitchen is a thermometer decorated with a picture of the Pope. The apartment is so church-like, I think about setting up a collection box at the front door as a way of skimming some euros back from the nun's extravagant rental sum.

Aside from Catholic accoutrements, though, the apartment is monastically austere. The bedroom looks like the antechamber of a mausoleum – cold marble with just a sliver of a clothes cupboard, the kind you could smash into

5

kindling with one blow. 'Are they kidding?' says Gill, eyeing the cupboard and then her gargantuan suitcase.

The beds are the killer. Since we're newlyweds, a *letto matrimoniale* (double bed) would have been nice. Instead, there are two singles made of frigid metal. They look like discards from an asylum. I half expect to find looped leather straps for the wrists and ankles, and a mute American Indian mopping the floor in the corner.

They're also impossibly heavy, but we manage to drag them together. There's a ten-centimetre difference in height where they join.

'On the bright side,' I say to Gill, 'at least when you want to have sex you can just roll over from your side and drop right on top of me.'

Gill feigns a laugh but I can see that she's glum. Perched on the end of the bed, she sheds a tiny tear of disappointment. I do what I can to comfort her (juggle, pretend to pull a coin from behind her ear, recite pi to forty places). But even I am gnawed by the realisation that our dream of an extended Mediterranean honeymoon spent in a modest but sunny bedsit next to a pebbled beach has, for the moment at least, eluded us.

At six pm we emerge from our clutter of half-emptied suitcases to forage for food. Our body clocks are saying it's three am and our last meal was two flights ago, somewhere over Istanbul.

It's our first saunter on Sicilian soil and the place looks excitingly different, albeit down at heel. One block north of

Via Gesuiti we strike Via G. Clementi, a busy road clogged with scooters and an unglamorous assortment of shops and services. The 'G' might well stand for grim.

Several outdoor merchants are in operation. On one footpath, a fellow roasts buttery chestnuts in a drum. He's the same shape as the drum and the same sooty colour. Chestnuts are popular in Catania. In a country lane not far from the city you'll find the world's biggest chestnut tree, four thousand years old with a girth of sixty metres.

Next, Gill and I spy a portable *chiosco* (kiosk). It's a small caravan – the kind found on countless urban corners in Sicily – serving takeaway drinks and pastries. Two oily mechanics stand there with beers.

On another footpath, a chain-smoking grandpa boils sheep's offal in a metal cauldron. Every few minutes, he dumps a ladle of steaming, squiggly organs onto a marble counter and hacks them into bite-sized chunks. I watch a man on a Vespa drive right up, spin a one-euro coin onto the counter, and slurp down a strand of hot, baggy intestines that he's picked up with his fingers.

'We could eat there,' I suggest to Gill.

Luckily for her, she's noticed a wood-fired pizza restaurant nearby. I've always equated Italian pizzas with simplicity: a smear of tomato sauce, two olives and a basil leaf. But this place, Pizzeria Pavone, boasts forty varieties of pizza and an astonishing array of ingredients: boiled egg, carrots, raw onion, salmon, peas, truffle oil, Emmental cheese, fried zucchini. One pizza has Nutella drizzled all over it. Another, called 'pizza fantasy', comes formidably topped with French

Shamus Sillar

fries, German sausage and ketchup. The only ingredient missing from the menu is pineapple, since Italians would be more disturbed to find a piece of pineapple on their pizza than, say, a pubic hair.

Ignoring the flamboyant offerings, Gill keeps things simple with a margherita (tomato, mozzarella, basil). She enjoys it so much it becomes her pizza of choice for our entire year in Sicily. One thing about my wife, she's loyal. When she finds something she likes, she sticks to it.

'Why don't you try something different?' I ask from time to time.

'Because I don't *want* to try something different.'

'But maybe you'll find something that you really, really love.'

'I really, really love margherita.'

'Yes, but maybe your perfect pizza is out there, just waiting to be ordered.'

'Well, it can wait as long as it likes.'

As an unabashed 'foodie', I'd rather see Gill push the culinary boat out from time to time, but at least her philosophy of allegiance augurs well for our marriage.

Meanwhile, I order a *pizza rustica*: salty olives, salty capers, *very* salty anchovies, and salt. It's the kind of pizza that doesn't put hair on your chest so much as peptic ulcers on your duodenum. I'm soon gasping for a beer.

As it happens, Sicily doesn't have a signature beer. The preferred drop is Birra Moretti, a Heineken-owned product from northern Italy. As lagers go, it's unexceptional. But the label is brilliant. It features a working-class man with

8

a handlebar moustache and porkpie hat, holding an enormous mug of frothy brew up to his lips. Apparently when the Moretti people saw this fellow in a bar half a century ago and asked if they could photograph him as the face of their beverage, he requested only one thing in return: that they buy him another beer.

I, too, order another. I figure a few drinks will not only combat the desiccating effect of my *pizza rustica* but allow a few hours' sleep in my asylum-issue bed.

It works. I don't move until six am. When I do wake, it's to the sound of a single loud *click!* followed by a strange drawn-out hiss. For about half a minute I'm utterly disorientated. Then the fog clears: we're in Sicily; we moved here yesterday.

Sicily. How very surreal. I take a tiny peek under my sheets for a horse's head.

Meanwhile, the hissing sound continues: '*Sssssssssss-sssssssssss . . .*' As I start to wonder what's going on, it swells to a terrifying roar: '*FUNGHI! . . . MELONI! . . . FRAGOLE! . . . SPINACI!*' Then there's just the hiss again, and the racing thump of my heart.

A minute passes. Suddenly: '*BANANE! . . . FINOC-CHI! . . . ARANCE! . . . MELE!*'

Gill has also shot up from her pillow like a stepped-on rake. Our two hearts thump as one.

I draw back the slatted curtain and peer groggily outside. The sun is already strong. Two feet away on the pavement, a well-bellied man in a flat cap (known in Sicily as a *coppola*, like the film director) is standing beside a wooden cart full of fruit and vegetables, clutching a loudhailer. Incredible. In a city of three hundred thousand people, this farmer has determined that our street corner – indeed, the very footpath outside our bedroom – is the perfect place to peddle his produce. The initial click that broke my sleep was his loudhailer being switched on; the roar that followed was his sales pitch.

'*MELANZANE!... POMODORI!... ANANAS!... PATATE!*'

There he goes again. *Mamma mia*, that's loud.

Our rowdy street seller has probably done us a favour in waking us so early. It's a gorgeous morning and our to-do list is a mile long.

First on the list is finding a *farmacia* (chemist): I desperately need eye drops. I suffer from pterygia, triangle-shaped growths on the membranes of my eyes. Pterygia are common among Aussies who spent too long at the beach as children. They're not cancerous, just red and ugly – especially when irritated by wind and dry weather. Flying is the worst. After fifteen hours on a plane, I look like Satan's spawn. Customs officials start lubricating their gloves before I even hand over my passport. Palmina must have got the shock of her life when she met me at the airport, especially with the superstition of 'evil eye' (*malocchio*) so entrenched in Sicily. So, if I want to become a regular functioning member of society, I'll need extra-strength Visine.

I'm not the only one with ophthalmological issues. A stray cat is sunning itself in the street outside our apartment. One of its eyes is ruptured and gooey, obviously from a fight. Catania is overrun with stray cats and most of them look like they've just gone twelve rounds with a milkshake blender.

The *farmacia* is a breeze – even my first attempts at speaking the language are a success. ('No, I'm not a Cacodaemon. I just need some eye drops.')

Next, we need to navigate our way to Gill's place of work, the Giga school on Via Rocca Romana. It will be a 'dry run' before Gill teaches her first class the next day. Palmina has shown us directions on a map.

It proves to be a simple fifteen-minute stroll along Via Antonino di Sangiuliano and up Via Santa Maddalena, near enough to the very heart of the city, the *centro*. As we walk, I mentally catalogue everything I see: black basalt streets; Baroque buildings of fading splendour; brief flashes of Euro-chic; a preposterous number of churches; corners of squalor; miniscule cars all dented and scraped; skinny teenagers riding in pairs on menacing scooters; baristas smoking outside their cafés; seven-foot Sudanese men hawking watches on foot-paths; palm trees and sandy squares (my diary entry for the day reads: 'Have we come to North Africa by mistake?'); tiny box-shaped altars cut into the sides of buildings for statues of Christ or the Virgin Mary; tired *palazzi*; red-tiled domes; difficult cobblestones; ferocious gargoyles; even more ferocious graffiti ('*POMPINARA!*' screams one wall: 'Cocksucker!'); tiny wrought-iron balconies filled with potted plants and laundry pegs; bright orange buses; Roman remains; and, hanging from the occasional window, a rainbow-coloured flag saying '*PACE*' (peace).

We find the Giga building but decide to stop for a coffee before going inside. There's a bar on the next corner.

As Gill and I walk towards the front door of our first Sicilian café, we hear the banshee screech of brakes from one block west. Spinning around, we watch a single grey hatchback travelling through the intersection of Via Roccaromana and Via Nino Martoglio. It approaches at a completely normal speed and trajectory – entirely conventionally, in fact – except that it travels through the intersection *on its side*. The car looks momentarily like a breaching whale, the road its ocean, before finally coming to a shuddering halt.

More extraordinary is what happens next. A couple of bystanders walk over to the car – a leisurely walk, not a dash or even a concerned jog – and help flip the vehicle back onto its wheels. At which point the car drives away in a sprightly fashion, as though nothing unusual has happened.

'Coffee?' I ask Gill, opening the door of the bar.

'Love one,' she replies.

We each order a macchiato. I also decide to sample Catania's most famous snack food, *arancini*. These have started gaining popularity in Australia, in the kind of pretentious cafés where prices appear with one number after the decimal point ('mini arancino with hommus: 9.5'). Here, though, they're more of a working-class snack – like an Aussie meat pie. *Arancino* means 'little orange', and that's exactly what they look like: palm-sized balls of gluggy risotto rice, stuffed with a spoonful of *ragù* or béchamel then lightly fried in breadcrumbs until golden. When the barman places a hot *arancino* in my hand, in a cupped serviette, with a nonchalant

12

'*Prego*', before turning to wipe the froth from his Gaggia coffee machine, I suddenly remember why we've chosen to live in Italy.

At the Giga building, we press the intercom and get buzzed in by the school secretary, Valeria. A dodgy elevator cage rattles us up to the fifth floor.

Gill is impressed with what she sees of the school. It's privately run, modest in scope, but decently equipped with resources. Plus, the vibe among the mishmash of English teachers – from Ireland, Canada, France, Scotland and the US – seems enthusiastic yet low-key.

After Gill is given her teaching timetable, we have a chance to check our emails on the school computers. Bad news.

'The police are looking for us,' says Gill, reading an email from her parents.

'Aussie police?'

'Yes.'

Bugger. They know I stole those beer coasters from the Regatta Hotel in Brisbane.

No, that's not it. Someone has racked up thousands of dollars on Gill's credit card in the few days since we flew out for Sicily.

It's all the Prada we've bought, we jokingly email in reply.

Actually, we've not purchased a thing, and Gill's card is safely in her purse. The fraud squad's theory is that a thief has stolen a document from our letterbox in Brisbane and subsequently gained access to Gill's credit card number. Thankfully the matter is resolved with a single phone call.

If only things were as straightforward when it comes to the Sicilian police.

We're required to report to police headquarters (the Questura) as soon as possible to apply for our *permessi* – permits to live in Italy. Without them, we're illegal aliens.

Getting documentation in this country can be a notoriously complicated process. Just buying a simple stamp in a post office requires various sittings before a committee and a host of signatures in triplicate (or something like that).

The Questura is five minutes from Giga. Palmina kindly comes along to help grease the wheels. In the stuffy waiting room, a dozen mostly African applicants sit in plastic seats looking glum. A clock ticks loudly and listlessly on the wall. Policemen drift about the place. One has a little moustache, his shirt unbuttoned to reveal a crucifix on a chain, and a lit cigar hanging out the side of his mouth. I count as many as seven signs on the walls saying '*VIETATO FUMARE*' – 'No Smoking'. Palmina wanders off to see if she can butter up the chief. Meanwhile, I'm not thinking too much about long delays. All I want is the chance, finally, to interact with the *carabinieri*.

Italy has several arms of the law and the *carabinieri* are arguably the most famous. They're the ones who lounge in patrol cars on street corners wielding Beretta semi-automatic machine guns.

They also have a reputation for being incredibly stupid. *Carabinieri* jokes are thrown around in Italy like blonde jokes everywhere else. So aware of this situation are the *carabinieri* that their official website includes a collection of jokes, 'The Carabinieri in Humour'. Listed in the section are old chestnuts like:

Q: How many *carabinieri* does it take to change a lightbulb?

A: 1001. One to hold the lightbulb, the other 1000 to rotate the barracks.

Then there's the one about the *carabinieri* car driving backwards up the narrow road to Mount Etna. When an onlooker asks why, the driver replies, 'In case there's nowhere to turn around up there.' Later, the same car comes driving down the mountain, again in reverse. The driver explains: 'I found a place to turn around.'

My plan, should I encounter the *carabinieri*, is to test this legendary thickness by gauging their response to a fiendishly easy question, *viz.*: 'It says I need four passport photos for my *permesso* but I only have two. How many more passport photos do I need?'

Unfortunately we end up dealing with the boring old state police, the *polizia*. Mind you, they aren't entirely boring. Female officers of the *polizia* are allowed to wear their hair down and get about in knee-high leather boots, and one such vixen happens to be working in the station while we wait. I watch the cigar-smoking cop glancing in her direction from time to time. I also glance in her direction from time to time. Gill, meanwhile, glances in my direction from time to time, lips slightly pinched.

Palmina works her magic and soon we're sitting before the police chief in the inner sanctum, our completed documents laid out on the table. I feel sorry for the Africans who are trying to do this on their own. In fact, the way it's panning out, we're on the verge of getting through the molasses of Italian bureaucracy in under an hour.

The officer is clearly flustered. This won't do. How can he let two new arrivals off the hook so easily? Naïve foreigners moving to Italy are meant to be so bedevilled by the *permesso* experience that they all go away and blog about it. What will his colleagues think if we saunter out after thirty minutes with a free pass? More crucially, what will his saucy long-haired colleague think – and will it jeopardise his plans to get into her pants?

He scans our documents again, almost furious now. Finally, after several minutes, I see his eyes catch on something and light up. A muscle tugs the corner of his lips into a smirk. He picks up a pen and homes in on the inventory of *permesso* requirements. There, where it says 'four passport photos', he lazily scribbles a line through the 'four' and changes it to 'eight'. Then he leans back in his chair and gives us his best 'checkmate' look.

Gill and I have only brought the four photos we thought we'd need. I begin to protest: 'But we don't have–'

'*Otto*,' he interrupts. Then, with what he obviously deems an exquisite flourish to finish, he repeats it in English: 'Eight!'

It means that our next two days are spent tracking down a place that will take passport photos, forking out a bunch of euros for the extras, organising a return trip to the Questura with Palmina, lining up again, hoping for no other last-minute procedural amendments, and, finally, getting the seal of approval.

We have discovered for ourselves why officialdom in Italy has such a bad reputation. We have also discovered the answer to my earlier query for the *carabinieri*:

> Q: It says I need four passport photos for my *permesso* but I only have two. How many more passport photos do I need?
>
> A: Six.

2. Adjusting

Lasciate ogne speranza, voi ch'intrate.

Abandon all hope, ye who enter here.
– Dante Alighieri, *La Divina Commedia*, 1308–21

How did we end up in Sicily?

The seeds were sewn a decade earlier when I dropped out of law school at the University of Queensland. Oh, the euphoria! Three years of tedium, over at last. It was, as the Tantric sex practitioners of my hometown, Byron Bay, like to say of their orgasms, a long time coming.

With a legal career happily in tatters, I saw out the rest of my university days in the musty, underfunded halls of the humanities department. There I learnt essential life skills, such as how to read *Beowulf* in the original language: '*Hwæt, we gar-dena in geardagum, Þeodcyninga Þyrm gefrunon, hu ða æÞelingas ellen fremedon!*' ('Lo, we have learned by tradition the majesty of the Gar-Danes, of the mighty kings in days of yore, how the noble men perfected valour!')

If you hang around in this environment long enough and grow plenty of facial hair, there's a good chance you'll land a scholarship to do a higher degree. I signed up for a PhD in Roman History.

Several years later I had a graduate's scroll, a silly black cap on my head and new initials in front of my name. It meant that if somebody asked, 'Is there a doctor in the house?' I could reply in the affirmative, before assisting the injured person by reading aloud from *The Annals* by Tacitus (in Latin).

Of course, with a doctorate in ancient history I was wholly unemployable. Faced with the prospect of ushering people to their seats in a suburban cinema, I trawled for academic positions overseas. One eventually came up – in China, of all places. I signed on as a 'Foreign Expert in Roman History and Latin'. The job was in a far-flung city called Changchun, a place buried in ice for six months of the year and rotting food scraps for the rest.

During this radical relocation, I proposed to Gill. We'd been together for six years, having met at university where she was a fellow law-school dropout. (We bonded over a mutual hatred of promissory estoppel.) Now, though, we were apart. Gill didn't follow me to China. She'd earned a swag of teaching degrees and was beginning to use them to great effect in some of Brisbane's best schools. It didn't seem the right time to suddenly abandon all of that. Also, China was well down Gill's list of preferred countries in which to live – not as low as Kazakhstan or Yemen, but far below the front-runners.

My proposal, then, was a long-distance one. I arranged for Changchun's most famous calligrapher to paint the Chinese characters for 'Will you marry me?' on a giant cardboard love-heart. On Christmas Day, in temperatures of minus twenty-five degrees Celsius, I stood on a frozen lake waving the cardboard sign above my head. A friend took photos as hundreds of mystified Chinese looked on. That night I emailed the photos to Gill. She couldn't read Chinese characters so at first she thought the message said 'Merry Christmas'. Luckily I'd painted an English translation on the reverse side. In the final photo of the email, I turned the sign around.

Gill said yes (perhaps because she was concerned about the lengths I might go to if required to propose a second time). I even twisted her arm to join me for my final four months in the Middle Kingdom. She got a job teaching English, and each of us earned four hundred US dollars a month.

We didn't sign on for a second year. Money wasn't an issue – on those salaries we were well off. But Changchun was brutally cold, not to mention filthy. And while my job – and China – had been a fascinating experience, the academic department where I worked was little short of shambolic.

More to the point, I was losing interest in my chosen field. In lectures, I would find myself droning on about amphitheatres and aqueducts, while stealing furtive glances outside to an old fellow in a Mao suit selling watermelons from a wooden cart. I wanted to travel the world taking photos of craggy-faced villagers. Maybe I could become a travel writer, and regale magazine readers with tales from Chinese provinces and beyond. Surely I'd be just what the dailies and the glossies were looking for!

Still, it would be folly to throw away all that study. So I pushed on. The British publishing house Routledge paid me an advance to write a biography of the Roman emperor

Caracalla based on my PhD dissertation. I applied for various university positions in the UK, Canada and Australia, including a lecturing role at my alma mater, the University of Queensland. I was short-listed for the latter and invited to a two-day interview.

As we packed up our Changchun apartment, we still needed to make a decision about the coming year. Even if I landed the position in Brisbane – and it would be months before I heard a yes or a no – the job wouldn't start for almost a year.

'How about we go back to Australia and get married, then go overseas again for an extended honeymoon?' I said to Gill. 'You could teach English while I finish the biography, try my hand at some travel writing, and wait for news about work.'

'You mean be a househusband?'

'In a nutshell, yes.'

'Sure,' she replied, without a second thought. It was like I'd asked her to pass the potatoes at the dinner table.

Only one question remained. Where?

It was a no-brainer.

Gill and I had dreamed of living in Italy for as long as we'd been together. She loved the lilting language, the stunning fashion and – most of all – the sheer *passion* of the Italians. I loved their readiness to take the best part of a day to roast a baby suckling pig over an open fire. Often we would talk about owning a villa with a coop of Tuscan chickens round

21

the back. In fact, 'Tuscan chickens' became a kind of two-word mantra during those days in China when the grime and general nuttiness were too much to bear – our own version of 'Serenity now!' from *Seinfeld*.

But why Sicily? And why Catania, a city we'd never heard of? Simple: it was the first place Gill found a job. Because she has a British-born mother, Gill's passport allows her to live and work in an EU country. I would just be tagging along, like a jaunty puppy, my visa stamped *familiari al seguito* ('following the family').

After sending applications to various language colleges across Italy, Gill received an offer from the Giga school in Catania, Sicily's second-largest city. We scarcely weighed up the pros and cons – we didn't even do a Google search to find out more about our destination. Gill accepted the job and out came the suitcases again.

Had we delved a bit deeper we might never have said yes. I've already mentioned Paul Theroux's unflattering assessment of Catania (Mafia, drugs, pollution, ugliness). At the time, I brushed it aside, telling myself Theroux hates everything. As it turns out, the queue of people lining up to condemn Catania stretches a long way around the block. Consider these comments from various articles and online forums:

'Catania in Sicily is a hole.'
'The most degraded city of Europe.'
'Rotting urban carcass.'
'Ugly, decayed and crime-ridden.'

Wow. Epithets this strong are usually reserved for places like Nairobi or Canberra.

And there's more. Each year in Italy, a daily newspaper named *Il Sole 24 Ore* publishes a survey ranking the nation's hundred major metropolises from best to worst, based on living standards, safety, environment, employment and more. Catania usually comes dead last. One year, though, it was voted the fourth-worst city in all of Italy rather than the worst. This was considered a triumph.

To Gill and me, Catania seems bearable enough – at least initially. Anyway, how can we complain? We're living in Italy! Sure, we have very little money (okay, *no* money) and we have some issues with the apartment (okay, *many* issues), but at least we're here.

The weather's perfect, too. Sicily is chokingly hot in August. But we've arrived in September when it's summery but manageable. We walk around in t-shirts. We slowly get tans – first a Berlusconi orange, then a chestnut brown. I alarm the locals (who, like all Italians, are obsessed with *bella figura* – 'dressing to impress') by wearing shorts instead of trousers and thongs instead of shoes. My thick beard leaves them flummoxed, too.

We even have mosquitoes in the apartment to remind us of summer back home. Gill stands on the hard springs of her metal bed each night, can of insect spray in hand, picking off the mozzies (pleasingly called *zanzare* in Italian) as they jerk through the jagged holes in our windows.

A routine develops. Gill's timetable is twenty hours of teaching a week, spread over the afternoons and evenings. She walks to the Giga school by herself during the day, but I always meet her when classes finish at nine pm. Catania after dark is no place for a young woman alone. Our own street, Via Gesuiti, is seedy enough. The Michael Dibdin thriller *Blood Rain*, a book filled with murder, crime and treachery, is set in Catania and one of its final grisly scenes unfolds in Via Gesuiti. So, Gill and I stride home at night along stony back alleys with arms hooked at the elbow.

As a private English-language college, Giga caters to Catania's elite. It opened three years before we arrived, the classrooms ritually sprinkled with holy water. Palmina, the director, is the glamorous face of the school. She lives with her plastic-surgeon husband and previously mentioned children in an impressive *palazzo* (a proper one) overlooking the entrance to the city's leafiest garden, Villa Bellini. Her brother is a local TV personality.

Gill's students – adults, teenagers and children alike – similarly come from wealthy families. The mature-age students tend to be lawyers, businesspeople or bored housewives. One woman, while recounting her summer holiday, explains to Gill that her big dilemma had been whether to visit Vienna for opera season or take the yacht to the French Riviera. ('Can you please fail her?' I implore Gill.)

Vocab drills with the teenage class invariably lead to exchanges like this:

Gill: 'How many bedrooms does your house have?'
Student: 'Which house? We own four.'

One boy turns out to be a descendant of Ignazio Paternò Castello, Prince of Biscari. The Prince was an eighteenth-century nobleman who collected rare artworks and artefacts, many of which are on display in Catania's civic museum. His lavish former residence, Palazzo Biscari, was used more recently as the setting of a music video by British band Coldplay.

'Judging by their surnames, you wouldn't guess they're filthy rich,' I say to Gill after scanning her class roll. I've found a 'Rat Eater' (Mangiaratti), 'Half Head' (Mezzatesta), 'Four Eyes' (Quattrocchi), and someone called 'The Unnamed' (L'Innominato).

Speaking of names, Gill's class of six-year-olds has been given the cutesy title 'Ladybirds'. It should be 'Terrors': they're spoilt and rambunctious. The leaders of the pack are a pair of boys, Filippo and Andrea, who quickly earn the nickname '*brattini*' (little brats).

The tone is set in Gill's first class, when the students are asked to introduce themselves to the group. In stilted English, Andrea says, 'My father's name is Cretino' – the class erupts into giggles – 'and my mother's name is Scemina' – even louder giggles. The words mean 'cretin' and 'little fool'. Filippo, meanwhile, adopts a studious expression and asks Gill things like: '*Come si dice "scoreggia" in inglese?*' ('How do you say "fart" in English?'). Then he and Andrea collapse laughing.

It's the first time Gill has taught young children. She's in for the scatological ride of her life.

While Gill pays the bills, I play hunter and gatherer. That's how I discover Catania's famous outdoor market, the Pescheria. As the name suggests, seafood's the thing here. But you'll also find every fruit and vegetable under the sun, vats of tomato paste, salted anchovies in barrels, forests of fresh herbs, cheeses galore, and an array of meats, from piquant sausages trussed up in red string to castrated baby goats swinging from ganghooks. Men in grubby white coats walk through the aisles in gumboots carrying slaughtered pigs across their shoulders.

As far as markets go, it's a confronting place ('almost frightening in its intensity,' says one guidebook). On my first visit, I watch a fisherman rip the spine out of a live calamari – *with his teeth*. Another fellow machetes the head off a swordfish and places it upright on a bloody bench like a trophy, with its sword pointing to the sky and its black-jelly eyes filling with milky death.

The Pescheria is set in a sunken quadrangle of dank stone, giving it the feeling of an open dungeon. Locals say that a mysterious subterranean river flows beneath the space. I stop and listen for it, but all I hear are the market's raucous vendors. They sing, joke and cajole, competing for attention. You won't see a better bit of theatre. I almost feel like David Attenborough the first time I observe the rival males, standing in front of their trays of squiggling marine life, making their unique calls.

My first attempt at buying something, however, is a disaster.

'Two blood oranges, please,' I say in my best phrasebook Italian to a croaky old farmer in a wife-beater singlet.

With a Tourette's-style bark, he punches open a brown paper bag and begins furiously filling it. Blood oranges topple out of his muddy hands – many more than two.

'Erm . . .' I mumble.

'Two kilos!' he says in a tone of voice which means: 'Hey, I'm simply giving you what you asked for.'

'No,' I reply, as politely as possible. 'I only want two *pieces*. Not two kilos.'

He pauses briefly, then: 'I'll give you a kilo of blood oranges. One euro.'

He makes it sound like a special discount, but a handwritten cardboard sign on the pyramid of fruit says '*€1 al Kg*'.

'I only want two blood oranges.'

The fellow stops in his tracks and gives me an exasperated look. It means: 'This isn't how we do things around here.' Slowly he removes the excess blood oranges from the bag, one by one, while continuing to stare at me. Still staring, he drops the barely filled bag on a set of scales. I read the measurement and hand over thirty cents. He accepts the coins like a detective removing a used prophylactic from a crime scene.

A similar thing happens at another stall when I try to buy lemons. 'Half a kilo, please.'

'*Half a kilo?*' screams a stout, hairy-armed vendor, causing everyone to turn and stare. 'What can you possibly do with half a kilo of lemons? Nothing! Here, I'll give you two kilos, *va bene?*'

'Oh. Okay.'

In the end, I begin agreeing with what they say, purely to avoid drawing more attention to myself.

A typical expedition to the Pescheria therefore sees me lugging almost twenty kilograms of produce back to the apartment. If Gill happens to be home, she'll peer at the booty and say, 'Why did you get so many tomatoes?'

'I couldn't help it. The guy wouldn't stop filling my bag. I only wanted a handful, but he insisted on three kilos.'

Another day she'll open the fridge to find a wall of green leaves filling the shelves. 'What are these?'

'Lettuce.'

'Why so many?'

'They made me buy six for two euros.'

'What are we going to do with six lettuce? I don't even *like* lettuce!'

Sadly, Catania's famous market mightn't be around for much longer. Nine out of ten people I see shopping there are middle-aged or older. Younger Sicilians prefer the ease of a supermarket, where they can get everything under one roof, with a single payment and no haggling. Catania isn't the only Sicilian city where change is afoot. Palermo's famous fresh produce market, the Vucciria, is almost wholly sustained by tourism these days.

During our time in Catania, the most popular super-markets seem to be SMA (owned by the massive Rinascente group) and a chain with the ominous name Despar. Soon after we leave, though, a gigantic new mega-market called Etnapolis opens its doors. It's hard to begrudge the creation of more than two thousand local jobs, but there's something a bit dismal in the thought of the sons and daughters of local fishermen buying their tuna in neat slices, one centimetre thick, on a polystyrene tray with a cling-wrap cover and a sticker with a fixed price.

On weekends, Gill and I take time to explore our new neighbourhood. Usually we start early, driven out of our bedroom at six am by the resident greengrocer: ('*BANANE!* . . . *FRAGOLINE!* . . . *LIMONE!* . . . *SPINACI!*'). The problem isn't just the din but the fact that he has no customers. This just makes him stay longer and plead more loudly. I'm tempted to sprint outside in my boxer shorts, jam the loud-hailer into his ear and yell, 'NOBODY WANTS TO BUY YOUR SHIT. PLEASE VACATE THE AREA.'

We soon discover that our apartment is surrounded by an extraordinary collection of Roman ruins. Within a hundred metres are the remains of two ancient bathhouses (*thermae*), one housing a steam room and eight marble bathtubs. A few minutes' walk further on are the significant ruins of a Roman theatre, with seating for seven thousand people, and a smaller stage used for minor productions and rehearsals. The theatre was previously Greek, the very spot where the Athenian general Alcibiades addressed Catania in 415 BC, urging its citizens to take Athens' side in the Peloponnesian War which had embroiled Sicily.

With me seeking to rediscover my Roman history mojo, we couldn't be better located. A sign on our street corner reads 'Archaeological Park – Zone of Limited Traffic'. (The first bit is excitingly accurate; if only the same could be said for the second. There seems no limit to the number of Vespas that zip through our intersection twenty-four hours a day. Still, in this, our first flush of Italian living, the chaotic traffic remains more a novelty than a nuisance.)

We're surrounded by more recent history, too. Seventy metres from our front door is Sicily's largest – albeit uncompleted – church, Chiesa di San Nicola, flanked by the second-largest Benedictine monastery in Europe. Construction of the church was permanently halted by the destructive earthquake of 1693 in which two out of three Catanese were killed. Despite an unfinished façade, the remains are colossal, covering almost the area of a football pitch, with a sixty-two-metre-high dome topped by flashing lights that guide ships as far as fifteen nautical miles away.

Annoyingly, the dome can't be seen for scaffolding. We keep waiting for it to come down, but it never does. So many of Sicily's monuments are scaffolded, it could almost be an architectural style unto itself: Baroque, Art Nouveau, Scaffold. I wouldn't have a problem if the crisscrossing timber was put up temporarily – say, for a few weeks. But Sicilian scaffolds are like barnacles.

The church was once famous for its organ, the largest of its kind in Europe. As big as a house, it consisted of three thousand pipes and was designed to be played by three organists at one time. When the German literary giant Johann Wolfgang von Goethe visited Catania in the 1780s, he raved about the instrument's range of sounds, 'from the gentlest whisper to the most powerful trumpet blasts'.

For the record, he was less impressed with dinner at his inn: 'A chicken boiled with rice is certainly not to be despised, but an immoderate use of saffron made it as yellow as it was inedible.'

While our neighbourhood might be rich with history and religious culture, it sure ain't pretty. The same goes for the city in general. One problem is Catania's primary building material: lava. Successive civilisations have mined Mount Etna for its volcanic stone. And why not? As long as there's an eruption from time to time, the supply is never-ending. Yet lava in its cooled state is black. It's a good colour for cocktail dresses and heavy-metal album covers, but not ideal for a city. Even on a fine day, Catania looks glum. When the skies are grey and the rain tumbles down on the black basalt streets, the effect is funereal.

The dark tones serve as a constant reminder of the volcano's presence. Etna's peak might be thirty kilometres from the city, but when you walk the streets, they still feel chiselled out of the mountain's flank. It's not far from the truth: our apartment is located near a once-active volcanic vent. How disconcerting to think that it could reopen one morning and lob molten rocks onto our Rice Bubbles (which, incidentally, don't go 'Snap, Crackle, Pop!' in Italy but 'Pif, Paf, Pof!').

Catania has been destroyed nine times – once or twice

by foreign invaders, but mostly by Etna. Each time, the city has been rebuilt from scratch from the very ammunition of the volcano itself. Will it suffer again and be reborn? Maybe. Or maybe Catania is like one of its many cats, and its nine lives are up.

While Gill and I quickly get to know Catania's landmarks, getting to know the people takes longer. Language is part of the problem, of course. Gill has studied some French and Spanish, and she spent a year speaking Portuguese in Brazil; I've had my head swirling with Latin for half a decade at university. It's easy enough to extrapolate rudimentary Italian out of that linguistic stew. However, most of the people around us, especially the older generations, speak Sicilian. That's like someone with no more than basic English trying to understand a Cornish farmer. (Consider the saying, 'February may be short but it's the worst month'. The Sicilian wording is, '*Frivareddu è curtuliddu, ma nun c'è cchiù tintu d'ddu.*' Looks more Romanian than Italian.)

During our early struggles with all of this, only the young manager of the internet café in our neighbourhood is spontaneously chatty. Older shopkeepers, like the family that runs our *panificio* (bakery), the owner of the nearby pizzeria, and the fusty *nonna* in the wine store, remain mysteriously aloof – even when Gill and I try repeatedly to break the ice.

'One of the women in the *alimentari* gave me a friendly nod when I walked past today,' I'll say to Gill.

'No! At the *grocery store*? Are you sure?'

'Well . . . I think so. It seemed like a nod. I nodded back but she turned away.'

'Was she definitely looking in your direction?'

'Yeah. I guess. Then again, there were lots of people on the street. Okay, maybe it wasn't meant for me. But I think they're slowly warming to us, don't you?'

'Nope.'

When it comes to strangers, Sicilians are suspicious – a mistrust built up over thousands of years of foreign invasion. That's the stereotype, in any case, but the locals are doing nothing to disprove it. Perhaps Gill and I can begin to erode the social barriers by mastering *il bacio* – the kiss.

It's no secret that your average Italian loves an open display of affection between acquaintances. Sicilians are the same. If both are male, no matter. D.H. Lawrence on Sicilian men: 'they pour themselves one over the other like so much melted butter over parsnips'.

For an Aussie male, this requires some adjustment. In Australia, the only tactile male bonding (tonguing, genital fondling) is carried out by the national cricket team at the fall of an opposition wicket. This is largely why I stopped playing cricket, on the infinitesimal chance I became good enough to make the national side.

The most famous all-male kiss in Sicilian history was allegedly planted by former Italian prime minister Giulio Andreotti on the cheek of Totò Riina, the Mafia's *capo di tutti i capi* (boss of all bosses), in Palermo in 1987. 'The Kiss' – if it took place – was considered confirmation of Andreotti's involvement with the Sicilian crime organisation. It became one of the key elements in a high-profile trial that saw the former PM up on charges of conspiring with the Mafia. At one point, Andreotti was convicted and handed twenty-four years in prison. This was later overturned. The acquittal was then appealed. The appeal was overturned. Finally, The Kiss was dismissed as 'a fiction'.

If only a single kiss between friends were enough. The problem is that many Sicilians insist on *three* – left cheek, right cheek, left cheek – which requires considerable technical proficiency. One day I watch Gill's colleague Brock, a Canadian, get horribly tangled up with his local greengrocer – not the most kissable of men, let me add. When we enter the store, the two of them lean in for a customary three-cheek greeting. Unfortunately, they start from an awkward angle and never recover: someone's lip ends up on a nose while a tongue finds its way into an ear-hole. It's a scene from a high-school disco.

The first man I kiss three times on alternate cheeks is Claudio, a Catanese painter whose English girlfriend, Sarah, does some teaching at Giga. Sarah's sister once dated Orlando Bloom. Presumably those two also kissed, though sadly I never uncover enough details to sell to the tabloids.

Claudio and Sarah live around the corner from our Via Gesuiti apartment. They own a funky three-storey joint with Claudio's art studio on the bottom floor. I like his paintings a lot. They're mostly dreamy nightscapes of Catania, the city's black-grey buildings transformed into blocks of brooding blue, with whispery Etna forever in the background, brightened by an oversized moon. The solemnity of Claudio's work seems to belie his cheery round face and happy nature. But that's an artist for you.

Claudio teaches me the cheapest way to buy booze in Catania. At the *enoteca* in our neighbourhood, the Cantina del Sol, he hands half a dozen empty one-litre water bottles to the black-dressed *nonna* behind the counter. She carries the bottles over to a large barrel in the corner of the room. Turning the tap on the barrel releases a flow of rich red wine. There's more than one barrel, too. The Cantina sells Nero d'Avola (a full-bodied red from Etna's slopes), Fragolina (strawberry-flavoured), Zibibbo (a yellowy, sweet white wine) and Rosata (a light red). And it's all stunningly cheap – less than a euro a litre.

Kiss Claudio? Jeez, I'll *sleep* with him.

Another local we get to know is Massimiliano – Massi for short. Like Claudio, Massi breaks the mould of male Catanese. He has long hair and a beard – ninety-nine per cent of young men in the city are short-haired and shaven. Massi plays guitar and sings in a band called Drift'n Blues. They play a weekly gig in a smoky sliver of a bar called L'Insonnia (Insomnia), close to Catania's famous opera house, Teatro Massimo Bellini.

Gill and I become regulars. Drinks aren't cheap but the music is excellent: wandering bass lines, tight drumming, harmonica solos from a hard-drinking guy in a wheelchair, and Massi's outstanding guitar work. He also sings, peppering his lyrics with exuberant shout-outs:

'GOT THE BLUES!'
'INCREDIBLE!'
'MOJO WORKIN'!'
'BLUES FOR YOOOUUU!'

All with a thick Italian accent, of course.

Massi actually speaks like this in normal conversation, too. 'INCREDIBLE!' he says whenever we run into each other, instead of 'hello'. Then he'll launch straight into some zany story, like how he woke up in the middle of the night to have a coffee and a cigarette, only to find that his pet goldfish was dying. So he massaged the fish back to life: 'Little fishy, do you want me to play you a song? On my guitar? BLUES FOR YOOOUUU, little fishy!'

One day Massi takes Gill and me on an impromptu tour of Catania. Watching him drive through the streets, we can tell he loves the place. It's a refreshing change – most locals seem somehow browbeaten. Massi, on the other hand, brims with enthusiasm. 'We are hot-blooded people,' he says.

He wants to know about Australia, too. With a deadly straight face he explains that he'd like to get to know all of our sharks, on a personal level. By the time we pull over at a drink kiosk, this has somehow turned into a discussion about living with Eskimos in northern Canada.

At the kiosk, Gill has a glass of Catania's famous thirst quencher, *seltz limone e sale* – soda water, fresh lemon and sea salt. Massi and I have a couple of Castello beers.

Back in the car, Massi's mobile is ringing.

'Ciao, Mamma! INCREDIBLE!'

His mother is calling to see if Massi can make it for lunch on Sunday.

'Sure, Mamma, lunch on Sunday. How about lunch in Australia, with my Australian friends? *Si*, Mamma, *si!* LUNCH IN AUSTRALIA!'

There's a pause while his mum speaks. Clearly she's asking him what on earth he's talking about. She lives in Catania. What's all this talk about Australia?

'INCREDIBLE!' he shouts down the phone, by way of explanation. Then: 'Okay, Mamma, I need to go. BLUES FOR YOOOUUU!'

Massi's girlfriend, Alaina, later tells us he can be hard work. 'He's always like this,' she says with a resigned but loving sigh. 'There's no downtime.'

Massi claims to suffer from something called 'humid hair'. This is why he carries a hairdryer around – in case his scalp gets too moist. He also believes there are ghosts in his apartment; he wakes up in the night and sees them at the end of his bed. Another time we're in his car when a sad song comes on the radio. Massi flicks his windscreen wipers on (it's a clear, sunny day), slows right down, and pretends he's driving along in the pouring rain, sobbing to himself after a bad break-up.

Massi's mad enthusiasm and general joie de vivre are useful for the times when Catania starts getting on our wick – whether it's from incessant car horns, gloomy architecture, too much scaffolding, our lack of euros, a misjudged kiss, getting pushed around at the Pescheria, or the rogue seafood lasagne that gives us *diarrea esplosiva*.

Indeed, once Gill and I have sunk knee-deep into our lives in Catania, our list of mild grumbles about the place seems to be growing.

But do we understand the justification for Catania being voted the very worst city in Italy in a survey of a hundred cities? Not quite yet. Not the *very* worst.

3. A trip to Taormina

Wealth unused might as well not exist.
— Aesop, c. 620–560 BC

Celebrities, rock stars, politicians and the generally well-heeled usually arrive in Taormina, Sicily's premier seaside resort, by helicopter or private yacht. Gill and I can't be bothered getting the yacht out, so we arrive instead on the 8.45 am bus from Catania (€3.80 a ticket).

It's our first escape from the city. I figure Gill could do with getting out of our murky apartment, so I arrange a daytrip. The one-hour bus ride to Taormina takes us north along a coastline of jagged dark rock formed by Mount Etna's fiery drizzle sliding into the ocean and hardening with a hiss.

Sharing our bus are five Africans, their skin as intensely black as the volcanic cone looming above the left-hand window. Gill and I, on the other hand, are still ghoulishly white from the Aussie winter we've just left. Together we make the perfect human chess set. (Our opening gambit: the Sicilian Defence.)

Each colourfully attired African manhandles a duffel bag overflowing with carved wooden giraffes. The knick-knacks are to sell to tourists in Taormina. Rather than living in the resort town with its extortionate rents and glamorous cafés, the Africans travel from Catania each day, returning in the evenings. I've already met some of them in the markets in town, selling everything from sarongs and Russian balaclavas to pirated DVDs and – if you ask in the right kind of whisper – hashish. Many of them live in a ramshackle crisscross of streets near Catania's main railway station, just along the waterfront from the port. By night they hang out at a club called Clear Moon. I've seen the flyers: *Every Friday at Clear Moon, from Africa to Sicily, the Cous Cous Clan! Midnight. Plus, DJ set from Momhar (Senegal) and live Djembe and African Percussion.*

One fellow on the bus sees me eyeing his duffel bag. He lowers his dark sunglasses, points a wooden giraffe in my direction, and breaks into an enormous toothy smile. 'Friend. *Vuoi una giraffa?*'

'No thanks,' I say with a return smile.

'*Tigre?*' he persists, holding up a tiger instead.

'Not today.' The last thing I want is a woodcarving, unless he can whittle me a life-sized replica of Monica Bellucci.

Not to be rebuffed, he fishes in his bag and retrieves a black case. 'Sunglasses? *Occhiali?*' he asks in his English-Italian hybrid, thick with an African accent. Inside the case is a pair of sunnies with iridescent yellow frames. They're grotesque. 'Look,' he adds, 'they match your *capelli.*'

Capelli means hair. Is he suggesting I have iridescent yellow hair?

'*Cinque euro*, friend. Special price!' And on it goes.

It's not just the Africans trying to sell stuff. When we jump off the bus at Taormina, signs crowd around us like paparazzi: *Pizzeria Bar. CAMBIA EXCHANGE WECHSEL. Lido. Snacks. Menu Turistico. Pizza and Beach! ALBERGO. American Express. We Speak English. Souvenir – Foto – Film. Visitate!*

Then there's Taormina's main pedestrian street, Corso Umberto I, with its interminable succession of high-priced shops. Each one is fronted by the kind of frosty middle-aged Italian woman who likely spends her siestas in a steamy tryst with a chiselled young pool cleaner from one of the town's resort hotels.

As we stroll along the Corso, Gill knowledgably assures me that the shops are 'insanely good' – the highest end cloth-ing boutiques, antiques sellers and jewellers. I'd be equally excited to see a string of dental surgeries.

'Thank *god*,' I yell abruptly, pointing to one of the boutiques.

'What is it?'

'A place selling luxury linen tableware – I was worried we wouldn't find one!'

Gill looks my way and harrumphs. This might seem like a pricey retail hell to me, but my wife is a fashionable woman who aspires – one day – to enjoy an occasional indulgence from a Taormina boutique.

To ensure it's not today, I divert her attention to Vicolo Stretto (Narrow Alley), a dark and slender passageway between two buildings, leading off the Corso to the right. At just sixty centimetres across, it's one of the narrowest official streets in the world. Tourists like to creep along its length and stop in the middle to take photos. Gill and I do exactly this. It's a tight squeeze. Don't try Vicolo Stretto after a three-course lunch. I can imagine the bellowed command of the emergency crew already: '*Presto, presto! Porta il* concrete cutter – *e Vaselina!*'

Piazza IX Aprile, meanwhile, may not be the largest square in Taormina, but it's the spiritual heart of the town. It's named for a date, 9 April, perhaps to honour the birthday of American porn star Jenna Jameson, or maybe for some other reason.

Lined with cafés and churches, ringed by flowering trees, and paved in elegant black-and-white squares, the piazza acts as a vast balcony overlooking the ocean below. Leaning on the bougainvillea-entwined railing and drinking in the panorama is one of those sublime moments that make all the negatives of travel seem worthwhile – the missed train connections, the visa dramas, the amoebic dysentery.

The weather today is postcard perfect, too. Even Mount Etna is unimpeded by cloud. It's our first clear look at the volcano. By January, the top half of the mountain will wear a white cloak of snow; for now, though, it's a pyramid of pitch black. Not a single wisp of smoke rises from its many vents and cones.

This, to me, is disappointing. 'Mount Etna's a bit lame,' I mention to Gill.

'Don't say that!' she snaps.

Gill's already a fraction nervy about living for a year in the shadow of an active and potentially lethal volcano. The last thing she wants is her husband jinxing the situation by being flippant about it.

It's too late though. I've issued Etna a silent challenge: *show me what you're made of*.

Several of Taormina's obscenely rich people have gathered to sip coffee from Botoxed lips in the world-famous Caffè Wunderbar in the corner of Piazza IX Aprile. Apparently it's illegal to mention the Wunderbar without using the names Liz Taylor and Richard Burton in the same paragraph – this is where the pair came for cocktails while holidaying in Taormina.

I'm surprised that one or two of the café's waiters, dressed impeccably in black slacks and red suit jackets, haven't written tell-all accounts of the megastars they've served. Everyone likes hearing intimate details of celebrities. What did they drink? How *much* did they drink? Did they tip? Did they wash their hands after using the bathroom? How many times did they use the bathroom in a night? Was it a lot? Was it a lot because they had some kind of uncomfortable bladder ailment or because they were forever snorting drugs in there?

A three-minute walk (or seven-minute drunken crawl) from the Wunderbar is the San Domenico Palace, formerly a fifteenth-century monastery but now a sumptuous hotel where Taormina's rich and famous visitors generally stay. When I show Gill a photo of one of the rooms, she sighs and glances at me – not for the first time in her life – with a look that says, 'When will you be able to afford to treat me to a place like that?' (I glance back at her with a look that says, 'Not in the immediate future.')

Taormina is full of staggeringly expensive accommodation. Aside from the San Domenico, there's the Villa Sant'Andrea at the foot of the town, a boutique hotel in a restored nineteenth-century residence with a garden by the sea. Another is the Grand Hotel Timeo, right next to the Greek theatre, with a courtyard full of centuries-old magnolia trees and a marble terrace surrounding a pool. A line of shiny BMW taxicabs waits outside the Timeo. *Timeo*, by the way, means 'I fear' in Latin. As in: 'I fear we can't let you into our hotel, sir.'

· Famous people have been coming to Taormina for centuries, especially artists, musicians and writers seeking inspiration (and good cocktails). If you're looking for someone to blame for this bohemian influx, turn to J.W. Goethe, who arrived here from Germany in 1787 and praised the place to the hills. Thereafter, the die was cast. In the nineteenth century, two more Germans – one a painter, the other a photographer – gave Taormina an even more desirable reputation on the continent.

Otto Geleng was twenty when he moved to Taormina to paint scenes of the sea, the Greek Theatre and Mount Etna. When he exhibited his works in the cities of France and his homeland, some critics refused to believe his paintings were of a real place. They insisted on visiting Taormina to see for themselves.

Following close on Geleng's heels was Wilhelm von Gloeden. He wielded a camera rather than a brush, and his photographs of naked Sicilian boys struck a chord on the continent. Today they'd barely escape the prying eyes of a censor. Fair enough, too. I've heard von Gloeden's photos described politely as 'arcadian', but it's not an arcade that I'm keen to walk down any time soon.

After Geleng and van Gloeden came the glut. The check-list of illustrious Taormina tourists since that time reads like a list of seminar topics at university: Brahms, Bernstein, Dali, Dumas, Klimt, Steinbeck, Dietrich, Fellini, Welles and Wilde. Arguably the most famous of the lot was D.H. Law-rence, who stayed in Taormina from 1920 to 1922. He was prolific, too, writing books and plays, and perhaps finding inspiration for *Lady Chatterley's Lover*.

By 1925, British author Louis Golding could cynically allude to the 'five thousand four hundred and thirty two' writers who had penned odes to the beauties of Taormina. Yet still the artists and authors came. Tennessee Williams was another, along with his 'close friend' Henry Faulkner (a Ken-tucky artist with a bourbon-drinking goat named Alice), and Truman Capote. It may have been this lot that inspired one description of Taormina as 'a polite synonym for Sodom'.

From the list of famous tourists to Taormina, the name that means the most to me is Roald Dahl, whose books kept me mesmerised for most of my childhood. I have no idea what Dahl wrote while he was visiting the town – or if he wrote anything at all. But I'd like to think that, amid all the literary pretensions of the array of characters mentioned above, he came to the Sicilian seaside paradise to polish his first draft of *The Twits*.

Behind Piazza IX Aprile, a dramatic cliff face rises up to a gleaming white cross at the top. This is Taormina's own little Corcovado. A mule track has been Zorro-ed into the cliff. I suggest to Gill that we climb it. I'm forever hauling my reluctant wife up to the highest point of a town for the views.

The steep path zigzags a dozen times. At each turn is a statue depicting Jesus in a different scene from his final hours – the Stations of the Cross, as they're known: 'Jesus falls the first time', 'Jesus is stripped of His garments', and so on. My own stations are more mundane: 'Shamus changes a memory stick', 'Shamus stops for a Snickers', 'Shamus listens to his wife explain that she was perfectly happy in the shops so why do they have to *climb some fucking mountain*'.

The white cross we saw from town turns out to be part of a rustic seventeenth-century church known as the Sanctuary of the Madonna of the Rock. This tiny sanctum, chiselled out of the chalky cliff, is the starting point of an annual procession in which a statue of the Madonna is carried down the hill and into the main square of Taormina, where wine flows and herbed lambs are roasted over a wood fire.

The front door of the church is closed, but I spy an open door at the back so I sneak inside. It's a church; what's the worst that can happen? Suddenly a crone in a cardigan appears from nowhere and sets upon me with her broom, pushing me out the door while spitting hostilities in a thick Sicilian brogue. I believe this is called excommunication.

Continuing to mutter, the woman follows me outside and wanders over to a bench seat that has clearly been installed for climbers to catch their breath and take in the views. She promptly upends a tin of glistening Whiskas onto the seat, whispering the word for fish, *pesce*, over and over again: '*Peshhh! Peshhh! Peshhh! Peshhh!*' A dozen stray cats emerge from the shade of some nearby cactus plants and start eating, spreading a rank sardine gel across the surface of the bench with their tongues.

'I *was* going to sit there,' says Gill, panting from the climb. The crone looks pleased with her work.

From the sanctuary, a final weed-covered stairway leads up to the remains of the Saracen castle, a windswept medieval fortress four hundred metres above sea level. I heave myself to the top in ten minutes, only to find the castle door is closed. I stand and stare at the lock, hoping the power of my gaze might bend it open, Uri Geller–style. It doesn't.

Before descending, I take a couple of photos of distant Castelmola, a village of one thousand people that sits high on another stony ridge across from Taormina. Castelmola is home to the notorious Bar Turrisi. This otherwise nondescript bar has become famous for housing a collection of ornamental penises: statues, trinkets, carvings, ceramics, posters and more – every corner cluttered with cock.

Who would bother visiting Bar Turrisi? I know *one* fellow: the Aussie backpacker I met in Austria's Hohensalzburg Fortress many years ago who, as we were being led on a tour of the historic royal quarters, raised his hand and asked the guide – in front of everyone – 'Where's the old dunny where the king used to shit?'

After zigzagging back down to town, Gill and I decide that it's time to visit Taormina's – and possibly Sicily's – most famous structure.

The Greek Theatre is to Sicily what the Opera House is to Australia. Hewn from the hillside in the Hellenistic age, with a view unrivalled by any outdoor performance area in the world, the theatre held as many as five thousand fans of the dramatic arts. They would sit and watch famous tragedies about men and gods, with Mount Etna as a suitably spectacular backdrop.

These days, when it's not besieged by tourists, Taormina's theatre is still used for live performances. Bob Dylan played there shortly before we arrived in Italy. Elton John was scheduled to perform the following June. It's also a favourite of film directors. Woody Allen chose the location for the classical scenes in his 1995 film *Mighty Aphrodite*.

There's opera, too. Only a month before our visit, a tenor named Franco Bonisolli made headline news after suffering a mid-performance hissy fit, giving two fingers to the audience and storming offstage to a chorus of boos. This kind of erratic behaviour earned Bonisolli the nickname 'Il Pazzo' (Madman). Another time, during *Il Trovatore*, his voice broke while singing the final high C in 'Di Quella Pira'. Enraged at his own poor form, he plunged his sword into the timber boards, walked to the front of the stage, and belted out a correct version of the note, unaccompanied.

Gill and I witness a few 'performances' during our own visit. The first comes courtesy of a whiny ten-year-old Italian boy who turns up his lip at his parents' praise for the theatre. '*È piccolissimo,*' he says petulantly. ('It's tiny.')

It reminds me of a story my brother-in-law Matt tells about his visit to Rome's Sistine Chapel. As he stood there contemplating the ceiling's visual feast, a puffing tourist stormed into the room with a video camera thrust into the air. Upon joining Matt in peering skyward he quickly and loudly proclaimed, 'Is that *it*?' (I think I said the same thing when I first saw the Mona Lisa in the Louvre, but that's justifiable – it's microscopic!)

Elsewhere in Taormina's Greek Theatre, a plump English girl with red curly hair is being positioned so her even plumper mother can take a photo. The nagging mum is relentless: 'Big smile now. Stand on that step. Why don't you take your hat off? Brush your hair from your face, dear – I can't see your eyes. Not that step, the other one. Hat off! Big smile now . . .' Lesser men than me would seize the camera and hurl it over the cliff into the Ionian Sea; even lesser men, the mother.

The whole family – mother, father, daughter – look red-faced and drained. Not just from the heat of the day, but from their holiday in general. The father lugs a leather pouch of passports and traveller's cheques over his shoulder. It leaves an imprint of sweat on his shirt. He's clearly sick of the Sicilian sun, the extortionate cost of everything, the demands of his fat wife, and the Africans pestering him to buy carved wooden giraffes.

Later I see the woman standing in front of a gap in the stonework, yelling out across the theatre, 'Quick, Clive, there's more of a breeze over here.' Everyone turns to look at Clive as he dabs at the perspiration on his forehead and acknowledges his wife with an embarrassed wave of his hanky.

We might sneer, but in truth the heat's getting to Gill and me, too. Eventually the expansive ocean views and the hypnotic glimmer of sun on water become too much to bear. 'Bugger this,' I say. 'Let's go down for a swim.'

Unsurprisingly, the two beaches at the bottom of Taormina, Mazzarò and Isola Bella, are among Sicily's most exclusive. First we check out Mazzarò to the north. Our feet have barely touched the pebbles when we feel the penetrating stare of a deckchair attendant. He asks for something obscene like twenty euros from us, just to lie on the beach.

'What part of *vaffanculo* don't you understand?' I say.

At least, I would've said it if I'd thought of it at the time; instead, I stammer for a bit, glance in my wallet as though twenty euros might be something I'd actually find in there, and at last lead Gill away from the hallowed deckchair area, trudging slightly in the manner of the resignedly impoverished.

Next to the beach is a small headland where we scramble out to a set of stony ruins. While Gill wanders, I speak briefly to a tanned American fellow in his sixties. He's wearing an impeccably pressed white-and-blue linen outfit, with gold watch and gold bracelet. His Japanese wife sits silently and awkwardly on a jumble of rocks, watching waves slosh around the crevices below.

The man explains what they're doing in Taormina. 'We just figured it'd be swell to have a simple holiday by the sea.' With a wave of the hand he indicates the simple place they're staying – the marble-pillared Villa Unaffordable, or whatever it's called, that maintains sovereignty over eighty per cent of the beach. It's the type of place where a young bum like me couldn't even poke a toe across the threshold without getting Tasered by security.

We talk briefly about Taormina and Sicily in general but soon I have to excuse myself before I'm blinded by the powerful shards of sunlight catching on the woman's jewellery.

The next beach along, Isola Bella, is postcard divine. It's so magnificent that when I email photos through to my office-bound friends in Australia, the tone of their replies isn't envious so much as *threatening*.

The 'isola' in question is a tiny dewdrop of an island, reachable at low tide by walking along a bank of pebbles. Sometimes referred to as 'the Pearl of the Ionian Sea', it's now a miniature nature reserve, full of birds and lizards. In the late nineteenth century, though, it was owned by a wealthy British woman named Florence Trevelyan who allegedly came to Taormina after a scandalous affair with the Prince of Wales (later to become Edward VII). Whether she left England of her own accord or was 'invited' to leave is open to debate.

Arguably the best thing about Isola Bella is that one small section is free of charge and open to plebs like Gill and me. We spend the next few hours lolling around on our towels in the sun and taking the occasional dip. The water is delicious, though the beach's large pebbles make wading in and out a chore. I enjoy watching glamorous Italians in bikinis rise like goddesses from their deckchairs then start stumbling about like drunkards when they get to the shoreline.

I also scrutinise the efforts of a funny man rowing around the bay in a boat, advertising trips to the nearby Grotta Azzurra (Blue Grotto) for ten or so euros. Despite pushing seventy, he is shirtless, wearing just a pair of pink shorts and a sombrero. He rows his boat right up near the beach and touts his trips by honking vigorously on the rubber bulb of a silver horn, as a clown might. When nobody takes the bait, he shakes his head in anger. Later I see him making his way towards the grotto with a family of four aboard. I hear the faint tones of amateur opera as the old fellow sings to his new shipmates, his boat bobbing around the headland and out of sight.

The afternoon unfolds languidly. One of the remarkable aspects of Isola Bella is the incredible colour of the backdrop. Staring out at the sky and the sea, I observe a vague seam where the two of them merge in the middle. Other than that, they're almost indistinguishable, just a canvas of wondrous shimmering blue. For Gill and me, this is probably our happiest moment since we stood on an ocean headland in Australia, surrounded by family and friends, exchanging marriage vows in a salty breeze.

Soon, though, the bus back to Catania is due to take off. When we're halfway home on the A18 freeway, Gill lifts her head out of her magazine and says, 'You know, I'm not delirious with excitement about leaving Taormina.'

'Yeah. Well. Could be worse,' I shrug. And with that, the sun dips below the looming blackness of Etna out my right-hand window.

4. Erupting

If it were my wretched fate to belong to Catania, I too would brave the terrors of possible hot lava and live high up on the slopes.

– Josephine Tozier, *Susan in Sicily*, 1910

'Who wants to climb the volcano?'

It's Gill's colleague, Brock. We're lounging around his apartment, ploughing through a cheap bottle of Nero d'Avola, and trying to learn an Italian card game called Scopa.

'Definitely,' I reply, without a moment's hesitation.

Gill isn't so sure. 'But . . . won't it *erupt*?'

'Maybe,' says Brock, dealing three cards with odd-looking designs on them to each player.

'And then . . . we would die?'

'Can't rule it out.'

Gill glances my way.

'Don't worry,' I say. 'Apparently the lava from Mount Etna flows very slowly.'

'But I *run* very slowly,' she protests.

'Well, I'm no Matt Shirvington either,' I say.

Brock looks bewildered. 'Who's Matt Shirvington?'

'Shirvo? He's an Aussie runner,' I answer. 'One of our

better sprinters – though that's not saying much. In fact, he's generally less famous for his results and more famous for wearing a revealing running costume.'

'Revealing in what way?' asks Brock.

'Grotesquely. Let's leave it at that.'

Beside me, Gill is shuddering at the thought of it.

'Hmm,' says Brock. 'The only Aussie athlete that Canadians know is that Steven Bradbury guy. The skater who was coming last in the Winter Olympics until everyone else fell over and he got the gold.'

'Steven Bradbury is an Aussie legend!' I say. 'Don't go knocking our Steven Bradbury or I'll bring Celine Dion into this.'

'Back to my question,' Gill interrupts. 'Will Etna erupt?'

'We should be okay,' says Brock.

Etna's last major 'episode' took place a year or so before we arrived, but there weren't too many rumbles in an eight-year gap prior to that. A sudden eruption does seem unlikely.

'Anyway,' I add, 'isn't there a story about the patron saint of Catania – what's her name, Brock?'

'Agatha.'

'Yeah, that's her. Legend has it that Saint Agatha stopped the lava flow with only a *veil*. So, how dangerous can it be? You wait. We'll be scooping that stuff up and throwing it around like snowballs.'

'Okay,' says Brock. 'How about this Saturday, then?'

Gill doesn't speak. She's staring at Brock's three goldfish, Slap, Darts and Barney. Perhaps she's hoping they'll vote against the motion.

'Lock it in,' I say, thumbing one of my Scopa cards onto the table with a triumphant flourish, only for Brock to shake his head and say, 'Shall I go through the rules again?'

Australians are volcano virgins. We do endure the occasional earthquake – like the unexpected and fatal tremor in Newcastle in 1989 (5.6 on the Richter scale, thirteen dead, a hundred and sixty injured, damage bill of four billion dollars). Yet, because the country sits in the middle of a tectonic plate rather than at the edge of one, seismically it's a very quiet place. Gill and I therefore have no idea what to expect from Etna.

For Sicilians – and particularly for Catanese – the relationship with the volcano is intimate and respectful. Consider what they call her: Mongibello (or Muncibeddu in dialect), a combination of the Latin *mons* and Arabic *gibel*, both meaning mountain. So: 'mountain of all mountains'. Sometimes she's simply *'a muntagna*, 'the mountain'. No reference to fire and brimstone at all, whereas the Greeks named Etna after the verb *aitho*, meaning 'I burn', and the Arabs in the ninth century termed her Jebel Utlamat ('mountain of fire').

She's much more than just a mountain though. In the list of the world's most active volcanoes, the fame of Etna surely outshines the rest. (Anyone know much about Klyuchevsky, Unzen, Ol Doinyo, Merapi, Sheveluch or Yasur?) Only her Sicilian counterpart, Stromboli, is a match for notoriety. Yet Etna is well over three times as tall. At around 3300 metres – her height varies as new eruptions alter the landscape of the summit – she's the tallest active volcano in Europe. Does that make Etna something to be proud of, or something to fear and despise because of the destruction she causes?

I ask a souvenir seller in Catania this question. He spies me riffling through his postcards and other tat one evening in his shop near the city's main square, Piazza del Duomo. When I pick up a bottle of undrinkable red alcohol labelled Fuoco dell'Etna ('Etna's Fire' – the bottle is coated in a layer of fake black rock), we get talking about the volcano.

'I'm not afraid of Etna,' he says. 'I like her.'

'In what way?'

'She's a good mountain.'

'Good?!'

'Yes. Good for my business!' He laughs and glances in the direction of a rack of Mount Etna tea towels. It's a fair point – I already have one in my hand, ready to send back to Australia as a gift (clearly for someone I loathe). 'Also,' he continues, 'so many things grow on her slopes. The soil is fertile. Oranges, lemons, pistachios, apples – all kinds of vegetables. The markets in town would be empty without Etna.'

The fellow keeps a myna bird in a timber cage at the front of his store. It's the noisiest bird I've ever heard.

'*Ciao*,' it says whenever I walk near it. '*Buona sera!*'

'*Ciao*,' I reply.

The bird gives a condescending high-pitched whistle. Then: '*Come fa il gatto?*' ('How does a cat go?')

I don't answer.

'*Miao!*' says the bird.

When Gill walks in, she receives a shrill welcome: '*Ciao, bella! Come stai?*'

As we farewell the shop owner and walk out the door with the tea towel, a handful of postcards and two bottles of Fuoco dell'Etna (couldn't resist), the bird shrieks, '*Hai pagato?*' ('Have you paid?') It's the kind of creature you'd love to take up to the summit of Etna and lower in its cage into one of the volcano's deadlier fumaroles.

On a blue-sky Saturday morning in October, we pack a picnic lunch and drag ourselves aboard the 8.15 am AST bus – the only daily service from Catania that goes remotely near the volcano's top half. With us is Brock, ringleader of the hike, and Natasha, another Giga teacher, also Canadian.

An hour later we reach Nicolosi, a pristine town of five thousand people that marks the last settlement along the Strada dell'Etna, the road to the volcano. The air outside, I notice, is considerably cooler than at sea level, even though we've barely climbed a quarter of the mountain's height.

While Nicolosi is still fifteen kilometres away from Etna's peak, it sits right next to one of the volcano's countless subsidiary craters. During the eruption of 1669 – the most destructive on record – a lava flow from this crater scorched its way down to Catania and wiped out much of the city. Nicolosi was obliterated.

Etna is a 'complex' volcano, meaning that eruptions aren't limited to a single fountain of lava spewing from the top – the kind that a kid draws with a crayon. Instead, there are hundreds of active craters up and down the slopes. More often than not it's these 'flank eruptions' that threaten property and endanger lives.

From Nicolosi, our bus climbs through a few final thickets of pine and beech trees, but then the landscape turns morbid as we start to cross solidified rivers of old lava. The charred corner of a farmhouse roof pokes through the rubble. Conversation draws to a standstill. Every set of eyes is trained on the eerie scenes outside.

It's another forty-five minutes before we reach the end of the road. Rifugio Sapienza, at an elevation of nineteen hundred metres, is the headquarters of the volcano's southern slopes. It's little more than a car park and a modest collection of rangers' huts, plus some souvenir stalls and a restaurant. The whole thing looks vaguely like a Swiss ski lodge, except that it's surrounded by jagged black rock rather than five feet of white powder, and there's no fondue in the restaurant.

Rifugio Sapienza literally means 'wise refuge'. It's a silly name. In 2001, the car park and a couple of huts were swallowed up by lava. The entire site would've been engulfed but for an armada of bulldozers working round the clock to divert the lethal flow.

I'm tempted to have a dig around the souvenir stalls before our hike, if only to replenish my supply of Fuoco dell'Etna. I've also heard you can buy ten-inch ornamental penises carved from black lava stone, though I imagine they'd look good on only a select number of mantelpieces around the world. But there's no time for shopping. Our bus is due to leave again at four thirty pm, so we have six hours on the mountain. According to guidebooks, we'll need four of those just to hike up to three thousand metres.

Like all climbers, we're required to visit the information centre to get an update on conditions at the summit. Inside, seismic readouts show Etna to be in a relatively benign mood. Despite this, there are plenty of savagely worded warnings concerning the dangers of approaching craters without a guide. To reinforce the message, photos show Rifugio Sapienza burning to the ground. There's also a reminder about high-altitude cerebral oedema, which has been known to strike mountain climbers from as low as two thousand four hundred metres. I glance over at Gill, who looks like she's about to tour an abattoir.

The ascent is easy going at first as we follow a graded slope of black rubble. Soon, though, the scree becomes steeper and less compact. Climbing on tiny volcanic pebbles is like walking up a marble ramp covered in ball bearings.

Every thirty minutes or so, a four-wheel-drive van comes winding along the impromptu track, taking a handful of tourists up to where the road runs out, at around two thousand seven hundred metres. Initially we scoff at the people inside, labelling them lazy spendthrifts (tickets for the van are thirty euros; we're walking for free). Within the hour, though, we're shooting envious glances as each passing van leaves us in a choking wake of ash.

A cable car opened here in the 1980s, but it's been buried by eruptions. From time to time we hike past an abandoned pylon, sticking out of the slope at a bizarre angle like Pisa's tower.

By the time we stop for a break, thighs appropriately molten, the landscape has become insidiously bleak. It's all steaming pits and craters. Tolkien is thought to have modelled Mount Doom on Etna's forbidding scenery. Adding to the eeriness, a large statue of the crucified Christ appears on the track, his gunmetal-green body offering the only splash of colour against the gloom, aside from the occasional patch of tenacious Etna violets.

After another hour of steep uphill climbing – during which time we coin a new word, 'trudgery' – we reach the point where the road stops and the four-wheel-drive vans are forced to turn around. From there, a makeshift handrail of knobbly sticks leads further up. The four of us push on.

Next we walk into a wet fog. The temperature plummets, sending us scrambling for warm headwear. Courtesy of our companions, Gill and I learn another word: *tuque*. It's Canadian for beanie.

At three thousand metres, we arrive at a sign hammered into the volcanic rock: 'IT IS DANGEROUS TO GO BEYOND THIS LIMIT BECAUSE OF EXPLOSIVE ACTIVITY'. Some kind of mountain sickness may be taking hold, because we all roundly ignore the warning and continue climbing. Even Gill pays it no heed.

The incline levels out to a plain of black sand dotted by heavy, football-sized chunks of rock. These are 'incandescent bombs' – blobs of molten orange that have lobbed out of the volcano and hardened. I kick one with my shoe, wondering if it might crack open and drizzle burning lava like a yolk. It would be a novel way to lose a toe. Finally I'd have a story to match my uncle Bob who accidentally amputated one of his pinkie toes in the crook of a step ladder, then tossed the useless digit to the kookaburras in his backyard.

It's now difficult to tell fog, cloud and smoke apart. Sulphurous tendrils rise from cracks and crags. Presumably we're right near the summit. Etna has three or four main vents at the top – we're somewhere in between. The vapours clear just long enough for us to spy one of them. It's two hundred metres away, rising to a brim of crusty yellow, with a steady funnel of grubby smoke drifting away on the breeze. But the ground has become virtually unnavigable, so we take one last look and turn back.

It would be lunacy to continue, especially as we're so ill-equipped. Lists of paraphernalia required to climb Etna have long been comprehensive. A passage from the nineteenth-century *Handbook for Travellers in Sicily* advocates leather leggings, a stout iron-shod stick, a green veil to shield the eyes from the sun's glare, a barometer and a geologist's hammer. Back at the information hut at Rifugio Sapienza, the list of recommended items includes a hand-held GPS, excellent hiking shoes, a thick winter jacket, plenty of spare food, a cell phone, and a torch with spare batteries. Our inventory is more modest: Gill's carrying lip-gloss and a hairbrush, while I've got a bus timetable and half a packet of Fonzies, Italy's far inferior version of Twisties.

Etna cripples us. Back in Catania, Gill and I convalesce for days. We press each other's stiff hamstrings to compare our respective agonies, the way we do with bruises and sunburn. Some might call it sadomasochistic; we call it the secret to our marriage.

Despite the pain, I'm soon contemplating a return journey to the volcano. But not Gill. She'd be happy never to walk on a gradient of more than fifteen degrees for the rest of her life. (And hasn't yet, I might add.)

Brock, like me, is keen to go again. We begin laying the groundwork for a more comprehensive exploration of Etna. The plan this time is to arrive by car, driving through the town of Linguaglossa to the mountain's well-forested northern slope. Parking at Piano Provenzana (similar to Rifugio Sapienza but less touristed) we will head west and do a two-day loop on foot. The night will be spent in one of the empty log huts that ring the mountain between fifteen hundred and two and a half thousand metres.

Brock has roped in a local friend of ours, Angelo. This is handy for two reasons: first, he has a good idea of the mountain's trails; second, he has a car. Angelo reminds me of one of those plastic action figures that ten-year-old boys collect. He's always wearing army fatigues. Brock has a penchant for khaki clothing as well, but Angelo goes the whole hog, adding a utility belt full of various tools, knives, torches and incendiary devices. Forever scheming about adventures – exploring caves, tackling dangerous summits – he's the type of guy who can talk for hours about how much damage he's done to a friend's ribcage in a recent game of paintball.

The weather report for the last weekend of October is perfect. Overnighting on the mountain will be cold, though, so I scurry around looking for thermal underwear and a sleeping bag. By Friday it's all systems go. I can almost smell the alpine air.

Then our intrepid guide – resilient, adventurous Angelo – comes down with *mal di stomaco* (a sore tummy). The hike is postponed. Gill is pleased. She hasn't warmed to the idea of me spending a night in an abandoned timber hut on an active volcano with two men wearing army fatigues. Now that I think about it, it does sound vaguely like *Deliverance*.

Instead of mountain climbing, I find myself moping around the city. On Saturday, Gill drags me to Catania's main boulevard, Via Etnea, to do some clothes shopping. Is there anything worse? Suddenly the idea of being hogtied by hillbillies seems inviting.

Early on Sunday morning, I open our bedroom window to the street and think despondently about the Etna adventure that has slipped through my fingers. Looking up, I'm surprised to see a streak of white-grey cloud.

'Hmm,' I say to Gill. 'I think it might rain.'

But the overcast conditions don't seem right. The newspapers predicted bright and sunny.

Our phone rings. It's Brock. He's just had word from a friend who lives higher up the mountain, in the town of Belpasso. Apparently the air is so clogged with ash and smoke, he can't see to the end of his street.

Sicily's acclaimed twentieth-century writer Leonardo Sciascia referred to Mount Etna as a huge house cat, snoring quietly (*un immenso gatto di casa che quietamente ronfa*): 'Every now and then it wakes, yawns, stretches lazily and with a swipe of its paw destroys a valley here or there, wiping out towns, vineyards and gardens.' Overnight, Sciascia's pussycat has woken up. The mountain's southern flank is erupting in devastating fashion. It started around midnight, when a series of loud detonations were heard and a one-kilometre gash ripped open on the slope, exactly where we walked a few weeks earlier. The four of us would've been instantly swallowed.

Now, boiling magma is spewing as high as two hundred metres, along with a gargantuan volume of ash. The latter has formed a 'pyroclastic column' rising kilometres into the heavens. It's what I've just seen in the sky and mistaken for storm clouds.

Things are even worse on the other side of the mountain, where Brock, Angelo and I were planning to spend the weekend. At two thirty in the morning, a crater on Etna's northeast flank began spouting lava. At Piano Provenzana, the ground ruptured and caused the partial destruction of a hotel, Le Betulle. Everyone in the area was immediately evacuated. The car park, meanwhile, was torn in two by a fissure – Angelo's vehicle would have slid into the crack. God knows the fate of the flimsy little timber hut where'd we hoped to occupy a night in the woods.

Gill and I sit tight, watch the darkening sky, and wait for further reports. There are no signs that the mountain may be mellowing. On the contrary, by midday lava is oozing steadily towards Rifugio Sapienza. The higher towns on the mountain's slope are shrouded in falling ash. 'Nicolosi's Black Sunday', reads the newspaper headline the next day.

Activity on the northeast slopes has also dramatically increased. A dozen vents have opened. The skiing facilities at Piano Provenzana are buried under molten rock. Incandescent bombs land on top of a restaurant and wipe it out.

Soon Linguaglossa is in danger. A few kilometres above the town, a forest of pine trees is incinerated. Squadrons of helicopters and special Canadair CL-415s fly repeat missions to stem the lava flow by bombing it with water – the aerial equivalent of trying to douse a bonfire by pissing on it.

In the early afternoon, Gill and I head down to the port for a clearer view of the pyrotechnics looming behind Catania. But the whole volcano is enveloped in a mushroom cloud four times its size, obscuring a clear blue sky. Choppers buzz around the edge like mosquitoes. Faint booming sounds can be heard in the distance, sometimes minutes apart, sometimes seconds. High in the sky, the mushroom cloud tapers into a trail of grubby smoke that floats above the city and away over the ocean.

Later, it's described as the most explosive eruption of Etna for a century and a half. More than a hundred earth tremors have rocked the mountain, too. Local vulcanologists, in an effort to quell suggestions they were ill-prepared for the disaster, refer to 'a lack of premonitory seismicity'. In plain terms: there were no warning signs. This gives me food for thought. Quite frankly, if it weren't for Angelo's bellyache, I'd be belly-up.

On Monday morning, Etna is the only topic of conversation anywhere in Catania. I pity anyone lying on a surgeon's table or expecting a lawyer to fight their cause in court. *Everyone* is distracted by news of the volcano.

It's hard not to be. Waves of ash have started raining down on the city itself. The eruption plume is being driven by the breeze in a southeast direction – in other words, over Catania. It's grown much thicker and darker overnight, too, and is even visible from the Aeolian Islands, a hundred kilometres the opposite way. Any skyborne material that doesn't settle on Catania drifts across the Mediterranean as far as Kefalonia in Greece, five hundred kilometres away, and even into North Africa. Stunning satellite photos of Europe streaked by a long volcanic cloud appear in newspapers across the world, accompanied by suitably flammable headlines: 'Etna spews lava onto Sicily', 'Mount Etna coughs fire, villagers pray', 'Etna state of emergency declared', 'Mt Etna eruption blackens sky'.

Ash and lava aren't the only worry. Earthquakes continue to strike, and they're strengthening. A chunk of the mountain is breaking away from the eastern slope and sliding towards the ocean. On Monday afternoon at Gill's school, teachers and students feel the building start to sway. Everyone is evacuated and the school closed until further notice.

On Tuesday morning, the earthquakes intensify again; a dozen are felt in Catania alone. The biggest one strikes at around eleven am. I'm sitting in our local internet café answering frantic emails from family back in Australia who've read all the Etna news reports, when the room goes woozy. I've only experienced one other earth tremor, in China's Jilin

Province a year earlier. It was a massive quake – 7.2 on the Richter scale – but damage was minimal because it struck so deep below the earth's surface.

This quake, on the other hand, measures just 4.4, but it's shallow and destructive. The epicentre is the village of Santa Venerina, north of Catania, where a thousand people flee their homes and a hundred buildings are wiped out. There are fifteen injuries, fortunately none of them serious. Other towns in the area get crunched as well. Many people sleep in their cars, fearing they'll be caught inside a flimsy building during an aftershock.

It's an odd feeling, being in an earthquake. For the first few seconds, you're convinced it's your own personal issue rather than something happening around you – an unexpected bout of dizziness, perhaps, or a mild fit. 'Too many wines last night?' you wonder to yourself. Or: 'Maybe it's my sinuses.' Then you see the looks on other people's faces and quickly realise that everyone's feeling exactly the same way.

By the end of the week, the tremors begin to settle. Despite the devastation at Santa Venerina and some other towns in the area, there is one happy statistic: zero fatalities.

On Friday, though, sighs of relief turn to national grief. This time, Etna isn't the culprit. Without warning, an earthquake (magnitude 5.4) strikes the region of Molise in the middle of the Italian mainland. It destroys a school and kills dozens of children. As the country mourns, fears mount that the geodynamic activity in Molise is related to the eruption of Etna, suggesting a great arc of instability from Sicily as far north as Rome. Will Vesuvius be next?

But the events are unconnected. Like the earthquake that struck Newcastle, the tremor in Molise is a lethal, one-off occurrence.

If you're lucky enough to remain untouched by the tragedy they wreak, volcanoes can be tremendously exciting things. The very word gets the heart palpitating. When I hear 'volcano', I think of cowering Romans snap-charred at Pompeii, of Krakatoa suddenly emerging from the bubbling ocean, and of time-lapse photography showing the obliteration of Mount St Helens.

Gill and I soon learn, however, that if you're close to the action, one thing quickly removes the gloss. Ash.

Before the eruption, I had a romantic notion of volcanic ash. I thought it consisted of fine, feathery flakes – the kind you could smear in lines across your cheeks to impersonate a Red Indian or Adam Ant. Maybe I could bottle some falling ash, mix it with water to make a lovely charcoal-grey paint, and start tinkering with a brush and canvas.

How wrong I was. Ash is horrid stuff. The word doesn't do it justice. Now I understand why scientists speak of 'tephra', 'pyroclastics' and 'scoriae' – anything but 'ash'. Perhaps the most accurate description is 'lava sand'. That's exactly right: volcanic ash is like a gritty, black, heavy version of sand.

When it first starts to fall, though, it's fun. On Sunday, when everything is getting covered by centimetres of dark grit, I go outside and scrawl messages on the pavement as though it's drying cement. 'ETNA!' I write, and 'Eruption,

27 October'. I fill a glass cup with the sand and hold it under the light to analyse the contents. I take photos.

Soon, though, it begins to block the drains. Our apartment has a strange internal courtyard, just a metre or so square, with stuccoed walls on all sides – it's like the bottom of a shaft that drops through the middle of the *palazzo*. We sweep this courtyard vigilantly to prevent ash pouring into the central drain, but to no avail. The only way to unclog the pipes is with industrial-strength cleaner. Our place smells like a cross between a hospital ward and a stagnant pond.

Outside is worse. Catania is swimming in filth. Streets, gutters, bins, window frames – everywhere is black with ash. Teams of street sweepers in bright orange outfits and face masks scramble as fast as they can to pile it into sandbags. I walk down to Catania's busiest square, Piazza Stesicoro, and the place is shrouded in grey dust kicked up by the workers' brooms.

I can understand the face masks. Apparently if you breathe enough volcanic ash, it mixes with the moisture in the lungs and creates a kind of liquid cement. This is perhaps why I start to see so many dead cats on the street at this time. In one courtyard alone, seven or eight dead strays are piled on top of one another, as though someone's collecting them for their pelts.

Driving on volcanic excreta is lethal, too. There is accident after accident in Catania. Motorbikes are banned for a time.

When it's raining ash, as it does almost constantly for the first fortnight of the eruption, an umbrella is de rigueur, regardless of whether the sun is shining or not. I hate umbrellas. I *never* carry one, not even in the worst weather. Gill says I'm like one of those leading males in a romantic comedy who stands outside the door of his love interest, soliloquising in a downpour, to the point where you start yelling at the screen, 'Get out of the rain, idiot!'

But in Catania an umbrella is essential, if only to stop ash from getting in your hair and beard. This isn't snow, remember – it doesn't sit on top of your curls where it can be easily brushed away. Volcanic ash is *heavy*. It sinks to the whorl of your scalp. To get it out, you have to bend over and vigorously run the fingers of both hands through your roots.

Still, an umbrella's not much chop in the wind – the ash simply swirls up and under, and into your eyes. Microscopic shards of crystal in volcanic material can carve up a cornea in no time. The pterygium in my left eye turns blood-red; I begin to look rabid. Gill feels like there's a beach behind her contact lenses.

It gets in your teeth, too, not to mention food.

'I'll have the *caponata*, please.'

'Certainly. Today it comes with tiny black rocks.'

Archaeologists working with mummies have discovered that the molars of ancient Egyptians were worn away over time by crunching on sand. It wouldn't surprise me if dental records of east-coast Sicilians revealed a similar phenomenon.

The ash is more than just a personal inconvenience. Catania's international airport, Fontanarossa, is immediately closed and all flights cancelled after news of the eruption on the first Sunday morning. With Etna's continuous emissions, it stays closed for almost three weeks. Flying through a pyroclastic cone in the air would be dangerous enough, but it's the skidding landings that authorities are most worried about. Tourist numbers plummet, Catania's *La Sicilia* newspaper starts printing estimated financial losses for the city and surrounding area.

One night, four weeks after the initial eruption, when the immediate threat of earthquakes is at least over, some friends plan a midnight viewing of the lava from close quarters.

Brock and Angelo come along, as does Claudio and his girlfriend, Sarah, and a handful of others. Gill not only says no, but adds that I'm a fool for saying yes.

'But, honey,' I say philosophically, 'I could be dead tomorrow.'

'You could be dead *tonight*,' she counters.

At ten pm, we set out from Catania in two cars. Already we can see Etna's ongoing eruption in the distance: vermillion squiggles halfway up the horizon, set against a forbidding blackness; even higher up, the occasional slow-motion spurt of molten rock being ejected into the sky.

After a stop at Nicolosi for beer and wild-mushroom pizza, we park the cars at a vantage point below Rifugio Sapienza and wait for the final sightseers to drive back down to the city. Dozens of carloads have been coming up from Catania each night, hoping to get a first-hand experience of the pyrotechnics. A police roadblock stops anyone going beyond a safe level.

We intend to hike past the roadblock without the police noticing. It's hard work, scaling a volcano in the dark while trying to keep the crunching of boots to a minimum, but we make steady progress.

Half an hour after rounding the fuzz, I can tell we're getting closer to the lava before I even see it. The air begins to warm dramatically. Angelo, who is leading the way in his army fatigues and headlamp, soon begins to glow faintly orange. A minute later he turns around with a smile, his face fully lit as if by a campfire.

We slowly make our way to his spot and peer over the edge of a trench. I feel an intense heat on my face. There before us is a five-metre-wide river of lava. Only, it's moving like sludge. The noise is incredible: a high-pitched crinkling sound of hot-'n'-crispy stones rubbing against each other and shifting forward, almost like a giant sheet of toffee being cracked apart. For an eternity I can do nothing but just stare at this thing. I strip all my extra layers of clothing off and, every now and then, walk a few metres away to cool down.

At some point I remember my camera. I take a whole bunch of photos, none of which look like anything other than a shaky blur of bright orange framed by darkness.

At three am, the headlights of a jeep round a corner not far from where we're perched.

'Shit!' says someone. '*Polizia!*' We duck our heads behind a ridge of black rock to avoid being spotted.

Now the cops have got their windows down and their torches out. The jeep is a hundred metres away. Suddenly I feel as if the crumbly rocks that I'm sitting on are about to give way and jettison me further down the slope. I have to move. I watch the sweep of the torch beams in the manner of *The Great Escape*, waiting for them to pan away so I can scramble into another gully. Darkness enshrouds me and over I go. I'm a bit too hasty, however; as I slide heavily into my new hiding spot, sharp rock slices into the top of my leg and rips open the flesh around one of my knuckles like a burst grape. I've learnt another lesson about lava: it doesn't cool into a smooth polished stone. It's jagged and sharp as a knife.

At least I've evaded capture. The jeep passes by and we continue to watch and listen to the lava, our faces burning in the glow.

Fifteen minutes later there's a kerfuffle further down the slope. The police are smarter than we thought. They've parked the jeep and come back on foot. Now they've got Claudio. They place him under arrest. One cop leads him back to the vehicle while the other rounds up a few stragglers in our group. The rest of us manage to stumble away to safety. Later we rendezvous with Claudio. The police have taken his ID card and recorded all his details. He's confident it will just be a warning though: 'Everyone in Catania has done this at some time or another.'

I slip into bed at five thirty am.

'How was it?' says Gill groggily.

'Good,' I whisper, trying not to fully wake her. 'Watched lava flowing from twenty feet. Cut my leg open. And my hand. Nearly got arrested.'

'Sounds stupid,' she murmurs in her half-sleep.

Gill's right. I find out later that most of the deaths on Etna have resulted not from the immediate eruption but from clowns like me who go up for a closer look. In 1843, a sudden blast of steam killed fifty-nine people who were watching the lava flows near the town of Bronte, fifteen kilometres west of the summit. In 1979, nine sightseers were killed in something called a 'phreatic explosion'. Eight years later, the mountain claimed two more onlookers.

As it turns out, we've been scarily fortuitous with our timing. The night after our visit, a new vent on the southern slope becomes 'vigorously' active. More ash rains down on the city. A school building collapses.

One week later, renewed activity forces the re-closure of Catania's airport – 'Prisoners of Etna', reads the headline in *La Sicilia*, because nobody can leave the place. Officials even close the airport of Reggio Calabria over on the mainland.

Six weeks after it started, Etna kicks into a third gear. Fresh eruptions destroy the highest man-made structure on the mountain, the so-called Torre del Filosofo. Here in the fifth century BC, the Greek philosopher Empedocles is said to have thrown himself into the volcano, hoping people would equate his disappearance with his transformation into a god. But Etna spat one of his sandals back up to the surface, thereby foiling the ruse.

Lava spills from a new seam above Rifugio Sapienza and threatens to engulf the whole area. The flow rate is one metre every twenty seconds – much faster than what we'd witnessed up close.

On the night of 17 December, lava comes into contact

with a cistern, resulting in a powerful explosion that injures thirty-two people. Three are hospitalised with burns and lacerations from flying debris. Steps are taken to ensure the danger zone is 'hermetically closed' to anyone without authorisation. I wonder if our little run-in with the law has led to a strengthening of security measures. If so, then we at least did something right. Right?

Just before Christmas, two months after the eruptions started, things finally begin to tail off. Even then, however, it's another whole month of ashfalls and slow lava flows before Mount Etna is officially said to be quiet. For now.

The poets of Greece and Rome attributed Etna's activity to great giants thrashing about under the mountain – Enceladus and Vulcan, and Typhon with his hundred heads.

Contemporary scientists tend to take the fun out of it. The eruption, they suggest, is caused by 'a dilatational strain on the footwall of an east-facing normal fault in the Siculo–Calabrian rift zone where WNW-ESE-directed regional extension takes place'.

All I know is that after ninety-five days of eruptions, with seventy million cubic metres of pyroclastic materials ejected into the sky – enough to fill ninety thousand Olympic swimming pools – and with estimated losses amounting to almost one billion euros, it's been quite a show.

5. A trip to Syracuse

> I was told that instead of going along the coast . . . I
> should cut straight across the interior. Though it meant
> leaving out Syracuse, [we] readily yielded to this tempt-
> ing suggestion because we had heard that little now
> remained of that once glorious city but its name.
>
> – J.W. Goethe, *Italian Journey*, 1786–88

Sick to the back teeth of ash on the streets and in our courtyard, and through our hair and in our undies, in November
we decide on a daytrip to Syracuse, fifty kilometres south of
Catania, ostensibly because it's a world-renowned destination, but mostly to escape Catania's interminable volcano.

I have an ulterior motive for the trip, too. Word has just
come back from my former university that I missed out on the
lecturing position I applied for. I'm not surprised: I completely
mauled the interview, gasping like a goldfish at even the most
straightforward questions. So, while I'll keep plugging away
at the biography of the emperor Caracalla (I don't have much
choice – the advance has been spent and we don't have the
money to pay it back), I'm going to concentrate more intently
on my travel writing. And the famous city of Syracuse sounds
like just the place to furnish me with ideas for articles.

When you talk about historical cities of the Western world, Syracuse looms large. For one thing, it's hard to imagine a city as old as this one. It was occupied from as early as the thirteenth century BC. That's more than *three millennia* ago. As an Aussie, I struggle to comprehend such a time frame. Canberra was built in 1908!

The city isn't just old; in its day, it was all-powerful. After Greek colonists from Corinth seized Syracuse in 734 BC, it quickly grew in strength thanks to abundant natural resources and an advantageous harbour. A string of nasty but effective despots ensured that Syracuse kept its teeth bared at its rivals, leading to the defeat of a Carthaginian force from Africa in 480 BC. When an invading fleet from Athens was crushed seventy years later, Syracuse became the supreme city of the Mediterranean, if not the Western world. The great military historian Thucydides (c. 460–400 BC) summed things up like this: '[The Athenians] were utterly and entirely defeated; their sufferings were on an enormous scale; their losses were, as they say, total; army, navy, everything was destroyed, and, out of many, only few returned.'

Times have changed. Today, Syracuse is a modest city even by local political standards – 'a peripheral player in Sicilian affairs', according to one guidebook. Consider the Syracuse soccer team. When Gill and I visit, we find the local team languishing in the lowly fifth division of Italy's national league, playing fixtures against other Sicilian towns like Belpasso in front of a few hundred people.

That's quite a comedown from world domination.

My wife and I arrive after a two-hour train trip from Catania one Saturday morning. Outside the station, we're met by a barrage of hotel-advertising signs of varying shapes, colours and sizes. They vie desperately for attention, savage red arrows pointing in all directions. These clumps of signage grow like wildflowers in every touristy town in Italy. We're only there for the day so we don't need a place to stay. If we did, we'd probably choose the Hotel Jolly. It has a cheerful ring to it.

Syracuse spreads across a limestone terrace rising gently from a natural harbour. There are two distinct halves – the mainland, where we now stand, which combines the hurly-burly of a modern town with a slew of ancient Greek and Roman remains, and Ortygia, a small island that drips into the harbour to the south and is home to the city's Baroque churches and piazzas.

The mainland, quite frankly, is ugly. It doesn't help that Syracuse suffered thirty-six Allied bombing raids during World War II – the 1950s architecture used in the rebuilding process hasn't aged well. This was the decade, after all, that gave us design icons such as flying ducks on a wall and Mr Potato Head. Yet no amount of bombs or bad design can account for footpaths full of dog shit.

Maybe Gill and I are just having one of those days. It soon starts to rain, for one thing. There's also the dodgy *arancino* I order from a bar on Corso Gelone, the main street. As I've already described, when they're good, these buttery Sicilian rice balls are manna from heaven; when they're bad, you wouldn't serve them in a prison. Even our coffees are below par – a rare occurrence in Sicily.

Next, we make the mistake of visiting Syracuse's newest landmark. Built in 1994, the towering Santuario della Madonna delle Lacrime (Sanctuary of Madonna of the Tears) must be the only church in the world shaped like an instrument for colonic irrigation. Locals prefer to say it resembles a teardrop. Either way, at almost a hundred metres in height, it dominates the city skyline in a rather ugly fashion.

On a brighter note, it does have some ingeniously tacky souvenirs for sale in the foyer. The souvenirs commemorate the year 1953, when a statue of Mary allegedly wept tears for five days on the spot now occupied by the church. Frenzied scenes followed as thousands gathered to witness the miracle. Sick grandmothers were pushed forward – carefully, it's hoped – to be cured. Delegates from the Vatican arrived to assess whether or not the weeping was genuine. Did the statue actually cry? Did the liquid consist of real human tears? Before long, Pope Pius XII issued an official announcement: yes, the weeping Mary was authentic. This was a lucky break for the Vatican. A 'no' might have seen them deprived of a whole bunch of associated income from souvenirs.

It's easy to be cynical about weeping statues. Well, I find it easy. In 1980, a statue of Mary in northern Italy was said to have cried bloody tears, only for rumours to emerge that the owner was using his son's water pistol to squirt red-coloured liquid onto the statue's face.

(Australia, by the way, is not immune from these episodes. In 1994, tears were said to stream from a statue of Our Lady of Fatima located in the Sydney suburb of Rooty Hill.

I'm not sure how many pilgrims flocked to Rooty Hill when they heard this news, but I bet they didn't stay long.)

Among the souvenirs, Gill takes a liking to the ceramic heads of the Virgin complete with glued-on plastic teardrops. I enjoy the collection of 'magic' portraits made from ridged plastic: tilt them left and they show the Madonna without tears; tilt them right and she weeps. I also pick up all the Mary snow domes and give them a good shake. After sifting through every item and raising the hopes of the sweet little nuns manning the stalls that we might actually buy something, we wander away and enter the church proper.

It's a cavernous yet soulless affair. Of mild interest is the crumbling Roman wall that remains in situ in the middle of the congregation space. I also like the fully automated confession booths: simply choose your desired language from a panel of labelled buttons and a pre-recorded message absolves you of your sins in words you can readily understand. (Sinners from Japan take note: there is no button for your language.)

The presence of these booths is indicative of a problem facing Catholicism in the world today: a shortage of priests. Young people are increasingly turning away from even attending church, let alone pursuing a career in one. As many as ninety-seven per cent of the Italian population might claim to be Catholic, but far less than a third of that number actually attend mass. Papal thermometer factories are cutting production. The Vatican isn't doing much to help overcome the scarcity of priests: not only does it refuse to allow women to do the job, but its own birth rate is a sluggish zero. Now might be the time to buy shares in automated confession booths.

I will say this for the Sanctuary of Madonna of the Tears: the rose garden out the back is delightful.

Across the road from the giant rectal pump sits a more traditional piece of religious architecture: the crumbling remnants of the Church of St John the Evangelist. As we pass by, two local teenagers are locking lips against one of its walls, inadvertently pressing a trail of powdered stone into their clothes for their friends to tease them about later.

The church has an eerie feel to it. Maybe it's the skull and crossbones carved into the lintel above an ancient archway, or maybe it's the memory of Saint Marcian, the first bishop of Syracuse, who was tied to a pillar on this spot and flogged to death by the Romans eighteen centuries ago. Back then, the Basilica sat atop a vast underground burial chamber for Christians. Bodies were laid on concrete slabs along a maze of passageways lit by oil lanterns. In Italy, only the catacombs in Rome cover a greater area than those of Syracuse. And for a couple of euros, anyone can go down and take a look.

Except today. A makeshift sign reads '*Chiuso*' (closed). I love creeping around in catacombs, so this comes as a crushing blow. Genuine tears well in my eyes. Later I realise there's no need to fret. English poet and writer Lawrence Durrell visited the same catacombs in the 1970s and left unimpressed: 'a coal-mine would have offered the same spectacle'.

In an attempt to turn our day around, Gill and I duck into a tourist office for some tips on seeing the best of the city. The place is a paragon of efficiency. When we approach the counter, an older employee with a heavy moustache plies us with brochures. She couldn't be more helpful.

Something about these brochures soon catches my eye: they seem remarkably frank. So, the endless petrochemical zone that lies to the north of the city is not only mentioned in detail, but criticised as a place of 'throbbing industrial noise'. The architectural styles of the post-World War II period are similarly lambasted. Other disappointments are listed, with the accompanying rationale that to deny these things would be 'useless'. What a refreshing change to see a city's dirty laundry aired in a tourist brochure. Normally the PR spin in this kind of literature can be measured in g-forces. Certainly that was my experience in China. There, even some two-bit, crumbling truck-stop town would be touted as worth a visit, lauded for its suspect local cuisine ('eight-treasure lotus-seed glutinous rice!') and given a meaningless accolade ('Designated among the Central Government's Fifteen Special Municipalities!'). A friend in northeast China once paid good money for an excursion to a border area near North Korea, including a visit to a 'Korean palace'. It sounded interesting. After a torrid ten-hour bus ride, though, he arrived in a dingy town which, while undoubtedly full of Koreans, didn't appear to have a palace in sight. When questioned, his tour leader explained that the itinerary contained a slight spelling mistake; they had arrived, as planned, at a 'Korean *place*'.

As I'm reading the frank descriptions of Syracuse's uglier side, I think of the oft-quoted words of Renato Guttuso, the island's most famous twentieth-century painter: 'In Sicily you can find dramas, pastorals, idylls, politics, gastronomy, geography, history, literature . . . in the end you can find anything and everything, but you can't find truth.' Actually, Signor Guttuso, you can. Try the ATP Tourist Office in Syracuse.

Buoyed by this bout of sincerity and freshly armed with info, we cross busy Viale Teracati to the most popular tourist attraction in Syracuse, the Neapolis Archaeological Park.

Typical of all the major sites in Sicily, the approach to the park has been transformed into a narrow alley (which I dub 'The Gauntlet') designed to funnel visitors past a series of shops and tents selling souvenir tat at astronomical prices.

The most popular item for sale seems to be a man's barbeque apron superimposed with a life-sized image of Michelangelo's David so that at first glance the wearer appears to have the physique of a Greek Adonis – albeit with an incredibly tiny penis. There's a similarly themed apron for the ladies, featuring an image of a busty Italian woman wearing nothing but a slice of vine-ripened tomato over each nipple and a bouquet of basil over her nether region. I subconsciously find myself ordering Caprese salads for the next week or so.

Mercifully, two-thirds of the shops in The Gauntlet are closed. It's November: the high season is well and truly finished. Even better, the archaeological park itself is empty. After handing over our four-euro entry fee and then wandering a short distance along a dirt path, we discover we have the fifth-century-BC Greek theatre entirely to ourselves.

What a stunning chunk of ruins. Hewn directly from the natural stone slope, the semicircular theatre is one of the largest and best-preserved of its kind. Almost twenty thousand audience members could fit into its wedge-shaped seating bays at a time.

What did they watch? The plays of Aeschylus, among others. Known as 'the father of tragic drama', Aeschylus made regular trips from Athens to Sicily, and to Syracuse in particular. But the island would be his undoing. The play-wright was killed here in 456 BC, when a tortoise fell on his head. More specifically, an eagle mistook his bald head for a rock and dropped a tortoise on it in an attempt to crack the creature's shell. Laughable as the tale seems (indeed, it's considered a myth), there's apparently a vulture called the lammergeier in this region which does exactly that – drops tortoises onto rocks to crack them open. So, a tip for bald readers travelling to Sicily: pack a wig.

Our silent reverie in the Greek theatre is interrupted by an American family of four. In what a playwright might refer to as dramatic irony, the first words I hear uttered on this stage where solemn choruses held capacity crowds enthralled two and a half thousand years ago are: 'GIT ON BACK HERE 'N QUIT YER HOLLERIN'!'

It's the father of the family, yelling at his young son who is playing the clown on the far side of the ruins. These people seem at odds with their surrounds. I wonder if what they actually booked was a holiday in Syracuse, Kansas – maybe for a Monster Truck rally being held there – only for the travel agent to press the wrong button on the computer.

What is it with my bad luck in ancient theatres? I've been to half a dozen across Europe, and each time my divine silence has been rudely shattered by fellow travellers. Worst was my visit to the theatre at Ephesus, Turkey: as I sat alone on a marble pew, contemplating the astonishing history of the place, an entire class of primary-school children walked onto the stage and started playing their recorders.

Gill and I leave the theatre to Cletus and his kids and continue along a sandy path to the Quarry of Paradise, a fertile hollow lined with cliffs and teeming with lemon groves and other vegetation. As we descend into the hollow, Gill says, 'It reminds me of that place in South Australia.'

'What place?'

'That little valley in the middle of Mount Gambier – the one with the flower gardens in it.'

'The Umpherston Sinkhole?'

'Right.'

Gill has an uncanny knack of comparing famous historical locations with Australia's most mundane country towns. Later when we visit Sicily's hilltop settlement of Enna – ruled successively by Greeks, Carthaginians, Romans and Byzantines – she takes one look and says, 'It's a bit like Toowoomba.'

The early afternoon weather is improving. We enjoy a somnolent stroll through the greenery of the Quarry of Paradise, following a series of winding paths, stopping occasionally to display our astounding ignorance with respect to botanical matters.

'These trees with the pink flowers, are they . . . almonds?'

'Not certain. Maybe. But where are the nuts?'

'Hmmm. They could be magnolias.'

'I thought magnolias had white flowers.'

'I think they can have both.'

'But don't magnolias grow in bushes, not on trees?'

'Trees, I think.'

How embarrassing. I feel completely inadequate when reading other authors on Sicily. They're always so descriptive about the native flora. The American Mary Taylor Simeti, who relocated to Sicily in the 1960s and has written reams about the place, lists enough flower types on a single page of *On Persephone's Island* to leave the reader sneezing: daffodil, hyacinth, calendula, bougainvillea, daisy, borage, campion, camomile, wood sorrel. Are there really that many flower varieties in the world?

Considering how it was employed in antiquity, the Quarry of Paradise is a misnomer. In the fifth century BC, the place served as a brutal limestone mine where prisoners of war toiled for years. The historian Thucydides writes of bodies 'heaped together on top of one another' and an unimaginable odour of death. Apparently, the only way to secure release from this hellhole was by proving your Greekness and reciting a verse of Euripides from memory.

Cut into a wall of the Quarry, Gill and I find one of Syracuse's most famous landmarks, the so-called 'Ear of Dionysius'. This giant man-made cave, seven storeys high and extending sixty-five metres back into the cliff, was allegedly used by Dionysius, tyrant-king of Syracuse in the fourth century BC, as a kind of eavesdropping device. The perfect acoustics allowed him to listen to the conversations of prisoners working the quarries. Presumably he heard lots of them practising verses of Euripides.

I can't help but test the renowned acoustics for myself. Off I run into the cave, clapping my hands, screaming curse words, and attempting to belch the alphabet all in one go.

Gill puts a stop to things: 'GIT ON BACK HERE 'N QUIT YER HOLLERIN'!'

Beyond the Greek theatre and the Quarry of Paradise, the archaeological park thins out into overgrown fields dotted here and there with pine trees. One field contains the remains of the Altar of Hieron II, a giant slab of stone employed by the ancients for appeasing Zeus with ritual slaughter. This was the largest altar ever built, as big as twenty tennis courts side by side. Four hundred bulls could be dispatched on the stone slab in a single day: that's a lot of steaming innards.

'Dare you to lick it,' I say to Gill.

If you've ever wondered what happened to the animals killed at a Greek sacrifice, by the way, be assured they weren't left to rot in a pile on the altar. They were roasted and eaten. Very little was actually offered to the gods – maybe a bone here and a lump of fat there. The rest was carved up and devoured by thousands of hungry people in tunics and sandals. Sacrifices in ancient Greece were part solemn ceremony, part community Sausage Sizzle.

Before leaving the archaeological park, we sit in the mossy remains of the nearby Roman amphitheatre for a ploughman's lunch of bread, cheese, prosciutto and fruit. We're joined by a pair of fat, greying hounds who fix their rheumy gaze on our spread. Like me, they've got eyes mostly for the prosciutto.

Back on Corso Gelone, Gill stops for dessert at a gelato van. She orders a scoop of *stracciatella* (chocolate chip) in a cup.

'Want one?' she asks.

'No, thanks,' I answer.

After she places her order, I add, 'Can you ask for two spoons?'

Gill's eyes narrow suspiciously. It's the same look I give her whenever we're in a fast food restaurant and she announces, 'I don't want fries,' only to end up reaching across with great regularity to take a handful from my carton. Marriage counsellors must hear a lot of this kind of thing.

Ten minutes later, we cross the Ponte Santa Lucia Nuova into Ortygia. The bridge is named after Saint Lucy, the city's patron saint. Lucy was a young, virginal and charitable woman who lived in Syracuse around AD 300. She was also a devout Christian, so the Romans stabbed her in the throat with a dagger and gouged her eyes out. She's now the patron saint of the blind – though, oddly enough, not of the sore-throated.

The name 'Ortygia' means quail, and was chosen by the ancients either because of the prevalence of the birds in the area, or because they thought the island was shaped like a quail. Can't see it myself. I prefer the description by travel writer Peter Moore, who with a nice Aussie flourish refers to Ortygia as a 'lamb cutlet-shaped appendix'.

Although barely a kilometre wide and a couple long, Ortygia has more amazing architecture and weighty history crammed into its tiny squares and alleys than some entire countries. In particular, it's a showpiece for two more recent epochs in the city's history – the Spanish Aragon period of the thirteenth and fourteenth centuries and the Baroque period of the seventeenth and eighteenth centuries.

The first stunning indication of this is at Piazza Archimede, a cobbled square flanked by elegant *palazzi* and studded with haughty cafés. Its centrepiece is a gushing Baroque fountain with a statue of Diana, goddess of the hunt, surrounded by sea nymphs, rearing horses and the kind of water jets that a dopey dog would snap at for hours.

The piazza itself takes its name from one of Syracuse's most famous citizens, the Greek mathematician Archimedes (c. 287–212 BC). He's the one who cried, '*Eureka!*' ('I've got it!') in the bathtub after discovering a nasty rash that clients of a local courtesan had been coming down with. Or so I remember from my studies.

Archimedes was a science whiz. He closely predicted the value of pi, explained how levers work, invented pulley systems to lift heavy objects, and developed the 'Archimedes screw' (the courtesan again?). He even calculated the number of grains of sand required to fill the universe: 8×10^{63}. That's a big number: an eight followed by sixty-three zeros. Let's be honest, though: as brilliant as Archimedes was, surely he plucked this figure from thin air. Can't you picture him now, sitting at his desk, jiggling his sandalled leg, glancing over a shoulder to check that nobody's watching, then adding a few extra zeros to the scroll?

Archimedes died at the hands of the Romans when they besieged Syracuse in 212 BC, but not before he devised a series of fiendish war machines to deploy against them. One was a pyromaniac's dream – an intricate system of mirrors designed to channel the sun's rays into a single powerful beam and destroy the enemy fleet by fire. I bet he practised on ants. These days, whole television programs like *Myth-Busters* and *Superweapons of the Ancient World* set about reconstructing models of Archimedes' various siege weapons and testing them to see if they really would have worked. I suppose this serves as an ongoing compliment to his many achievements – even if, just quietly, it turns out that his fire ray was a bit of a dud.

Three minutes' walk from Piazza Archimede is an even bigger, even better public space, Piazza del Duomo. If some cruel overlord allowed me to drink only a single cup of coffee during my time in Sicily, I'd probably choose to have it in one of the expensive cafés lining Piazza del Duomo. When Gill and I first walk across the square, we do so in a kind of dazed pirouette.

Occupying one side of the square is the *duomo* itself – Ortygia's cathedral – perfectly representing the rich tapestry of Syracusan history. It's astounding how many successive invaders have had their mitts on this building. There are hints of a Bronze Age altar, a Greek temple, an early Christian church and a Saracen mosque; the apse is decorated with Norman mosaics; the chestnut-wood ceiling is Spanish.

Despite all this, once we pass beyond the flamboyant wedding-cake façade (Baroque, by the way), the interior seems disappointingly drab. Making up for the lack of colour is the crowd gathering for a baptism. You've never seen so many impeccably outfitted and beautiful people together in one location. I know Italians go out of their way to look the part, but this is like a scene from an Armani catalogue. The baby looks like it's been crafted from the best bits of other perfect babies. The women, meanwhile, are all in stilettos. How they negotiate Ortygia's hundreds of severely cobbled lanes, I've no idea.

Gill and I hobble down one such lane, emerging a hundred metres later at the ocean promenade on Ortygia's western edge. Here, where the Ionian Sea washes against the sand-coloured walls of the tiny island, is the famous Fonte Aretusa (Arethusa's Spring). This freshwater pool, about twenty metres across, sinks like a broad well into the middle of the promenade. Locals walk around it like a manhole in their path; tourists stop for photos.

The wine-dark water of the pool is fed by a spring that has flowed since antiquity. You can lean over a railing, watching fat ducks skim across the surface below, or walk down a flight of stairs to water level and feed them. Gill and I do the latter. I'd like to go on the record and say that feeding ducks is an entirely soothing and underrated experience and I wish I did more of it. Gill enjoys it, too – enough to forgive me for eating most of her gelato half an hour earlier.

A thatch of bedraggled papyrus rises from the water and flutters in the breeze. Syracuse is the only place outside Africa where papyrus grows wild. As recently as the eighteenth century, it was cultivated for paper. If you enjoy whole museums dedicated to grass, by all means visit Syracuse's Museo del Papiro for more information on this. We don't, so we didn't.

According to Greek myth, the waters of the Fonte Aretusa derive from the tears of a nymph who became distraught after her mistress Persephone was abducted by Hades, God of the Underworld. On a later daytrip, Gill and I will stumble upon the spot where this abduction took place, a hundred kilometres inland near the town of Enna.

That's what happens in Sicily. You'll casually wander past a modest hill or an unprepossessing patch of grass that turns out to be the setting for one of the most influential myths or episodes in world history. Brock and I played a game of basketball one afternoon on a seaside court north of Catania, only to learn later that it was where Odysseus moored his ships before encountering the one-eyed giant, Polyphemus.

Gill has wandered away. I toss a final chunk of bread to a hungry duck and leave the pool, too. The weather is brighter now. A shaft of autumn light finally finds a gap in the mottled late-afternoon sky, revealing Ortygia's pink-and-peach *palazzi* in all their splendour. Yet the sunshine also spotlights centuries of wear and tear – cracked architraves, rusted balconies and leprous stucco. Somehow, though, the blemishes only enhance the beauty. Meanwhile a schoolboy rowing crew drifts around the southern tip of Ortygia, where a medieval castle sits like a sentinel on the point. Sparrows orbit the clock tower of a desiccated church.

Suddenly I realise why the travel brochures are so candid about the ugly outlying areas of Syracuse. They can afford to be.

I find Gill again, sitting on a harbourside bench, basking

under the newly emerged sun, and examining a map of Syracuse.

'Wow. There's something I don't see every day,' I comment.

'What?'

'You looking at a map.'

'What's so strange about that?'

'You *hate* maps. Imagine coming home one day and finding me playing one of your *Sex and the City* DVDs.'

'Okay. That *would* be strange.'

I plonk myself beside her with the local newspaper and flip through the sports pages. It's all football, of course. Syracuse's fifth-division team is about to play against Cavese, from Campania on the mainland. Cavese appear to be fielding a team of the city's best bakers, judging by the names in their squad – I see a Panini (Bread Rolls), a Mangiapane (Bread-Eater) and a Quattropane (Four-Breads).

'I've heard you can make lots of dough playing fifth-division football,' I remark to Gill.

She wanders away again.

We catch a five pm bus back to Catania. It's full of excited young Syracusans heading for the big smoke, priming themselves for a night in the clubs and bars of Sicily's second-biggest city. The bus driver plays a soundtrack of Europop to get everyone in the mood.

Our mood, on the other hand, is best described as dark – and not solely because of the Europop. Contemplating our day, Gill and I realise that Syracuse has completely won us over. As Italian towns go, it's much closer to the vision we shared for our year abroad than busy Catania.

Plus, our apartment is *really* beginning to give us the shits.

6. Renting

> I woke up one morning and my girlfriend asked me if I
> slept good. I said 'No, I made a few mistakes.'
> – Steven Wright, American comedian and actor

Gill and I should be at it like rabbits. We've only been married a couple of months. Sicily is our honeymoon! Now, though, we've stopped sleeping in the same bed.

Technically we haven't slept in the same bed since leaving Australia. But the situation has deteriorated. Gill now regularly spends most of each night not in her cold single metal bed in the bedroom but in a sleeping bag on the floor of our L-shaped corridor. And while occasional sex on cold tiles is fine with us, the elbows tend to suffer. More often than not, Gill avoids our apartment entirely and instead sleeps on a couch at our friend Natasha's place. An abstinent honeymoon isn't what we'd envisaged. Italy, after all, is a fairly lusty place.

It has always been so. Consider the Romans: I've read passages of Roman literature that even today would win 'Letter of the Month' in *Playboy*. While other civilisations were still struggling with the notion of fire, educated men of Rome were reading scrolls of the most blush-inducing nature, for example this from Petronius' *Satyricon* (written in the first century

AD): 'Oenothea brought out a leather dildo: this she rubbed with oil and ground pepper and crushed nettle seed, and began inserting it gradually up my anus . . . The vicious old woman then sprinkled my thighs with this liquid. She mixed the juice of cress with some southern-wood, and after soaking my genitals in it, she took a green nettle-stalk and began whipping me steadily everywhere below the navel.' In similar vein, anyone who has gazed upon a wall at Pompeii near Naples will have noted a predisposition in antiquity for the painting of phalluses; one memorable image portrays the god Priapus with his enormous cock flopped fish-like onto a weighing tray.

Italians emerge as a randy lot in more recent history, too. One name: Giacomo Girolamo Casanova de Seingalt. Casanova's career as one of the world's great womanisers reputedly began at the age of eleven at school, when he got a hand-job from the sister of his teacher.

Italian cinema is also pretty saucy. I'm thinking, for instance, of the pleasingly dimensioned Sophia Loren performing a smoky striptease for Marcello Mastroianni in the 1963 film *Ieri, Oggi, Domani* (*Yesterday, Today and Tomorrow*). And how about Cicciolina, the porn-star-turned-MP who tried to end the Gulf War by essentially offering herself to Saddam Hussein? Blimey. There aren't too many politicians like *that* in Australia.

It's presumably for these reasons that Italy – rather than, say, North Korea – is regularly described as 'the sexiest country in the world'. Foreigners flock here seeking a slice of this passion. Often they find it. From the travel memoirs I've read, it seems a foreign woman need only ask for help with the plumbing in her Tuscan villa and before she knows it a brooding worker named Salvatore is cleaning out the pipes, so to speak.

It's the same for male authors. Off they toddle to Tuscany, only to be immediately hit upon by a leggy waitress after ordering *bruschetta* at a restaurant in the village square. (The waitress usually turns out to be the daughter of a local official, with riotous ramifications!)

Gill and I are admittedly in a different position. For one thing, we're a newly married couple with no intention of having our pipes inspected by anyone but each other. There's also the issue of money: we have none. Those villa owners and Tuscan 'sea changers' tend to be flush with cash, hence the endless champagne lunches and their libidinous aftermaths. And it's not like we want to replicate the sex lives of the Roman elite; certainly I'm not lining up to have my anus penetrated by a dildo dipped in nettles.

All I'm saying is that it would be nice if Italy's long history of rigorously pursued passion brushed off on Gill and me. Instead, we find ourselves in an apartment that renders sleep – and, with it, romance – an impossibility. It's less a case of 'That's Amore!' and more a case of 'What's Amore?'

At first we don't really notice the noise problem. Certain quirky sounds are only mildly irritating, even amusing: our rusty bed-springs that yelp like a lonely dog with every movement; the over-zealous fruit vendor with his loudhailer each morning; the woman upstairs who gets around in her clogs every day.

Oh, haven't I mentioned Clog Woman before? Just back from vacation in Holland, it seems, with a wearable pair of souvenirs. *Clomp*, *clomp*, *clomp*, for hours on end. When it gets too much, Gill takes our broom (the one we use to sweep all the volcanic ash from the internal courtyard) and bangs the handle on the ceiling to send a message through to the second floor. I stand in the background with a grimace, hoping the lady's husband isn't a 'man of honour'.

Usually, though, we can't hear the clogs over the traffic. I did hope to avoid harping on about Italian driving. It's tricky though. Do you remember playing that game as a kid where you close your eyes, spin around a hundred times, and attempt to walk in a straight line? Italians, it seems, like to play that game just before they drive.

With eccentric speed and direction comes an overuse of horns. Drivers in Catania don't settle for a simple *meep! meep!* either. They lean on the button for so long you begin to think they might be slumped against the dashboard with blood leaking out of one ear.

Our apartment cops it more than most. Via Gesuiti isn't a main road by any means; in fact, as our street sign indicates it's been designated a 'zone of limited traffic' because of the surrounding archaeological sites. Yet this only encourages the more impatient locals to use the road as a shortcut. Now, when you've got speedy Italian drivers coming towards a blind intersection from four directions with no 'Give Way' sign, the result is inevitable. It's a *festa della honk*. Every car, scooter, van and truck passes our apartment with its horn depressed.

And depressed is the word. We're fairly stoic people, Gill

and I. Before coming to Italy, we lived in a city of millions in northeast China – not the quietest place on the planet (China is the land of chopsticks, giant pandas, and workmen using power tools between midnight and five am). It will take more than a tootle or two to throw us off our game. And during the day we don't particularly care that our apartment sounds like pit lane at a Grand Prix circuit.

At night, though, things are different. Late in the evening, traffic naturally becomes much lighter, the beeping more sporadic. Yet this is inestimably worse. As we drift off to sleep, a shrill blast of horn pierces the darkness; we shoot bolt upright like Uma Thurman after her adrenalin injection in *Pulp Fiction*. Five minutes later, the same thing happens; again and again, throughout the night.

We live right on the intersection – and I mean *right on*. Italian *palazzi* are built virtually flush against the road, with almost no footpath. Our bed is a single metre from the rumbling exhausts of passing traffic. Closing the windows doesn't help. The ancient glass panels are wafer-thin for one thing, but they're also badly cracked and the seals have crumbled away. (Don't get me started on the issue of security.) One window is actually missing a plate-sized piece of glass at the top. Our apartment sucks great columns of street noise in through this hole, like it's inhaling a cigarette.

The final straw, though, is the Ultras Ghetto.

The word 'ultra' comes from the Latin term for 'beyond'; in Italy it refers to a football fan whose zeal in supporting a team is beyond the norm. That's saying something. Here, even a run-of-the-mill football fan is called a *tifoso*, a word etymologically linked to *tifo* (typhus), suggesting a feverish attachment to the game. Ultras take this devotion to a whole new level. In English, we might say 'hooligan', but your average ultra would possibly be offended by the comparison. And you do *not* want to offend an ultra.

Ultras band together in groups of different names – almost like Roman legions – each with its own flag, symbol or catchcry. On game day, they gather in a particular section, or *curva* (curve), of the stadium. There, they light flares, chant, fight with opposition supporters, and occasionally skirmish with police. Many Italian ultras hold strong political views, usually as far right as you can get. Seeing Nazi salutes and swastika logos isn't out of the question.

Supporters of Catania's team, Club Calcio Catania (the Rossazzurra – 'Red and Blues'), are no less zealous than elsewhere in Italy. Each home game, played at the city's notorious Cibali Stadium, attracts tens of thousands of ultras. I go along to one such game – Catania versus Naples – and watch as a mob of ultras, many of them in makeshift balaclavas, smash a hole in the five-metre-high plastic barrier between the crowd and the playing surface, prompting fifty police to set upon them with truncheons and snarling German Shepherds.

Most of the groups have violent names: Drunks, Thugs, Kamikaze, Feroci, Virus, Lobotomy Boys, Sharks, Falange d'Assalto (Phalanx of Assault). Unluckily for Gill and me, another of these groups, the Ultras Ghetto, maintains its headquarters in a noisy garage just thirty metres from our bedroom window.

We soon learn that one of the conditions of joining the Ultras Ghetto – aside from a love of Catania, a knowledge of football and, if possible, a college degree in explosives – is an appetite for regular, late-night parties. Night after night, these guys celebrate like strikers after scoring a goal. At two am, one of them will be busy letting off firecrackers while another cranks his motorbike into action so he can perform *un doughnut*.

It's even worse on game night. Catania scored a 3–1 victory over Salernitana shortly after we moved into our apartment. The Ultras Ghetto went ballistic. Police were called that night; in fact, they are routinely called. Many times I peer out our window at midnight to see a *carabinieri* car parked on the street outside the headquarters, lights flashing. Maybe they're members.

Why don't I just bang on their door and tell them all to shut their mouths? Quite frankly, because they'd kill me. If the actual Ultras Ghetto members resemble the fellow portrayed in their logo (menacing eyes, long knife scar down one cheek), then they must all have done jail time at some point. On a wall near the headquarters is a line of graffiti reading, '*ULTRAS. ODIAMO TUTTI.*' ('Ultras. We hate everyone.')

So, we endure. Or try to.

Studies have shown that sleep deprivation reduces cortisol secretion and stirs activity on the hypothalamic-pituitary-adrenal axis which, among other things, regulates a person's moods.

What does this mean in practical terms? It means that someone as mild-mannered as me (I've never thrown a punch in my life) can lie in bed listening to the morning tolling of church bells – generally considered one of the more pleasant sounds in the world – with teeth grinding and sweat dripping, before finally hurling the covers aside and announcing, 'If those bells don't stop ringing, I swear I'm going to march over to that church and SMASH SOMEONE'S FUCKING FACE IN.' This is a *House of God* I'm talking about. What's happening to me? I'm displaying enough rage to qualify for Ultras Ghetto membership.

Gill's exhaustion manifests in different ways. Each day I see her skin grow paler and her expression more desperate as the hours of lost slumber add up. She tries earplugs; they don't work. She tries buying a fan to see if the drone of the motor might subsume the street noise; no luck. She tries, as I've mentioned, dragging a sleeping bag into the L-shaped corridor near the bathroom. But it's far from comfortable out there, and the incessant drip of our antique showerhead has the effect of a Japanese water torture: *Plink . . . Plink . . . Plink . . . Plink . . .* The plinking forms a chorus with the clomping of the clogs upstairs; and then another Vespa zips by, horn blaring.

I hold a crisis meeting with Gill's boss, Palmina. She's the one who lined up the rental apartment before we arrived. She's our conduit to the landlady. After consultation, the nun finally agrees to have our bedroom windows repaired, with better seals and no holes. This is duly done, but the decibel levels barely change.

So we start sleeping around, pouncing on the merest

whiff of alternative accommodation. First, a few nights in one of Palmina's spare rooms. It's a kind offer, especially as things are a little frosty between us over the apartment debacle. Gill finds it a little weird staying at the boss's place, but it's a blessed relief to catch some zees.

We also sleep over at Claudio's place, or Brock's, if they happen to go away for the weekend. This is variously successful. At one place, I get six solid hours but Gill is eaten alive by mosquitoes. At the other, Gill is fine but the metal crossbar of the bedframe burrows directly into my spine, causing some kind of neurological impairment whereby, for the first thirty minutes after waking, I speak like Rocky Balboa.

Most nights, though, Gill sleeps on Natasha's couch.

It's no sanctuary, either. Tash has some apartment issues of her own. Initially she was put up in a studio apartment even smaller than our L-shaped corridor. Desperate to move, she said yes to a two-bedroom place not far from Via Gesuiti.

Tash's new landlord is a forty-two-year-old local sculptor who has decided to live in Amsterdam for six months 'to find inspiration'. If only he'd taken some of his crap with him. Every corner of the place is cluttered with metal knick-knacks, pointy African titbits, heavy djembe drums and jagged crystals. It's a battle not to lose an eye. One piece of his 'art' even swings from the ceiling by a string. The temptation to swing at it like a piñata almost overwhelms me.

I won't say much about Tash's other apartment nightmare – a recurring (and odorous) plumbing problem – or she'll die of embarrassment. Tash is prone to prudishness. It's something I enjoy exploiting. One day we're discussing a colleague, an English teacher who is struggling to find students for her private home classes.

'Yeah,' says Tash, 'her privates have completely dried up.'

'They have a gel for that now,' I reply.

Tash turns bright pink and whacks me in the shoulder. 'SHAMUS! I mean her private *classes!*'

Meanwhile, I stay alone in the Via Gesuiti apartment, listening to the loud staccato of horns and the shouts of raucous football supporters, waiting for the sun to come up and the church bells to toll and the greengrocer to start bellowing into his loudhailer.

The only permanent solution is to sever the rental agreement and move. Thus begins our search for new digs. Every Tuesday morning I wander up to our neighbourhood general store on Via G. Clementi and pay €1.85 for a weekly newspaper called *Il Mercatino* – the equivalent of a *Trading Post* in Australia.

For some inexplicable reason, the front page of each issue features a section called '*Animali*' – pets and animal accessories for sale – as though these are the most important things that one can trade in Catania.

'We could get an Alaskan malamute,' I say to Gill over breakfast.

'How much?'

'Two hundred euros.'

'Hmm. Maybe.'

'Or a *pappagallo* – excellent condition, eighty-five euros. Comes with a cage.' We look up *pappagallo* in our dictionary. It means parrot.

Then we get back to the task at hand. Page two is our page – '*Immobili*' (real estate) – including a list of places for rent. At first it's a confronting jumble of abbreviated Italian: '*Bivani e 1/2 + accessori, III piano, affitasi €260 mensili.*' But we soon become accustomed to the lingo of house hunting.

'This could be us,' one of us says. '*Ideale per single o coppia*. Plus, it's just been *ristrutturato*.'

'Yes,' the other chimes in, glancing across at the ad, 'but it also has a *terrazza panoramica*. Too expensive!'

Once we know what to look for, out comes the red marker pen and we circle any properties that sound worthy of investigation.

Apartment 1: 'Secure neighbourhood'

The truly interesting thing, I discover, is not the type of phrases that are listed in the paper but the ones that are omitted. For example, it would have been helpful if the first apartment we visited had included in its *Il Mercatino* blurb the words 'prison views'.

The apartment itself, on Via Ala in the north of the city, is lovely. But from the kitchen window I can see Catania's biggest high-security prison just fifty metres away, with its rolls of razor wire and black-booted guards packing machine guns. Gill is horrified. I try to look on the bright side. 'Perhaps I could start a little cigarette racket; you know, make some money on the side.'

'And what if there's a mass breakout of murderers?' she asks.

I give this some thought. 'Look,' I reason finally, 'if someone escapes from jail, he's hardly going to knock on the door of the closest house – he'll be too busy trying to get away. So, this is probably the *safest* place for us to live.'

Gill fails to connect with my logic.

Apartment 2: 'Quirky interior'

The second apartment we circle in *Il Mercatino* is a stuffy little box that hangs from the side of a building like the toilet of a Red Sea dhow. It's also close to the prison, though thankfully out of eyeshot. Gill is teaching at the time, so I inspect the place alone. Something rubs me the wrong way from the start; maybe it's the shadowy individuals lurking on the street corners outside. I figure they're on day release. Or it might be the anarchy symbols spray-painted onto either side of the front door. Or perhaps it's just the apartment itself, nothing more than a stained living room with a sink in one corner, a bed in another, and a toilet in a closet. A shared door in the middle of one wall leads to someone else's premises. I see movement in the gap beneath the door and try to imagine what's happening in there – it's a bit like a virtual Rorschach Test. My guess? Two hoodlums rolling a corpse in a carpet.

The clincher, though, is the tattered and yellowing poster on the wall with a picture of New York's Twin Towers and a slogan written in cheerful cursive across the middle: 'The Big Apple!' Just what everyone wants in an apartment: a creepy little reminder of the war on terror every time they come home from work.

Not that I work.

Apartment 3: 'Renovator's dream'

The third property is right up in the northwest of the city, where the ambling ascent to Mount Etna becomes steeper and the volcano a little closer. From Piazza Duomo it takes forty-five minutes walking uphill at a decent clip. But I enjoy rising out of Catania's claustrophobic *centro*. Turning around to look back over the city, I spy a blue band of ocean above the black-stone *palazzi* and cathedral domes. What a tonic, the Mediterranean! I feel invigorated, like the ancient Greeks finally reaching the coast after marching through Mesopotamia, and shouting, '*Thalassa! Thalassa!*' ('The sea! The sea!')

It's a good thing the walk gives me pleasure, because I have to do it twice. The landlord doesn't turn up on the first day. The following day, at my insistence, he arrives on time. He brings a bunch of flowers by way of apology. (Not really – he just gives me a terse look and unlocks the door to the apartment.)

Inside, we clamber over piles of plastic piping and stacks of tiles and into a dusty hole filled with workmen's tools.

'So, when will it be finished?' I ask the landlord.

His eyes narrow. 'It *is* finished.'

I can smell sawdust and open cans of paint. Bundles of electrical wire sprout from concrete walls.

'Okay,' I say. 'When will it be *more* finished?'

I don't mind 'industrial chic', but this guy is taking the piss.

Apartment 4: 'God bless this home'

The fourth apartment belongs to an elderly gentleman who deserves a mention in the Guinness Book of Records: 'World's

Biggest Collection of Religious Iconography'. (He might also challenge for 'World's Deafest Man'.) Every inch of wall and mantelpiece is occupied by a holy painting, poster or plaque. If I were Catholic I'd be crossing myself for an hour.

'I like all your ornaments,' I comment politely when the man welcomes me inside.

'*Eh?*'

'I SAID, I LIKE ALL YOUR ORNAMENTS.'

In fact, they make me feel uneasy: like the time in Shanghai when I interviewed a woman with the world's largest private collection of snow domes. Yes, those round plastic baubles filled with fake snow. Terrifying!

Thankfully, this particular apartment is the fellow's own home – the one for rent is back downstairs and across a courtyard. It's on the bottom floor, austere and windowless. You've never seen a whiter apartment. Every surface is white formica. The only pieces of furniture – a plastic table and chair in one corner – are white. ('Picture the set of *Gattaca*,' I tell Gill later.)

I don't mind the sci-fi vibe, to be honest, but unfortunately the cons far outweigh the pros. In any case, the old man wants a full-year contract and won't budge at anything less (once I've yelled the question at him a few times). We'll only be in Catania for another nine months.

More never-to-be-repeated opportunities!

We'll be in Catania for a lot less than nine months if the right apartment doesn't come along in a hurry. But the disappointments continue to stack up. Most frustrating are the times when we actually say 'yes' to a place, only to be denied for one reason or another.

Gill meets a Sicilian–Australian girl who says she has a spare room in an apartment on Via Consolazione – miles from Gill's work, but by now we don't care. We take a look and like it. But when Gill calls the next day to confirm, the girl has changed her mind. The offer is off the table. Something must have bothered her at the inspection and I can only assume it was me. Maybe it was the leftover bits of breakfast cereal in my beard.

On my next solo mission, I find the perfect place.

'Excellent,' I say to the owner. 'So, it's three hundred and eight euros, right?' Eight euros over our budget, but worth the extra expense.

'Three hundred and eight?' he says. 'No, no, no. It's *three hundred and eighty-eight*.'

The '308' was a printing error in *Il Mercatino*.

A few days later, I find an even more perfect place. This time I actually shake hands with the landlord and scamper off to the bank to withdraw the first month's rent. While I'm gone, a leggy blonde happens by the apartment and asks if it's available. She's already paying the advance when I return. The oily landlord gives me a glance that says, 'I had no choice, my friend. Take a *look* at this *signorina*!'

The situation is getting desperate. We're now heavily sleep deprived, almost narcoleptic. (For the record, 'narcoleptic' is an anagram of Eric Clapton, whose music causes the disorder.) One day we even decide to leave Catania. In my diary I formulate an escape plan that involves flying to

London to stay with Gill's brother Matt while we both look for work. Not ideal – London is hardly our first choice; we've come to Europe seeking Mediterranean sunshine, not daily drizzle and Marmite and people saying 'jolly good' and 'guv'nor'. But what do we care? So long as we sleep.

Finally, Claudio the painter comes to our rescue. He knows the owner of an apartment in the southwest of the city, on Via Garibaldi, near the corner of Via Plebiscito.

'Via Plebiscito?' Gill pricks up her ears when I tell her the crossroad.

Few streets have a worse reputation than Via Plebiscito. Guidebooks warn against straying into its vicinity at night. When Palmina gave Gill a map of Catania after we first arrived, she circled Via Plebiscito and suggested we avoid it. Rumour has it that cars parked on this particular street are so likely to be vandalised or stolen that insurance companies make a point of excluding Via Plebiscito from any policy they draw up. I'd even heard that the neighbourhood around Via Plebiscito is Europe's second-poorest urban conglomeration after some part of Albania. Gill's concern seems reasonable.

Having said that, the personal recommendation of a friend is not to be sneezed at, and the price (three hundred and twenty euros per month) is only just over our budget. In the end, I agree to go with Claudio for an inspection.

Before seeing the apartment, we collect the key from the landlord, a Signor Pulvirenti. Intriguing character. His primary business – at least, it looks that way – is a small man-chester store with a front window full of pillows. Seems like a modest way to make a buck. Perhaps he has his fingers in other financial pies. I don't ask. Pulvirenti is probably sixty, though it's hard to tell because he chain-smokes cigarettes. Maybe he's fifty. His cheeks seem permanently ruddy, like those of a wind-chapped Tibetan. But he's an elegant dresser, with a penchant for tweed. He likes to wear his coat like a cape, draped off his shoulders at the back rather than buttoned at the front. Whenever he turns to address someone, his whole body swivels from the waist up, as though his head, neck and spine are all fused in the one position. His eyes blink in slow motion and they never quite fix on you in a conversation. Yet they are flinty with authority. Same with his voice – even when Pulvirenti speaks about trivial matters in his soft, semi-smiling drawl, the message seems clear: *I'm telling you how it is.*

Later, back at our Via Gesuiti place, I give Gill a rundown. 'There's good news and bad news.'

'What's the good news?'

'The apartment's nice. I mean, it's *small* – just a tiny living room with attached kitchen and bathroom, but there's a decent-sized bedroom. It's set back from the road on the bottom floor of a big cobbled courtyard. The interior is newly renovated – peach-coloured stucco walls with some hand-painted geometric designs, a couple of heavy wooden beams in the roof, wooden ceiling fans, tiled floors. There's a weird shower recess that you need to duck down to get into, but once you're in you can stand up.'

'Okay. That all sounds liveable to me.'

There's just one more roadblock to negotiate. 'And it's across the road from a cinema,' I say quickly.

'Great! I haven't seen a film in ages.'

'Yes, well . . .'

Gill fixes her gaze more firmly on mine. 'Go on.'

'It shows adult films.'

'Adult? What, like *Howard's End*?'

'Not quite. More like *Howard's Bell-End*.'

Turning to the cinema listings at the back of *La Sicilia*, I find the theatre in question, the Eliseo. It's filed under '*Per adulti*'.

'Here's what's currently screening there,' I say, then read aloud from the newspaper: '*La magica erotica di Alessandro Perrella, con Annette Van Soren, la regina dell'hard anal, 100%.*'

'Ew.' A minute of silence ensues. Gill is thinking. I'm also thinking, mostly of Annette Van Soren.

'Does this mean it's a no to the apartment?' I say eventually.

Gill ponders for half a minute more. 'I'm not sure.'

I figure if she isn't overly deterred by the presence of a triple-X movie theatre within metres of our front door (and I'm certainly not – how else will I fill my unemployed days?) then we might be home and hosed. I'm desperate to agree to the apartment. Another failed property inspection could break me.

'It's a long way from school,' she says. She's right. It's three times further from Giga than our current apartment.

'There are plenty of buses on Via Plebiscito,' I say. 'If they don't work out, I can walk you to school. And I'll definitely walk back with you in the evenings. The extra mileage will be good for us.'

'Until we get mugged.'

'Actually, Via Plebiscito didn't look too bad to me. There were little stalls out on the street – lots of old Sicilian guys roasting onions and artichokes on barbeques. Seemed pretty harmless. I did see one needle in a gutter, and lots of graffiti. But it wasn't very different from what we're used to already. No ultras nearby, as far as I could tell.' Hardly a flawless sales pitch. 'I tell you what,' I say finally. 'Why don't we both go down there, check out the apartment, and we'll see if you like the vibe.'

So, off we go, together, to take a look. I introduce Gill to Signor Pulvirenti ('How red are his *cheeks*?' she exclaims to me later). He comes with us in person to show us the ins and outs of his little courtyard apartment.

Later that day, we're back in his pillow shop signing a deal and handing over two months' deposit and the first month of rent. From that moment on, Signor Pulvirenti is rechristened 'Signor Pull-the-Rent-in'.

Actually, he's a very decent bloke. He even insists on buying a round of drinks at a nearby bar after the contract is finalised. It's my first taste of *corretto* – espresso coffee that has been 'corrected' with a shot of grappa.

Gill, whose documentation has been used to fill out the forms and whose earnings will pay the rent each month, is not invited to the bar. This is Sicily, and this is men's business.

7. A trip to the interior

> The houses in some of the villages hang so immediately
> over the edge of the rocks, that, as a measure of precau-
> tion, the young children are tied to the doorways, or
> some other parts of the building, during the temporary
> absence of their parents.
>
> – Penry Williams, *Recollections of Malta,*
> *Sicily, and the Continent,* 1847

Many years ago, I watched an extraordinary Greek film
called *I Tembelides Tis Eforis Kiladas*, made in 1978 by Nikos
Panayotopoulos. An approximate translation of the title is
Slothful Men of the Fertile Valley. It played on SBS Television
in Australia one Tuesday night at about eleven pm, as 'Late
Night Movie of the Week'. In his introduction to the film,
a young-looking David Stratton suggested that only very
patient viewers would watch to the end. Half an hour later,
I'd worked out why.

Nothing happens. I mean *nothing*. The story of *Slothful
Men of the Fertile Valley* loosely revolves around a father and
his three sons living in a remote country villa. And that's it.
They lie in their beds, under a swishing fan, with a view to
olive groves outside. I do remember there was a maid in the

villa, and I think I watched to the end because I couldn't imagine that she wouldn't suddenly remove all her clothes at some point, this being a film from Europe (and, let's be honest, this is the reason I was watching SBS at eleven pm on a weeknight). But she didn't. From memory, the men's lives became so entirely sedentary that they simply passed away where they slept.

Some of the towns in Sicily's interior remind me of that film.

Most Sicilian 'must sees' are found beside the ocean. A recommended tour of the island usually takes in Palermo, Taormina, Syracuse and Agrigento, all on the coast. Catania's on the coast, too, though it never gets a mention – it's like the Adelaide of Sicily. (In fact, Adelaide's urban layout was modelled on Catania, thanks to Colonel William Light, first Surveyor-General of South Australia.) The only thing left for the traveller to decide is whether to go in a clockwise or anti-clockwise direction. Lawrence Durrell travelled clockwise, for instance, and documented the trip in his book *Sicilian Carousel* (1977).

Tourists enter the interior only occasionally. More often than not, it's to drive to Corleone to photograph the town's sign, thereby triggering a spate of woeful Marlon Brando impressions when the holiday slideshow is shown back home. Someone needs to corral the world's Vito Corleone impersonators and make them an offer they can't refuse.

Despite its notoriety, Corleone is unexceptional. The rest of the interior, on the other hand, is worth a look. It's like a well-cooked lasagne: tough and bumpy on the surface, with rich, tasty layers below.

Over the course of the year, I visited more than a dozen towns in the Sicilian interior – sometimes alone, sometimes with Gill. And each one would work brilliantly as a location for *Slothful Men of the Fertile Valley II*, in the unlikely event that a sequel gets made.

Here are some travel notes from the handful of sleepy places where I was able to summon enough energy to take the lid off my pen.

Enna

If you throw a dart at a map of Sicily and hit the town of Enna, you've scored a bullseye. Enna lies smack-bang in the middle of the island. Hence its nickname, *ombelico* (belly button).

The town has a second nickname: *belvedere* (beautiful view). On a clear day, the panorama from Enna – which, at around a thousand metres, also happens to be the highest provincial capital in Sicily – is majestic. Apparently. When Gill and I visit Enna for the first time, one Sunday in November, the mist is so thick we can barely read the time on our watches, let alone enjoy a view. Not that we're complaining. A pea souper mightn't be ideal for Test Match cricket or for driving your wife to hospital when she's five centimetres dilated, but it's perfect for moseying along the streets of an ancient Sicilian town carved from stone.

Enna's bigger than most places in Sicily, but that's not saying much. A six- or seven-minute walk from the bus depot will get you to the main piazza. First, though, poke your nose into the town's enormous and extraordinary cemetery. You can't miss it. It stretches for half a kilometre across a hilltop adjoining Enna, almost like a second city. It's as if the only thing anyone does out here is die.

The cemetery isn't a grassy field dotted with flat gravestones like you might find in Australia. Rather, it's a mini-metropolis. The dead are buried in thousands of church-like tombs between one and four metres tall. Some even have Doric columns at the front and a tiny *cupola* (dome) on top. The tombs line up like terraced apartments and the alleyways are signposted like streets. It feels so much like a shrunken city that you almost expect a miniature set of traffic lights at each intersection and a bar selling thimblefuls of coffee.

In profile, Enna looks like a stone boat that has run aground on the top of a hill. The cemetery is at the 'stern'. After half an hour among its fungus-covered graves, Gill and I walk through the tightly clumped town to reach the 'bow', a small shelf of stone called Rocca di Cerere (the Rock of Ceres). A sheer drop on either side of the rock falls to the floor of the valley below. Standing there in a circling fog, you do get the distinct feeling of being at the front of some enormous ship, about to plunge into the rolling waves of Sicilian countryside.

Ceres was the Greek goddess of grain – hence our word 'cereal'. Her daughter Persephone was abducted and carried off by Hades, god of the underworld. One minute she was merrily picking flowers by the banks of a lake, then the earth split open and she was slung into the back of a chariot. The myth explains the annual growing cycles on earth: Ceres abandons the crops to search for her daughter and the land grows barren (winter). Persephone's return signals regrowth (spring).

I mention the myth because the lake at which the Rape of Persephone took place is generally identified with Lago di Pergusa, Sicily's largest natural lake, just ten kilometres south of Enna. If not for the fog, we'd be looking at it from where we stand.

The banks where Persephone once plucked flowers are today covered by a motor-racing circuit; the lake is brackish with oil, threatening its role as a stopover for migratory birds. Mary Taylor Simeti calls Pergusa 'a brilliant example of the Sicilians' best efforts to ruin their landscape'.

Next, Gill and I slither through the fog up to Enna's Castello di Lombardia, one of Sicily's largest castles. The central square is overgrown with lush, wheat-like grass and ferns, and towering dewy pines. Everything drips.

When erected by Frederick II in 1233, the castle boasted a whopping twenty towers. Crumbling remnants of six remain today. Gill and I climb to the top of the best-preserved tower and peer through the crenellations. Again, all we see is a whiteout. We feel like members of an '80s rock band battling a smoke machine.

A resilient defence existed at this location well before the time of Frederick II. In the ninth century AD, it took invading Saracen armies two whole decades to capture Enna – and even then they only succeeded by crawling single file through the town's sewer system. One hopes the victory celebrations included a long hot bath with plenty of soap.

Back in the heart of town, we grab lunch at Grotta Azzurra (Blue Grotto), presumably named after the sea cave off the coast of Taormina and offering cheap and hearty homestyle fare: minestrone, veal scallopine, baked chicken. It's all far more appetising than the recommendation I saw earlier at Enna's tourist information office: 'Visitors to the town should sample the very particular taste of boiled lamb's head coated in egg and breadcrumbs and baked in the oven.'

Gill and I get into an argument about the proprietor's name, Giuseppe Umbriaco. I'm convinced that it translates as 'Joseph the Drunkard'. Gill's not so sure. She wins. The word for a drunkard is *ubriaco* not *umbriaco*. Which isn't to say Giuseppe isn't one, because I couldn't think of anything else you would do if you lived in Enna but drink yourself silly. One of the town's many pluses.

One of its minuses is a lack of proper rubbish bins. All I find, while hunting for a place to dump a couple of empty gelato cups, is a metal box with a sign describing it as a receptacle for the collection of used batteries. The sign is accompanied by an insistent array of cartoons urging people to throw away their batteries once they run out. It seems very specific. How many times do you suddenly find yourself with pocketsful of flat batteries that need tossing out? At least it can be said that, while the streets of Enna are generously littered with plastic bottles and food wrappers, there isn't a single spent AA battery to be seen.

Enna's Easter celebrations are renowned. I see details on various billboards around town. The pictures make it look like a local theatre adaptation of *Mississippi Burning*. On Good Friday, fifteen different *confraternite* take part in a procession, wearing capes and pointed hoods that smack rather eerily of Ku Klux Klan outfits – holes for eyes and everything. Equally disconcerting are the very young boys and girls who are dolled up to look like fifty-year-old nuns.

For a celebration of a very different nature, try the Spring Reggae music festival in the countryside out of Enna. The yellow flyer that I pick up for the festival as we wait for a bus back to Catania features little illustrations of marijuana plants in each corner. The line-up of bands includes Stone Mama and Ganja Lover.

Calascibetta

Disappointed that in the whiteout I've barely laid eyes on Enna, I decide on a second daytrip the following May. This time, though, it's a solo jaunt. ('I'm not sure I need to rush back there,' is Gill's polite yet resolute reaction to my plan.)

Thankfully, the fog stands no chance against a murderous springtime sun, so I'm able to appreciate the view. The first thing I notice is a mirror-image town perched high on its own rocky crag just two kilometres north of Enna. This is Calascibetta. It's so close you could probably stand in the piazza of one town and pick off somebody in the other with a sniper rifle, if you were that way inclined.

Local buses regularly shuttle between the two towns, so I decide to pop over to Calascibetta for a look. If I'd known how long the bus was going to take, I'd have reconsidered. We cover the two kilometres in a stuporous twenty-eight minutes.

'Does the trip always take this long?' I ask the only other passenger on the shuttle as we finally pull into Calascibetta.

'No, no,' says the woman. 'It's usually a couple of minutes longer.' She's right, too. I check the schedule – it says half an hour.

The reason, of course, is that the two kilometres between Enna and Calascibetta is measured 'as the crow flies', whereas the coiled intestine of road is closer to ten kilometres. The bus dribbles down from Enna like treacle and takes even longer to ascend again. Still, to spend an age going nowhere very fast is great preparation for an afternoon in Calascibetta.

After the bus drops me at the main piazza and disappears around a corner, I'm left with just the sound of the occasional cicada and the flap of sheets drying in the warm breeze. Once, I think I detect the mellifluous tones of a *nonna* singing to herself in her kitchen. That's it.

Across the piazza, a traffic warden is making a vain attempt to look busy. The current complement of 'traffic' in Calascibetta consists of one electrician's van, a farmer on an antique motorbike, and a cart full of artichokes parked on a corner. There's a cord hanging around the warden's neck with a shiny metal whistle attached to it. These whistles, I fancy, are issued to all traffic wardens in the Sicilian interior, to be blown lightly in precautionary fashion whenever they find themselves falling asleep on the job.

In the middle of the square, a pigeon coos.

Nearby I see a metal sign with an arrow: '*Direzione da seguire in caso di terremoto o calamità naturale*' (Direction to follow in case of earthquake or natural disaster). And then I have a nasty thought. I find myself hoping that Calascibetta *is* afflicted by a natural disaster during my visit – just a little one, preferably with no casualties. It would make for a more interesting day. Even the name of the nearby church promotes inactivity: Chiesa del Buon Riposo (Church of Good Rest).

With my body in real danger of petrifying, I break away from Calascibetta's main piazza to explore the town. Here's how the next half hour unfolds: I take a photo of a medieval door; I take a second photo of the door, this time using the ten-second timer on the camera so I can be in the picture; I sit next to a woodpile and peel a mandarin; I look back to the square to see how events are unfolding down there – a few of the pigeons appear to have flown away temporarily (something for Calascibetta's blogosphere to report on); I take a third photo of the door, this time using the 'sepia' setting on my camera; I eat the mandarin; finally, I'm overcome by the sudden urge to flee, lest I lie down at the very spot where I stand, metamorphosed into a slothful man of the fertile valley.

Necking a quick coffee provides a welcome pick-me-up, but Calascibetta even seems capable of nullifying the effects of caffeine. It's time for a hike in the countryside instead. I begin marching in the direction of a nearby Neolithic tomb, the Reale Necropolis.

A strange moment follows on the outskirts of town when I come across a community billboard erected in the grass beside the road. It's covered in various ageing flyers with out-of-date job offers and messages about items for sale. In the middle, though, is a fresh note, showing a love heart, hand-drawn in pencil, pierced by a diagonal arrow. It reads 'Carmelo *e* Maria Grazia, *oggi sposi*' – 'Carmelo and Maria Grazia, just married'. And it has today's date on it.

Who drew this? Where were these two married? Is Calascibetta deathly quiet because everyone's at the wedding? Who drove by and stuck a note about it on a disused billboard in overgrown grass? *Why?* These are the thoughts I ponder during my one-hour walk to Reale Necropolis.

How appropriate that the best-known sight in Calascibetta is a city of the dead. The necropolis consists of a series of mini-caves cut halfway up a limestone hill and used twenty-five centuries ago as burial places.

To me, the necropolis is mildly chilling – like the mysterious, out-of-place notice about Carmelo and Maria Grazia's wedding – though it doesn't exactly get the adrenalin pumping.

What *does* get the adrenalin pumping are bees. I'm driven out of the gorge by a nasty great swarm of them within ninety seconds of arriving. I think it was Albert Einstein who stated that if all the world's bees were to die out, mankind would perish within four years. Almost worth it, no?

In Calascibetta, I feel better for the eight-kilometre walk. At least it means that the next three hours (thirty minutes waiting in the main piazza, thirty minutes on the bus to

Enna, thirty minutes waiting for a bus from there to Catania, and ninety minutes getting home) do not constitute the very lowest ebb of my life to date. That honour is still reserved for the time when, as an eight-year-old, I won a freestyle swimming race at a school carnival and pumped my little fists in triumph as hundreds of parents cheered from the grandstand, only to turn around and see the other competitors in the race all doing breaststroke. It was a breaststroke final. I'd forgotten, and swum freestyle the whole way. People weren't cheering: they were laughing – laughing at my sticklike frame, my tiny Speedos and my blushing face. And they continued to laugh at me all the way from the pool to the changing rooms.

Caltagirone

Caltagirone desperately needs an expert in Arabic language to go there and sort out the mess with its name. While reading up on the place, I find four wildly divergent suggestions as to its Arabic root and meaning: *qal'at-al-ganom* (Castle of Genies), *kalat gerun* (Castle of Caves), *Qalat-Jerun* (Castle of the Burial Grounds) and *cal'at ghiran* (Castle of Vases). The latter would be the most appropriate: the town's main claim to fame is its terracotta industry. This is Sicily's City of Ceramics (and a nightmare for anyone with a lisp).

Consequently, Caltagirone is full of pottery shops. I'd rather eat handfuls of ground glass than see any of those. I've hated pottery ever since someone made me sit through *Ghost*. But it's also known as a beautiful hilltown in its own right, so I'm happy to accompany Gill on a visit there one glorious day in mid-December. The sky is a flawless, stained-glass blue. During the ninety-minute bus ride from Catania, we pass orange trees so full of fruit that each orchard looks like a box of ping-pong balls.

Caltagirone's most famous sight, the Scala di Santa Maria del Monte, begins right where the bus stops. It's wonderful: a dramatic seventeenth-century stairway of one hundred and forty-two steps decorated with individually hand-painted majolica tiles. The scenes on the tiles illustrate the town's medieval past: soldiers on horses, hunting dogs, noblemen and -women, mythological creatures, religious motifs.

I like that nobody in Caltagirone seems too precious about 'the Scala'. Tiles are chipped to reveal dull terracotta below, weeds sprout from cracks, and the whole thing looks like it could do with a rag run over it. Apparently it gets a spit and polish in July, when four thousand oil lamps are placed up and down the length of the stairs for the Feast of Saint James.

I can't hold Gill back any longer. After attempting to get her to come along and see the town's Bourbon Prison (which sounds like the perfect place to be incarcerated), I resign myself to my fate. We're going shopping for ceramics.

Amid the one billion plates and tiles, I find a series of famous Teste di Moro (Moorish heads) – vases in the shape of a human head, all decorated with the face of the same moustachioed Moor. The story goes that this fellow fell in love with a Sicilian girl but then dumped her, so she hacked off his head with a knife. His infamy lives on in the form of a vessel in which to place geraniums.

Somewhere between the twentieth and thirtieth ceramic shop of Caltagirone, you'll find yourself overcome by a sudden urge to purchase a delightful handmade vase (nothing too expensive – say, five euros) then walk straight outside, place the vase in the middle of the street, and wait for a car – or, even better, a truck – to thunder past and crush the thing into a fine mist. Or put it this way: I don't intend to rush pell-mell to the Caltagirone Museum, whose exhibition at the time of our visit is called 'A Magical Journey through the History of Ceramics from Prehistoric Times to the Present Day'.

Anyway, rather than in a shop or museum, Caltagirone's ceramics are best seen in their alfresco settings around the town itself – the steps of the Scala, park benches studded with majolica tiles, and the wondrous gazebo in the public gardens, where terracotta vases with mossy gargoyle handles overflow with bougainvillea.

Caltagirone's second claim to fame is its crèches, or *presepi*. These are collections of figurines placed together to make up a three-dimensional nativity scene, depicting Jesus in a manger, Joseph and Mary nearby, the surrounding farm animals, and whatever else might take the artist's fancy. Saint Francis of Assisi is thought to have introduced them to Italy after a voyage to Palestine in 1220. Nobody had the good sense to tell him to take them back.

That's mean of me. Some of the larger *presepi* are unexpectedly impressive: they fill whole rooms and feature hundreds of figurines and working electronic parts, like the enormous toy train sets of plump, middle-aged nerds.

While we're wandering around one of the *presepi* workshops, I notice that the owner looks exactly like Art Garfunkel. Later in the afternoon, I run into a dead ringer for Paul Simon. Is there something going on here that I don't know about?

A stroll out of Caltagirone to the nearby hillside proves an agreeable diversion, until I tread on the ripe fruit of a prickly pear lying on the ground – it explodes underfoot like a tomato and sprays red pulp onto my jeans. Sicilians harvest these prickly pears, called *fichi d'India* (Indian figs), for food and wine. Curious, I pick a chunk of flesh from my clothing and taste it. It's pleasant. Watermelony.

The side of the hill whose summit we reach has been dug away, exposing grey clay presumably used in the ceramic-making process. In the sky above, a majestic sunset has begun, with Mount Etna visible seventy kilometres away to the northeast. It reminds us we have a bus to catch, back to the foothills of that very volcano.

A few months after our visit, a story in *La Sicilia* about a mother and son in Caltagirone catches my eye. According to the newspaper report, the mother didn't like the way her son was behaving, so she took away his house keys, cut off his daily allowance, and even dragged him in front of police when he stayed out late at night. He responded that his allowance wasn't big enough and that – gasp! – he didn't like her cooking. Police intervened and settled the dispute, and the two were reunited at home.

At the time of the complaints, the son was sixty-one years old.

Agira

Agira, fifty kilometres west of Catania, is reached via a minor
country road called the SS121, arguably the prettiest drive
on the island – especially in April, before the sun applies its
blowtorch. Gill and I visit on Palm Sunday (Domenica delle
Palme), our bus passing paddocks of lush grass uninterrupted
but for the occasional furrow of tractor trails. In each village
we drive through, children wave woven palm fronds against
a sky of duck-egg blue.

Agira feels strange. There are no women. For the first
thirty minutes, we don't see a single *nonna*, *donna* or *ragazza*
anywhere. Finally we work it out: they're all at home, cooking the Sunday lunch.

'Something you could do more of,' I say to Gill. Her
response is justifiable, if not entirely befitting a sacred occasion like Palm Sunday.

We start our tour of the town in the main square, Piazza
Garibaldi. Objective A is to find a nice spot for a coffee, but
it takes a while. Gill puts the kybosh on the first three bars we
enter. She doesn't like the proliferation of men, all of them
smoking, spitting and shouting.

I don't really like them either, but I don't tell Gill that.
It's better in this instance to appear like the patient but long-
suffering partner. Then you can use it as leverage later. For
example, if Gill suddenly wanted to look in a fashion boutique, I could say, 'But you've already dragged me into three
different bars!' Not that Agira is flush with fashion boutiques.

Finally we find the Biondi Luigi Café and enjoy a pair
of excellent macchiatos. In terms of clientele, it's not much

better than the other places. The men are younger, with treated denim jeans, outrageously gelled hair and dark sunnies. One of them hammers away at some kind of electronic gambling machine. All of them stare at Gill for the duration of our visit.

The weather is perfect: I wonder why these guys aren't out enjoying the day. Then again, I'm not about to challenge them on the point. In any case, they have the perfect defence: 'What about you? You came to Agira.'

Here's a surprise: Agira is full of churches. We pop our heads into one of them, the Church of St Philip, its pretty minaret covered in lines of turquoise tiling, with the occasional sprig of grass between the grouting.

Philip was a Syrian hermit, traditionally regarded as the first Christian saint to visit Sicily (first century AD). The story goes that he fought the devil at Agira and imprisoned him in a nearby cave. God knows what Satan was doing at Agira, but locals say that even now, on windy nights, you can hear his hellish cries. Philip is not only the patron saint of Agira, incidentally, but also of the United States Army Special Forces. Truly!

The church is empty except for a priest who's recently finished a service. He approaches and shakes my hand in both of his, before giving Gill a barely perceptible nod of the head. 'Where are you from?' he asks me. He doesn't once look at Gill during our conversation. It's the exact opposite of the Biondi Luigi Café.

'We're Australian,' I say.

'And you're Catholic?'

'Absolutely.'

I'm not sure what behaviour constitutes the minimum indiscretion to guarantee infinite damnation, but lying about your faith to a priest while inside a church on Palm Sunday must come close.

'Good,' he says. 'Welcome to Agira.'

I wonder what would've happened if I'd said no? Perhaps nothing. Or perhaps the floor would've dropped away beneath our feet, sending us tumbling into a pit to be trussed up in rope and dragged off to Satan in his nearby cave.

'And you're here for the Via Crucis Vivente?' says the priest, snapping me out of my vision.

'Sure!' I say, but I'm thinking, 'Via what-now?'

'Good,' says the priest. 'Enjoy your day.'

And so we escape. Talking to locals on the street, we discover that the Via Crucis Vivente (Living Way of the Cross) is a recreation of the events of Easter by living participants. In various locations around town, amateur actors in togas play out Bible scenes: Gethsemane, the Last Supper, the trial before Pontius Pilate, even some fake flogging and a fairly grisly recreation of the crucifixion. It's taking place on this very day in Agira. Being a university graduate, the concept of someone dressed in a toga doing anything other than binge drinking from a cheap bladder of wine is, to me, a novel one. So I'm glad we're here.

Next, we walk past a bust of Agira's famous son, Diodorus Siculus. Diodorus was one of the more tedious writers of antiquity. Born in the first century BC around the time of Julius Caesar, he spent most of his life preparing a history of almost everything, the *Bibliotheca Historica*. This collection of forty volumes, written in Greek, was impressive in size but less so in content. It lacked originality and was prone to geographical errors. Diodorus thought Rome was a coastal village in New Zealand.

Okay, that's not true. In fact, scholars are generally thankful for Diodorus, irrespective of his writing abilities. For some periods of Greek history (the fifth and fourth centuries BC, in particular), his books are almost all we've got as a written record of the times. They also work well as doorstops.

Gill and I climb to the castle at the very top of the town. Towards the summit we run into a local, an old man who asks if we're French. After Gill has revived me with a wet towel, we clarify our nationality.

'You're travelling at the best time of the year,' he says. 'April and May.'

He asks if we have any children. No, we explain, we're just married.

'Children are what life is all about,' he says, before beginning a detailed seminar covering the various branches of his family tree.

It's not until description of grandchild number seven that we are able to extricate ourselves and ask directions to the castle. He points up the path towards a stone arch and tells us to go through it and turn left at the *semafori*. Traffic lights? In this place? Surely not.

We say goodbye and wish the man a pleasant day. He replies: '*Buon pranzo!*' ('Enjoy your lunch!'). It's a stock phrase, rather like the Chinese greeting: 'Have you eaten yet?'

It turns out the old chap is right. We reach a crossroads of two steep lanes and find a single set of traffic lights, blinking away to nobody. Why? Perhaps they've been installed for decorative purposes.

It brings to mind the story of the former mayor of Naples who, when quizzed many years ago about the utility of the city's newfangled traffic lights, apparently explained that green meant 'go', red indicated 'proceed if safe', while the amber light – and here he stumbled briefly – was 'for gaiety'.

Soon we're at the summit. The view from the ruined castle at the top is as good as any in Sicily, complemented by warm sunshine on our faces, the aroma of grass and wildflowers (and just the littlest bit of dung), and the distant, drifting sounds of cowbells and bleating sheep. We stay on top of the hill, on top of the world, for hours.

Finally descending into town, we stop at a bar for *spremute* – cold juice from oranges crushed in a hand-pulled metal press and served in fifties-style fluted glasses. Across the road, outside a building labelled 'Society of Saint Philip', twenty elderly gentlemen spill onto the footpath in tweed *coppola* caps, grey suits, woollen vests and ties, and oversized sunglasses, to warm themselves in the late afternoon sun. The wall they're leaning against looks like it's been strafed with machine-gun fire. It probably has. The Allies fought a tough five-day battle for control of Agira in July 1943 as part of Operation Husky, aimed at liberating Sicily from German occupation. Earlier, on the hilltop, I'd spied the white crosses of a nearby war cemetery, a couple of kilometres out of town.

It contains the graves of four hundred and ninety men from the 1st Canadian Infantry Division and the 1st Canadian Army Tank Brigade.

In keeping with the military theme, a troop of Roman legionaries suddenly marches past. They must be starring in the Via Crucis Vivente. They look spiffily authentic, with everything from leather shin guards to long spears that hold their shape nicely, not like the wobbly things you see in *Ben Hur*. Their tunics, though, are daringly short. I'd hate to be walking up a flight of stairs behind these guys.

'Hail Caesar,' I say as they pass, kind of as a joke to Gill, but they hear me. Rather than running me through with a *pilum*, though, they promptly break formation and crowd around, smiling, while we take some photos.

Unfortunately we can't stick around for the show. Our bus is leaving for Catania again. Back on the delightful SS121 – more a rural laneway than a road deserving of a number – the sun lowers slowly behind us. Up ahead, Etna's snowy screen plays a slideshow of pastel shades, from yellow through to orange, then pink and finally blue as evening approaches.

Gill and I are emanating our own new colours, sunburnt from hours of life-affirming repose – okay, *slothful* repose – on the castle-crowned hilltop overlooking Agira.

8. Moving

I'm happy now, with a fireplace and a house that isn't
too elegant to be smudged with a little smoke, and a
lively spring, and a yard that's never mowed.
                                      – Marcus Valerius Martialis (Martial),
                                                  Epigrams, c. AD 40–104

My favourite show on Italian television is the nightly news
bulletin on RAI Uno. The female newsreaders are *dynamite*.
With blonde locks and half-unbuttoned blouses, they drape
themselves over the desk, ogle the camera, and read headline
stories about Taliban insurgencies and stock-market fluctua-
tions in the kind of husky tone you'd expect of someone on
the other end of an adult hotline.

Gorgeous babes are all over the country's wildly popular variety shows, too – usually as co-hosts next to sleazy old
men spouting double entendres. In fact, every female on
Italian TV looks like a model. Gill frowns whenever she sees
these leggy hosts. 'Where have the *normal* women gone?'

'I'm not sure,' I reply. 'But please don't bring them back.'

Elsewhere on the telly you'll find soap operas, *Wheel of
Fortune* (*La Ruota della Fortuna*), football matches, fifteen-
minute advertisements for abdominal tighteners, lotto

draws, *Buffy the Vampire Slayer* (*Buffy: l'ammazzavampiri*) and, with a bit of hunting around, more leggy blondes with great tits.

Not that we have a TV for watching any of this stuff. In fact, in our Via Gesuiti apartment, we have no TV, no phone, no radio and no internet. The landlady's a nun, you'll recall.

We read instead. After dinner, we sit in our L-shaped corridor and battle through the Italian newspaper, *La Sicilia*, or whatever books Gill manages to borrow from the modest library at her school. I work my way through Hemingway's *Fiesta*, then a John Grisham throwaway, then *The Dice Man* by Luke Rhinehart ('Seems a bit racy for a school library,' I say to Gill), then Ian McEwan's *Enduring Love* – anything I can get my hands on for free.

We have music, too, but only the dozen CDs I brought from Australia. There's no stereo, so I play them on my laptop. It's no Bang & Olufsen. And hearing the same albums over and over again starts to become a trial. Don't get me wrong: The Beatles' *Revolver* is a classic. Yet even *it* sounds dull after enough spins. If Paul McCartney were to appear at our door, I'd hurl the CD like a ninja star into his forehead. (He deserves it, anyway, for 'Mull of Kintyre'.)

It doesn't help that the CDs frequently skip in the disk drive of my dying laptop. The computer served me admirably at university. Now, though, it's desperately low on RAM and the battery compartment is leaking ferrous goo. What's more, all the letters have worn away from the keys. Typing is guesswork. My name comes out as 'Shanud Sillat'.

Worst of all, the laptop seems obsessed with trying to go online, even though we have no phone line and no internet account. Every minute or so, a new browser window opens: *The page cannot be displayed. The page you are looking for is currently unavailable. The website might be experiencing technical difficulties, or you may need to adjust your browser settings.* As fast as I close each window, another pops open. I try everything to fix the problem, from deleting all web-related programs to carrying out a complete reinstall – even smashing the undercarriage of the machine with a brick. Nothing works.

Playing CDs on the laptop is tricky enough, but the DVDs that Gill occasionally brings back from the Giga library are especially troublesome. On wet or cold nights, we prop ourselves up on our two metal beds with the laptop in front of us as a makeshift cinema. By the time the opening credits are over, the film is sticking every five seconds. The only way to overcome the glitch is to put my finger on the side of the DVD tray and push it back and forth repeatedly for the duration of the show. It's like my own movie-length insight into life with Parkinson's disease.

Slowly but surely, Gill and I begin to covet the idea of a television in the apartment – she to watch *The Bold and Beautiful* (simply called *Beautiful* in Italy), me to watch the news on RAI Uno.

'We've got a spare set,' says Brock one day when he hears us bemoaning our lack of home entertainment options.

'Yeah?'

'Yeah. It's kind of . . . *old*. And big.'

'The bigger the better!'

The next day, Brock comes by in a friend's car to unload the TV. It's a three-person job. This is the biggest piece of electronic machinery since IBM created Deep Blue to beat Gary Kasparov at chess. It looks like it was built in 1955 by a team of carpenters with sheets of cork and veneer and some lengths of plastic vacuum hose.

Since we only have twenty-four hours left in the Via Gesuiti apartment, we decide to wait and unveil the telly in all its glory in our new place. The excitement is palpable. Gill is especially happy. My days are pretty much filled with leisure already, so I don't crave TV. After a full day of teaching, though, Gill looks forward to the kind of mindless downtime that only television can provide.

So it's a shame for her when I go and drop the thing on the road, smashing it beyond repair.

It happens during our move. Palmina kindly offers to drive Gill and me and all of our belongings to the new apartment. Together we battle the TV into the car. By the time we get to Via Garibaldi and find a park, however, the heavens have opened. In a moment of ill-advised chivalry, I tell the two ladies to stay in the vehicle while I lug the television across the busy street. I reckon that by wrapping my arms around the back of the set and hugging it like a medicine ball, I'll be able to crab-walk thirty metres.

I reckon wrongly. After five metres, my legs buckle. Then I slip on a scud of wet ash on the road. It's a textbook 'banana-peel' fall – head back, legs up, and *slam* onto my back. The TV crunches into the bitumen with the sound of shattering cathode-ray tubes, before toppling over onto my lower half and pinning me to the puddly ground. For a few seconds I think I'll have to hack a limb off like that rock climber in Arizona in order to roll away from the television and avoid the oncoming traffic. Thankfully the drivers see me and slow down – slow right down, in fact, so they can stare at my predicament.

I crawl from under the television to assess my injuries. A corner of the box has gouged flesh from my shin. The road has grated my arm like *parmigiana*. And a piece of metal – either the aerial or the on/off knob – has dug into my right hand, leaving a perfect red circle in the middle of my palm. For the next two weeks, I will endeavour to hide this mark from people in the neighbourhood lest they proclaim it a sign of stigmata and inaugurate an annual festival in my name.

Other than that, the move goes smashingly!

In the end, we turn the broken television into a coffee table by covering it with a throw rug and putting a pile of magazines on top. Occasionally I'll walk inside to find Gill sitting on the edge of a chair, staring wistfully at the TV-cum-table, perhaps wishing the scrambled electronics would magically piece themselves together like the car in *Christine*.

The biggest test, though, is our first night in bed. Would we get eight hours or would Via Garibaldi curse us with its noise as well? I'm so nervous about sleeping, it keeps me awake. Finally I drift off at around four am, but not before hearing the clip-clop of a horse making its way up the street. Mounted police, I guess. The horse finds its way into my dreams – in the saddle is the Pope, swinging a lasso; he hogties Gill and me and drags us back to Via Gesuiti to complete our unfinished lease with the nun.

I don't know if Gill dreams, but she certainly sleeps – sleeps very, very well. The move has worked. Sanity is restored. Tuscan chickens!

It's not entirely smooth sailing, mind you. Take the dodgy electricity. The wall outlets of our new apartment have less current surging through them than a potato-powered clock. Blackouts are commonplace. If Gill or I flick one switch too many, *vooomp!* – the lights go off.

We're forced to juggle our energy consumption. This proves a challenge. Running one or two appliances at the same time is fine; adding a third is precarious. Example: while it's safe for me to use the laptop at the same time as recharging the mobile phone, if Gill then turns on the electric fan in the bedroom, we're plunged into darkness. Moreover, if we want to illuminate the bedroom and living room at the same time, the bathroom light has to stay off. I solve this problem by going to the toilet in the dark, leading to divorce threats from Gill when she discovers splashes of poorly aimed piss on the seat.

Then there's Gill's hairdryer. Wow. That thing could shut down the entire Sicilian grid for a month. The room lights go dim even as she's unwrapping the cord to plug it in.

'I'm just going to blow-dry my hair,' she'll announce, before turning off every switch in the apartment as a precaution.

I soon learn that if I'm working on the computer and my wife walks past with wet hair, I should automatically press

Ctrl+S. I even start saving documents at the very sound of Gill turning on the shower. I'm like Pavlov's dog.

Fixing the blackouts is painful. It means dragging a chair across the courtyard and climbing up to peer into a rusty, ratty circuit box. There I'll stand, torch in my mouth, holding the box open with one hand and searching for the appropriate circuit switch with the other. Flipping the wrong one elicits a scream from someone in another apartment as their shower turns cold.

Whenever we do have a power failure – and it's at least three times a week – Gill and I silently fume at each other for disturbing the electrical equilibrium. She'll give me a glare that says, 'I *know* you were secretly recharging your camera battery,' and I'll glare back with, 'Just how dry does your fucking hair need to be?'

Occasionally I'll run into a neighbour when I'm outside at the circuit box. They're generally a quiet lot: elderly, reclusive. Nearly all are single or widowed. They live on the second, third and fourth floors of the *palazzo* and rarely venture onto their Juliet balconies overlooking the courtyard.

An exception is the octogenarian living above us to the left. 'Happily batty' is how I'd describe her. She's always hanging over her railing, surveying the scene – and she keeps an especially close eye on our front door. Every time Gill or I emerge, she asks the same question: '*Che ora è?*' ('What time is it?') She even says this on our first encounter – not 'What's your name?' or 'Welcome to your new home!' but 'What time is it?'

I answer then leave to buy some fresh bread. Ten minutes later as I walk back across the courtyard she spies me again.

'*Che ora è?*' This time she points to her wrist for added effect. I provide an update.

Why such eagerness for knowing the time? Perhaps it's to do with a timepiece-related trauma from her past. Maybe on some breezy autumn night back in the 1940s she made a pact to be at a particular place at a particular time but never quite made it, with tragic consequences. That or she's senile.

The repetition is only occasionally annoying. If I'm struggling home, laden with shopping and fumbling for keys at the door, I find myself having to bite my tongue.

'*Che ora è?*'

'Time you bought yourself a watch, lady.'

Mostly, though, she's nice to have around. On sunny mornings we hear her singing to herself on the balcony. Or singing to her cat. The cat is the woman's reason for living. Fat beyond belief with a coat of pure white, it has a thunderous purr and is seemingly unfazed by its owner's insistence on posing chronometrical queries to strangers.

Each day, the cat sleeps on the precarious edge of the balcony railing. It wouldn't take much, I sometimes think, for the creature to slip and fall five metres to the concrete courtyard.

Which is precisely what happens. One day, Gill and I hear a strangled cry from outside, followed by three seconds of silence, and then a loud thud – the kind of thud made by a cat that should, in theory, be able to correct its fall in mid-air, if only it didn't gorge on so much food.

We race out the door and look up at our grief-stricken neighbour. She's staring over the balcony with head in hands.

'*Che ora è! Che ora è! CHE ORA È!*'

('Time to scrape your pet off the courtyard?')

In fact, the cat's okay. No broken bones or minced internal organs, just a set of especially wide eyes.

The next morning I see the fat feline sitting in the winter sun, perched on the railing, lesson not learnt. The old lady sweeps her balcony and sings. She peers down at me with a bigger smile than usual, overjoyed to be reunited with her pet.

'*Che ora è?*'

The only set of neighbours we get to know well is the family in the other ground-level apartment: Carmelo and his wife, Angela, plus their sons, Davide and Orazio (Horace – like the Roman poet), and daughter, Desideria ('Desi' for short). The parents are in their early fifties, the children in their mid-to-late twenties. Orazio and Desi have families of their own, with apartments elsewhere in Catania. But like all young adults in Italy, they spend plenty of time at Mum and Dad's.

We first meet Carmelo, the paterfamilias, on the Saturday after moving in.

'Mmm . . .' I murmur to Gill in the early afternoon. 'Smell that?'

It's the wonderful charry aroma of a barbeque lunch. Tendrils of smoke curl out from the corner apartment. Minutes later, a face appears at our door. It's Carmelo. Nice name: makes me think of 'calm' and 'mellow'. And that's Carmelo to a T. He communicates mostly in a language of friendly grunts, accepting shrugs and the occasional cheeky grin.

His appearance, however, belies the soft-sounding moniker. Carmelo is a leathery fisherman, sun-baked and gaunt. Thanks to a life of jarring boat trips and a permanent lit cigarette in his lips, he'll never be the new face of L'Oréal. You could write a book about his craggy hands alone – hands which, at that precise moment, clutch two plastic plates of freshly caught and perfectly grilled swordfish. It's a lunch offering for Gill and me.

'This must be the Sicilian equivalent of taking a cake around to the new neighbours,' I say to Gill.

We spend the next few minutes *grazie*-ing profusely. Carmelo only shrugs, digging around in a crumpled pack for another Marlboro Rossa.

We're still swooning with appreciation for the swordfish when we see Carmelo again the next morning. This time he's with his two sons. The three of them were out in the boat last night, off the coast of Syracuse; they've just been at the Pescheria, the seafood market, selling their catch. We find them sitting in a sunny rhombus of the courtyard unfurling a pile of red netting from the back of a car, running it through their hands, looking for rips and frays. I can smell the old net and its crust of salt and scales from our front door.

'*Buongiorno!*' I say.

When they look up from their work, I add a friendlier '*Ciao!*'

The eldest son, Orazio, shrugs in the manner of his father. 'Same thing,' he says. '*Buongiorno* and *ciao*.'

It's the first time we've met and already he's giving me a grammar lesson. What's more, it's a lesson that flies in the face of every Italian phrasebook I've read: *'Buongiorno' and 'ciao' are different; never use the informal 'ciao' with people you don't know – it's impolite; greet them with 'buongiorno' instead.*

Orazio couldn't care less about formalities; greet him however you want.

The rest of the family spills out to take advantage of the early winter sun. Angela comes first. She's fleshier than her husband, with paler skin, and mid-length auburn hair framing a round, friendly face. Yet, like Carmelo – like everyone in our new neighbourhood, in fact – her face shows signs of hard toil, perhaps even disillusionment. Her eyes smile, but it's a weary smile.

Angela works part-time as a hairdresser, giving cheap cuts to women who live in the area. She doesn't have a studio, just a chair, a mirror and a broom in the front room of their apartment. Often when Gill is away teaching, I'll look out and see a customer enter the courtyard from the street, before leaving an hour later with a fresh do. One afternoon I watch as the mother of a girl with severe cerebral palsy slowly leads her daughter into Angela's apartment for a cut. Angela and Carmelo don't have much money, but I bet she charges a paltry fee – if anything. She does community work, too. Sunday nights are spent looking after an elderly lady in the woman's home up near Cibali Stadium. She's salt of the earth, Angela.

'Occupata,' she says whenever we ask how things are. *'Sono sempre occupata.'* Always busy.

Angela also makes a point of telling us that she doesn't drink alcohol and doesn't smoke cigarettes. She doesn't even drink coffee. With the mention of each vice she takes a sideways glance in the direction of Carmelo. He's puffing away as usual.

Desi emerges from the corner apartment next, with her fiancé Gaetano in tow. Gaetano looks almost out of place in this down-at-heel neighbourhood. He wears trendy shades and plenty of denim, and has the styled haircut of a Serie A footballer. He's no show pony, though, just a genuinely decent bloke with a penchant for a practical joke. Desi has burgundy curls spiralling halfway down her back and a more laconic sense of humour. Her favourite expression is '*boh*'. It's a popular piece of Italian slang that lies somewhere between 'whatever' and 'dunno'.

Gaetano speaks the occasional word of English – the rest of the family, virtually none. When he tells us he works as a 'disc jockey', I have visions of him playing golden oldies at a retirement village crowd, with Angela cutting hair in the background. Later I see his Technics turntables and his mixing boards and realise with relief that he's the real deal. Desi works in a wedding-dress shop.

Desi and Gaetano are planning for their own wedding. They've been together for years – they even have a six-year-old daughter, Erminia. Finally, though, they've decided to make things official.

'It's costing us ten thousand euros,' says Gaetano, looking equal parts proud and petrified.

It seems a silly amount of money for this family, who

clearly don't have a lot. But weddings are a big deal in Sicily, no matter where you're from. It must be hard to skimp.

The ceremony will take place in one of Catania's most famous churches, Chiesa di San Domenico. The reception is booked for a villa on the slopes of Mount Etna. Carmelo will supply the fish for dinner.

Lastly, a young girl skips out into the courtyard, awkwardly clutching a pair of small dogs – wispy-haired Maltese terriers, one under each arm. She has lively, obsidian-black eyes and straight dark hair down to her waist.

'What's your name?' Gill and I ask in unison.

'Erminia,' she says with the studied drawl of a child under interrogation from adults.

'How old are you, Erminia?'

'Six.'

'And what are the dogs' names?' I ask.

'Minnie and Maggie.'

Desi chimes in: 'Minnie after Minnie Mouse. Maggie after Megan Gale.'

'Megan Gale? The Australian model?'

'Right.'

Megan Gale is *huge* in Italy. In 1999, she appeared in a sultry advertisement for an Italian mobile phone company and was virtually embraced as a local celebrity overnight – particularly, it must be said, by the men.

Meanwhile, the dogs are still hanging from Erminia's noose-like arms. Finally she lets them down and they scamper off to the grubby corners of the courtyard to find a place to shit.

Erminia, we discover, is a delight. But she can also be a handful. One day during the week we see her playing in the courtyard rather than at school. When we ask why, Desi rolls her eyes and says, 'Because she's an *asinella!*' A little donkey. No other explanation. Another favourite word that our neighbours use for Erminia is *monella* – 'scamp'.

One day, Gill and I hear Desi's voice out in the courtyard: 'Erminia, get off the bike.' A pause, then: '*Erminia!* Get . . . off . . . the . . . bike!' Desi then pops her head around our door and says, 'Whatever you do, don't have a daughter.'

Our neighbours are forever popping their heads around our door. Being on the bottom floor of the *palazzo* means our lives are very public. Anyone in the courtyard – and it serves four storeys worth of occupants – can see straight in at what we're doing.

Erminia, in particular, spends half of each day with her face pressed between the bars of our metal grille, giving us updates on the whereabouts of the two dogs: 'Maggie is over there near the front gate. Minnie is inside because she's in trouble.'

This kind of casual nosiness, known as *invadente* (you'll detect the root of an English word there), is common in Italy, particularly among young people. Yet it's not just Erminia who comes and goes. One weekday while Gill is teaching, Angela pays a visit.

'Here,' she says, handing me an enormous English–Italian dictionary, dusty with yellowing pages. 'This might be helpful. It belongs to the boys, but they never use it.'

When she's gone and I'm sifting through the book, it drops open at the letter 'F'. Sitting there, pressed into the page next to appropriate entries such as 'fern', 'fertilise' and 'fibre', is a seven-pronged marijuana leaf, twenty centimetres long, perfectly preserved. Seems like the dictionary came in useful after all.

Only a few days later, little Erminia stands at our door and hands over a different book. It's one she has innocently plucked at random from the family library.

'It's so you can practise your Italian,' she says.

I glance at the cover. The title is *Perché tuo figlio si droga* ('Why your son is using drugs').

'Erm . . . thanks, Erminia,' I say. 'But we've actually got plenty of books to help us. Maybe it's best if you take this one back inside.' I hate to disappoint a helpful six-year-old, but imagine if Angela, Carmelo or one of the sons walked into our apartment and found two of their books on the bench – the first providing a window on the issue of teenage drug use and the other being used as a kind of illicit press.

Still, none of this is remotely surprising. Do young people in Catania use drugs? Of course they do. There are joints being smoked at every party Gill and I go to. Anyone can buy a stick of local weed (Sicilian Sativa) or a bag of pills from the skinhead kids hanging around Castello Ursino in our new neighbourhood, or the seedy-looking characters on the steps outside a pub called Nievski, or even in the relatively salubrious surrounds of the city's opera house, Teatro Massimo Bellini.

Catania might be different from your run-of-the-mill European city, but it's not *that* different.

One afternoon while Gill's working, Angela asks me for some tech advice. 'Can you fix a photo for me on your computer?' she asks. 'Make it brighter?'

'Maybe. Let me take a look.'

Angela slips back to her apartment and returns seconds later with a thick photo album under her arm.

'Do you have the photos on a disk?' I ask.

'*Disk?*' she echoes, rolling the word around like it's the first time she's heard it.

I attempt to explain that the photos will have to be in digital format if I'm going to edit them for brightness or colour. But I'm struggling for the right terminology in Italian. I'm terrified of consulting the dictionary lest it flop open at the double-page spread of cannabis.

'Don't worry,' says Angela eventually. 'Some other time.' On her way out the door, though, she turns back to me. 'Do you want to see some photos?'

I get the feeling this was the idea all along – to show me the family snapshots. 'Sure,' I reply.

Plonking the heavy album on our dining table, Angela turns to a section showing photos of Desi and Davide participating in dance competitions as teenagers. The two of them are wearing a dazzling variety of tight, bright tango-style outfits with keyholes, mesh and sequins.

'Wow,' I say, and mean it – I hadn't pictured Desi and Davide as dancers.

'They danced for fifteen years,' says Angela. 'They used to win *everything*.'

Next she shows me some of Davide's stunning young

dance partners. 'She's a lawyer now,' says Angela, pointing to one of the girls. 'And this one was voted most beautiful teenager in Italy.'

The final photo shows Davide in a dance hall in Rome, accepting a gleaming national trophy in front of an appreciative crowd. Angela stares at the picture for almost half a minute.

'*Belli tempi*,' she says softly. Wonderful times.

Truth be told, this kind of interaction between Angela and myself is rare. She's indisputably kind – one time after I've battled to hang a load of wet clothes on our flimsy plastic clothes rack in the courtyard (not my forte), she walks over and re-pegs the whole lot without so much as a word. Mostly, though, she's a closed book. Part of this distance is because I'm a foreigner and I'm male. It's an unnerving combination for a middle-aged Sicilian woman in suburban Catania. But there's also the fact that I don't have a nine-to-five job. Like most of the neighbours – and, occasionally, Gill herself – Angela can't figure this out.

'Where's your wife?' she'll say in the middle of a week-day, knowing full well that Gill is at work. When I answer, she'll gaze into my eyes for a few seconds, as though trying to unlock an ancient puzzle. Finally she'll give a half-nod, half-shrug and wander away.

The difference when Gill walks across the courtyard is absolute. '*CIAO, BELLA!*' yells Angela, her face brightening.

Angela becomes very protective of Gill. She worries that Gill's working conditions aren't right and that, as a foreigner with no experience of Sicilian bureaucracy, Gill might be getting taken for a ride.

'Are you getting a stipend at Christmas?' Angela asks one time.

'I don't think so.'

'Well, it's the law. They have to pay you a bonus every Christmas.'

'Oh. Maybe it's different because I'm a foreigner.'

'Hmm, I don't think so. Bring me your employment contract and a payslip and I'll get a friend of mine to check it out.'

Angela also keeps an eye out for Gill's physical wellbeing. One morning when the two of them are nattering away outside, Angela pauses in mid-conversation and steps back to look Gill up and down. Finally she says, 'You're pregnant.'

If Gill had been drinking something, she'd have sprayed it out of her mouth in a violent cloud of mist. 'Sorry?'

'You're pregnant.'

Trying to remain composed, Gill says, 'Why do you think that?'

'I can just tell. Mostly because of your star signs.'

('At least it wasn't because she thought I looked fat,' Gill tells me later.)

'You and the husband are a perfect combination,' explains Angela, bumping her outstretched index fingers together to signal the partnership. Angela never calls me by my actual name; I'm simply *il marito* – the husband. 'You're a Gemini,' she says, pointing to Gill. 'And the husband is a Libra, right?' Then she drops her voice to a whisper. 'Do you know what that combination means?'

'No, what?'

'*Fuoco!*' Fire. Angela continues, '*Fuoco e . . . sesso!*' Fire and sex.

How flattering that Angela looks at me, a flabby, bearded, unemployed former academic, and sees me for what I really am – a no-holds-barred sex machine.

Gill blushes deeply, but Angela persists: 'My eldest son Orazio and his wife are pregnant with their second. He's Libra; she's Gemini. Same as you two.'

The logic isn't exactly watertight. Does this mean that every couple in the world with a Libra–Gemini combination is currently expecting a child? But Angela isn't finished. 'There's another reason I can tell.'

'What's that?'

'You look hormonal.'

Gill is about at the limit of her Italian language skills. An in-depth discussion about how or why she might look hormonal would be difficult indeed. So she simply says, 'Angela, I'm certain I'm not pregnant.'

Our friendly neighbour pauses, raises an eyebrow and shrugs her shoulders. It means: *Let's just wait and see about that.*

That evening, Gill says to me, 'Angela thinks I'm pregnant.'

The walls close in momentarily. 'Um . . . are you?' I scramble to remain emotionally neutral, in case this is something that Gill really wants. We've only been married for a few months. I certainly know where *I* currently stand on the ladder of childrearing (firmly on the 'DEAR GOD, NO!' rung). And I'm fairly sure Gill is on my wavelength. But you can't always tell.

'*Of course I'm not pregnant!*' she yells.

I make a mental note to buy a lottery ticket. Several booklets of them.

It does seem unlikely that Gill could be up the duff. We've only just moved into the Via Garibaldi apartment. Before that, at the nun's place on Via Gesuiti, we weren't even sleeping under the same roof. An immaculate conception, perhaps? It wouldn't surprise me, considering all the religious paraphernalia on the walls.

No, we have no intention of having a child in Catania. Can you imagine how many forms we'd have to fill out and how many queues we'd have to join, just to get a birth certificate?

A couple of days later, Gill walks past one of the older neighbours from an upstairs apartment. The woman shouts out, '*Auguri!*' ('Congratulations!')

'What for?' asks Gill.

'*Il bambino!*' The woman smiles, patting her stomach.

It's ten am on a Tuesday. I'm standing in the local green-grocer's store when Carmelo walks in. He's been out in the boat again. Now he's on his way home for a snooze, before another night at sea.

'*Ciao, bello!*' he says. Just as Angela calls Gill *bella*, Carmelo calls me *bello* (handsome). You wouldn't get away with it in Australia, but I figure it's an accepted idiom in these parts. I've been called worse.

Before I know it, Carmelo has dug two cold beers out of the fridge and handed one over. To reiterate: it's ten am on a Tuesday.

'No, Carmelo, I couldn't.'

'Not *no*,' he announces. '*Yes*.' To get the point across, he says this last word in English – it's the only one he knows. Then he leans over and pops the cap of my bottle with an opener.

I shrug. '*Cin cin*. Down the hatch!' I haven't drunk beer this early in the day since most of my first year and all of my second year at university.

Pubs aren't a big thing in Sicily so, like many local *alimentari*, this one serves a dual purpose as a fruit-and-vegetable outlet and a tavern for middle-aged and elderly men. We lean against a wooden crate of lilac-coloured cauliflower, sip our beers and make small talk. Talk tends to be *very* small with Carmelo, but I do get one or two sentences out of him. I ask him about his apartment, next to ours. How long has he lived there?

'I was five when my family moved into the Via Garibaldi place. It was just after World War II. I've been there ever since.'

Photos of the city dating from after the war show streets ravaged by gunfire and bombs. The Battle for Catania in 1943 had been a hard-fought one. I've also seen sepia pictures of trams travelling up and down Via Garibaldi. The tramlines are still there, embedded in the asphalt.

'They stopped running a long time ago,' says Carmelo. 'I remember riding them as a boy. It was fun.'

He's almost done with his beer already. I decide to exit before he opens the fridge again. One alcoholic beverage during the day is fine, but a session of beers before eleven am might be difficult to justify to the wife as she readies herself for an afternoon and evening in the classroom.

As I'm leaving, Carmelo calls out, 'Do you want some lunch? We're having *polpette di mucco.*'

'Sure.'

Actually, I'm *not* sure. *Polpette* are meatballs. But what was the second word? Was it *muco*, meaning 'mucus'? Ew. Or is *mucco* a made-up, masculine version of *mucca*, a cow? If so, have I just signed up for a lunch of harmless beef meatballs, or is *polpette* a colloquial expression for . . . you know, cow's *balls*?

Suddenly I'm suspicious. Didn't Carmelo give a funny little laugh when he mentioned the meal just now? And Sicilians certainly don't baulk at eating every bit of a beast they can find, so I wouldn't put it past them to dish up a wobbly pair of testicles.

Contemplative, I shuffle home. (Gill: 'You smell like . . . *beer.*')

A couple of hours later, Desi appears at the door clutching a plate of food. I feel like I'm on death row and the priest has arrived.

The plate is full of crispy round fritters, just out of the pan. I pick one up and juggle it in my fingers. When it's cooled, I break it open to look inside. Bad news: the flesh is white. These are definitely not traditional meatballs. Gill is watching from a few metres back, with her head turned slightly away like someone waiting for a firecracker to go off.

'What are all those black bits?' I ask Desi. Inside each ball, the white flesh is dotted with tiny dark specks. Already

I'm jumping to conclusions – and the conclusions aren't pretty. My guess is they are the itty-bitty heads of the moo-cow's sperm.

'What black bits?'

'*Those* black bits!'

'Oh, they're the eyes.'

'What do you mean *eyes*?'

'Eyes. Of the fish.'

A moment passes. 'Fish?'

'Yes.'

'From the sea?'

'Yes.'

The penny drops. This stuff is whitebait – juvenile fish. Probably sardines, to be precise, though baby mullet is also popular in Sicily. I've seen whitebait on sale at the Pescheria under a sign saying *neonata* (newborn). A popular method of preparation is to take a clump of tiny fish, combine it with a sprinkle of flour, egg, cheese and parsley, roll it into a ball, and pan-fry it. That's what I'm about to eat.

'So, how do they get their name?' I ask Desi.

'*Boh!*' She doesn't know. But I think I get the joke. Whitebait fritters and bull's testicles are pretty much the same thing: round balls filled with tiny little babies.

The fritters, at least, are salty and delicious.

Eating Carmelo's food doesn't get any easier. Another time, he appears at the door holding a square of butchers' paper in his hand with a pile of fresh, uncooked prawns in the middle. Their flesh is translucent, veiny and grey.

'*Ciao, bello,*' he says. 'Here, eat some of these.'

'Thanks,' I reply, prodding one of the slimy curls of seafood. 'So, what's the best way to prepare them?' I'm guessing he'll tell me to roast them on a pizza or perhaps pan-fry them and toss them through linguine.

'No, no, no. Eat them now. As they are.'

This marks the first time in my life that somebody has literally come the raw prawn with me.

'Really?'

'*Si, si, si!* They'll make you strong,' he says. 'And virile.'

Across the room, Gill looks torn. Clearly she abhors the idea of me putting an uncooked crustacean in my mouth, yet the glint in her eye suggests more than a passing interest in the promise of extra virility.

'Okay,' I say with a hint of uncertainty. 'Here goes.'

The prawns are gluggy but not unpleasant; I expect a powerful taste of the sea, but the flavour is subtle. No sudden tingling in the loins though.

The even happier news is that I feel fine the next day. I've escaped all four variations of shellfish poisoning (amnetic, neurotoxic, diarrhetic and paralytic) regularly contracted by people who do something foolhardy like consume raw, untreated prawns caught in the vicinity of Sicily's enormous petrochemical industry north of Syracuse.

Newly hatched sardines and raw prawns: Carmelo is keeping me on my toes with his weird seafood menu. And then it gets weirder.

'*Uova di seppia*,' he announces at our door a few days later, holding a plate of creamy, heart-shaped items, each one as big as a thumb. According to Carmelo, they were 'caught' this morning. He has gently fried them in a bit of olive oil and onion.

The term *uova di seppia* translates to cuttlefish eggs, though these don't look anything like roe. They look like large filled-in sacs of . . . *something*. Later, I go to an internet café to get to the bottom of the matter. But there's no definitive answer. I've either eaten some kind of entrails or a plateful of gonads. Or perhaps they were the half-developed embryos of new cuttlefish? I have no idea. All I know is that they're nicely textured, mildly flavoured, and entirely pleasing to the palate.

As usual, Gill politely declines Carmelo's offerings and instead watches every morsel go in my mouth, if not in horror, then certainly bemusement.

Cities around the world are defined in myriad ways. One is by the stereotyping of different social groups: in various places you'll find bogans, Sloane Rangers, soccer moms, yuppies, Volvo drivers, pikies and rednecks. The same applies in Italy. Depending on whether you're in Rome, Milan or Naples, you might hear references to *burino* (hick), *coatto* (chav) and *truzzo* (try-hard).

Catania has its own unique stereotypes, namely the *mammoriani* and the *monfiani*. The terms define two radically different groups of people on two opposite sides of the city. *Mammoriani* – the expression comes from the phrase '*mammoriri me omà*' (damn my mother!) – refers to Catanese who live in the impoverished southwest quarter of town. According to the stereotype, *mammoriani* are poor, rough, lower-class members of society; the young men tend towards petty crime; the young women wear heavy makeup and sleep with anyone. *Monfiani*, on the other hand, are the upper-class Catanese: cosmopolitan and metrosexual men, and snobbish women in expensive clothes. The name derives from Via Monfalcone, a street in Catania's wealthy northern suburbs lined with upmarket fashion boutiques.

Our new apartment is in the heartland of the *mammoriani*. And our neighbours are proud of it. Often they'll stop me while I'm speaking broken Italian to tell me I'm using the 'wrong' word. The first time it happens is when I make a comment about the '*aroma*' of something (the word is spelled the same in Italian as in English).

'No,' says Desi, in the middle of my sentence. 'We're *mammoriani*. We don't say *aroma*. We say *odore*.'

Even in their English equivalents – aroma and smell – it's easy to get a feeling for the difference that Desi is alluding to. Why speak poetically of something's 'aroma', 'scent' or 'fragrance' when you can cut through the bullshit and say 'smell'?

One day, just for a laugh, Gill and I take a bus up to the northeast of the city, home of the *monfiani*. We get off on Corso Italia and walk up to Via Monfalcone. Sure, there's the occasional luxury boutique of gleaming glass and steel in the area – the kind of thing you never see in Via Garibaldi or Via Plebiscito. To be honest, though, it all looks like the same old Catania to us: black stone, rutted streets, peeling posters, enraged graffiti, darting Vespas, and a whole lot of wary people looking over their shoulders.

9. A trip at Christmas

The man who has no sense of history is like a man who
has no ears or eyes.

– Adolf Hitler

Four Aussie friends – Richo and Kirsty, Simmo and Franki –
fly down from London for Christmas and a one-week jaunt
around Sicily. I'm given the task of preparing an itinerary.

Thoughts turn to the south coast. Gill and I haven't been
there yet, and it boasts some of Sicily's best-known destina-
tions, including Agrigento and Selinunte.

A few years ago, my brother Ferg drove along this same
frayed ridge of coastline in a Kombi. I phone him to ask what
he remembers about it.

'Poverty,' he says. Ten seconds of silence follow.

'O-*kay*,' I answer. 'Anything else?'

Another long pause. Finally he adds, 'Dead dogs on the
road?' He says it with an upward inflection, like he's wondering if it's what I want to hear. Frankly, I'd have preferred
'stunning ruins' and 'rustic pastas'. But the clock is ticking:
poverty and dead dogs on the road will have to do. I pencil
southern Sicily into the diary.

First, though, we have a Christmas to enjoy.

Although we're a long way from home, Gill and I attempt a little Yuletide joy. We find a two-foot plastic tree in a market and cover it with tinsel that our families have sent in a gift box from Australia. Also in the gift box are macadamia nuts, Santa-shaped lollies, a packet of Allen's Snakes, silver baubles, a stubby cooler and various other items of Australiana. The accompanying card features a koala dressed as Santa: he's driving a team of kangaroos across the sky and saying, '*Bewdy!*'

But Christmas is strangely muted in Catania. Even six-year-old Erminia seems unexcited. Then I discover why. Sicilian kids don't get their presents until 6 January, the Feast of the Epiphany. On that day, a witch-like character called La Befana flies in on her broom to fill children's stockings with surprises. Good children are given gifts. Bad children are given lumps of coal (which they presumably use for starting small fires in the neighbourhood).

Gill and I and our four Aussie mates are probably in line for lumps of coal in view of our drunkenness on 25 December. We join a party at a friend's place where festivities start innocuously enough with an exchange of gifts at the lunch table. Everyone dons silly paper hats and reads the terrible jokes from the Christmas bonbons ('Why was the mushroom invited to the party?' 'Because he's a fungi to be with'). Then a cork pops. My last memories, from around one am, include someone falling down a flight of stairs, a funny incident between Richo and a potted plant, and the unsafe yet exciting detonation of illegal fireworks on the outside balcony.

Christmas is a big boisterous blur. *Bewdy!*

Centuripe

The six of us wake up on 26 December feeling like we've been repeatedly punched in the head. It's Boxing Day, after all.

But we'll need our wits about us if we're to survive Sicily's infamous roads in our cramped hire car. Richo and Simmo have agreed to share the driving. I'll sit up front and navigate. The plan is to follow the A19 to the middle of the island, before taking a dogleg left to Agrigento on the south coast. I have a couple of interesting diversions in mind, too.

We negotiate the first hour safely and arrive at the hill-top town of Centuripe. It's one of several settlements on the island to claim distinction as the 'Balcony of Sicily' and rightly so: the views in every direction are phenomenal. An enormous half-arc of rainbow spouts from a bank of black clouds, bending across the saddle of a nearby hill and landing in the middle of the valley below.

Centuripe thrived under the Romans, but its subsequent fortunes were bleak. Virtually wiped off the map by the Normans in the thirteenth century and again by the Spanish in the sixteenth century, the town was then copiously bombed during World War II. Judging by the main square, where almost every establishment is padlocked shut behind a rusty roller-door, you'd think the inhabitants were still cowering under their desks.

Fortunately there is an open bar. As we're ordering coffees, one of the locals sidles up to me and asks if we'd like some lunch. All of us. At his mamma's house. Now. But there's something about the suddenness of the invitation and the eccentricity of the fellow's demeanour that rubs me the wrong way. I politely decline.

Isn't it a shame that the world is in such a parlous state that one can't accept at face value what is, in all likelihood, a genuine, off-the-cuff and heartfelt invitation? Instead, one ponders how one might wake up trussed to the wall of a basement the next morning, stripped of passports and money, and – if Hollywood films can be believed – soon to be operated on for black-market body parts.

In any case, we can't stay. There's a long day ahead.

The fellow looks disappointed. 'If I can't treat you to lunch,' he says, 'then I must pay for your coffees. To show you the hospitality of Centuripe!'

He hands a wodge of cash to the barman. I feel like an ungrateful swine (albeit one who's just saved himself seventy cents).

The Vulcanelli

Back on the highway, we pass beneath the hilltop town of Enna then turn in the direction of Sicily's southern coast. Half an hour later we leave the highway again, at a signpost for the village of Aragona.

My reason for the detour is to find the Vulcanelli di Macalube. A *vulcanello* is a miniature volcano. I've read about an eerie lunar landscape in the countryside here, full of cones of bubbling gas and mud.

Because they're tiny – a couple of feet high at best – the Vulcanelli are extremely difficult to locate. There's no distant peak to aim for. So, we drive in and out of Aragona, still with no clue, until finally Richo pulls up next to a rotund villager lumbering along the road. I wind the window down to ask for help.

'*Buongiorno*,' I say from the passenger seat.

The response is unexpected. The villager turns to face me, gives a giggle, and proceeds to mimic my voice – '*Buongiorno! Buongiorno!*' – only in the high-pitched tone of a Bee Gee.

This is startling, especially in view of his gigantic bush-ranger beard. And now he's advancing towards me. To think I was concerned about the guy in Centuripe inviting us to lunch at his mum's house.

Still, I'm not about to back down, otherwise we may never find what we're looking for. 'Erm . . . do you know the way to the Vulcanelli?'

While continuing to advance, the man hits me with another of his trademark squeals: '*Vulcanelli! Vulcanelli!* . . . *Buongiorno!*'

'Riiiiight,' I say slowly.

Having clomped up to the window, he now starts craning his neck into the car. I simultaneously lean back towards Richo in the driver's seat. The lummox is searching for something. A hand emerges from his pocket and begins to reach up. For a millisecond, I honestly believe he is attempting to eat my brains.

But I'm wrong. Now he's making the universal sign for cigarette smoking. '*Buongiorno! Vulcanelli!*' he intones in the manner of Tiny Tim, while tapping two nicotine-stained fingers to his lips.

I quickly grab a half-packet of someone's cigs from the dashboard and thrust it into his meaty hand. Then I start rolling my window up as fast as it can go, while simultaneously yelling at Richo, '*Go, go, go!*'

'Thanks for your help,' I add through the gap at the top of the window as our tyres spin on the clay laneway.

'*Buongiorno!*'

Our getaway route fortuitously leads us directly to a muddy parking bay and a rustic wooden sign for the Vulcanelli di Macalube.

After all that, they're shithouse. At least, they smell like one. Stretched like a grey, weeping scab across several acres of a flat plain, the site isn't quite the miniature Mount Etna I'm expecting. There are no volcanoes, no steaming geysers, and certainly no diminutive lava flows. Instead, I spy two or three crusty pools of silt and mud with the very occasional bubble breaking the surface. It's as endearing as diarrhoea.

We stay ten minutes. Another tourist pulls over in a car. I watch him wander tentatively onto the sprawl of grey mud, stare fixedly at the Vulcanelli for sixty seconds, then, with a resigned shrug of the shoulders, undo his fly and piss all over them, before returning to his car to drive away.

Back in our own vehicle, I say to the team, 'Not quite what I was expecting.'

But I can just imagine what they're thinking: 'Did we really come all the way from London for *this*?'

Perhaps the hangovers from Christmas Day are to blame, but there seems to be a mild edginess among our group. Already I've been given the title of 'Trip Nazi'. This is primarily because it falls upon me to keep everyone to a schedule. It was me, for instance, who insisted on an eight am departure from Catania. In retrospect, this did have an element of the Goebbels about it. So, while the nickname is certainly intended as a joke first and foremost, it feels ever so slightly accusatory as well.

Fortunately I have an ace up my sleeve: Agrigento.

Agrigento

For more than two millennia, visitors to Agrigento have raved about the place. Pindar, a poet of ancient Greece, called it 'the fairest city inhabited by mortals'; Goethe said, 'we shall never in our lives be able to rejoice again, after seeing such a stupendous view in this splendid valley'.

Recent press has been less effusive. Acknowledged as one of the poorest towns in all of Italy, Agrigento's modern-day reputation is of a Mafia stronghold, rife with illegal drugs. Shortly after our own visit, a businessman gets gunned down as he sits in a barber's chair in town waiting for a cut. When questioned by police, the barber claims to have seen nothing. Maybe he was over at the sink, washing some combs.

Despite the town's contemporary reputation, its number-one sightseeing attraction continues to make every list of must-sees in Sicily, if not all of Europe. The Valley of the Temples is not a valley at all, but a kilometre-long ridge halfway between the city and the ocean, lined by a stunning collection of ancient temples. I'd be tempted to compare the bleached columns to the ribcages of decomposed dinosaurs, except that every writer before me has done the same. I like

Lawrence Durrell's description of the temples – for him they were dinosaurs, too, only they were *alive*: 'One by one these huge mythological beasts came up to us, as if they were grazing, and allowed us to pat them.'

There are seven temples on the site. Three of these, the Temples of Concord, Hera and Hercules, are either wholly or partially standing, with a bit of help from various restoration projects undertaken since the eighteenth century. And they're gigantic. Twenty people standing in a circle, shoulder to shoulder, would barely wrap around the base of one column. These are colossal chunks of stone. It's perplexing to think about ancient workers moving even a single piece, let alone the thousands that dot the site. The columns of the Temple of Olympian Zeus – which, before a Carthaginian invasion halted construction in 406 BC, was set to be the biggest Doric temple ever built by the Greeks – were seven storeys tall.

As we wander through the site taking all of this in, the light fades and a glorious sunset wells on the horizon. A final touch is the sight of flowering almond trees in the fields surrounding the ancient ruins. Normally this doesn't happen until March, but a unique pattern of weather over the previous year means the blossom has come early.

'It's beautiful,' says Gill as we stand together looking out over the fields.

I nod in silent agreement. It *is* beautiful. 'And it's incredible to think,' I add at last, 'that on this very spot in the sixth century BC, a tyrant named Phalaris used to roast his enemies alive in a hollowed-out bronze bull.'

'Nice,' says Gill, in a tone that suggests I may have ruined a moment.

Our accommodation in Agrigento, the Hotel Concordia, is described in one guidebook – in one *sentence*, in fact – as 'dingy', 'depressing' and 'yucky'. But at the ridiculously cheap rate of twenty euros for a room, what's not to like?

The bathroom tiles, that's what. They're poo-brown with a geometric pattern like an optical illusion. When I stare at them for thirty seconds then look away, a fluorescent spiral starts dancing in front of my eyes. At least it makes up for the lack of a television set.

Gill and I have a routine in bad hotels – and we've stayed in a few. I act as guinea pig, testing out the particular quirks of the amenities so I can prepare a checklist. For example: 'Drain clogged with hair'; 'Don't touch showerhead (electric shock!)'; 'Dead rat in soap tray'. As chivalrous as this sounds, it also means that in the case of a dodgy hot-water system, I tend to get the warmest shower.

'If I'm not out in fifteen minutes, call the manager,' I say, entering the bathroom of our Hotel Concordia room armed with toiletry bag, Swiss Army knife, torch, can of beer and peanuts.

But the shower is fine. I've had worse – the cold, fetid dribble on offer at the Yellow Rose Hotel in Çanakkale, Turkey, for instance. I've never been stripped naked, hand-cuffed, and hosed down on the cold floor of a prison cell, but if it was offered as a bathing alternative at the Yellow

Rose, I bet all the hotel guests would rush to join a queue, clutching their little bottles of shampoo.

At least the Concordia's shower comes with a complimentary bar of wrapped soap, even if it is one of those thin white rectangles of mysteriously lather-less and odourless soap that have almost come to define cheap hotels.

An hour later when the six of us convene in the lobby to go out for dinner, I notice some of the others with damp hair and a startled look on their faces.

'I see you've showered,' I say.

They nod gravely.

Dinner is appalling. There's not a single memorable dish. I don't even make a note of the food in my diary, which is saying something. I write about *every* meal in my diary – often in great detail. Gill gives me a hard time about this. She reckons it's a strange habit, and it probably is. She'll ask, 'I wonder if we'll ever find ourselves in that romantic little French restaurant in Lorne again? The one where we stopped for dinner during our driving holiday along the Great Ocean Road.' And I'll say, 'I don't know. But if we do, I'm not ordering the gnocchi – *or* the rabbit.'

Our suspicions that we've chosen Agrigento's worst restaurant seem confirmed when we push our meals aside and stumble up the street only to find a large statue of some Greek god or other staring at us in a mocking fashion, one fist held aloft in our direction, the middle finger slightly but perceptibly raised.

We wake to a delightful winter's morning, feeling refreshed by a decent night's sleep – apart from a period between one and three am when a troop of stray cats decided they liked the look of the Hotel Concordia as a place to convene for urgent, violent sex.

We go for coffees and *cornetti* (Italian croissants) in Agrigento's main square. Some have their croissants plain, others with Nutella; some dip them in cappuccinos, others opt for espressos; one person even shocks three months' life out of the barman by requesting a pot of tea. It's like someone has just asked, 'Do you sell dildos?'

Simmo then surprises everyone by announcing his intention to have a quick rummage in the main shopping street – for business shirts, of all things. You'd think his guidebook says, 'Agrigento is renowned for Greek temples and menswear.'

Sadly it isn't. Simmo returns empty-handed. Meanwhile a couple of us nose about in a white-tiled fish market, admiring the perfectly looped eels and the boxes of shiny mullet and reflecting on our poor culinary choices from the previous night.

In general, there seems to be a mild reluctance to get back in the car and on the road. This may be because Agrigento looks so pleasant this morning. But I'm guessing it's really out of fear of being taken to the Vulcanelli again.

Eraclea Minoa

Thirty kilometres west of Agrigento, we turn off at a signpost for Eraclea Minoa. The road creeps for four kilometres through sandy olive plots, eventually stopping at a small parking bay on a crest above the ocean. Ours is the only car.

Eraclea Minoa flourished in ancient times, first as a colony of Greeks from Sparta, then later under the Romans. I've brought the group here because the remains of the ancient town are said to be worth a wander, accompanied by some delightful sea views.

The fellow in the ticket booth looks shocked at the presence of tourists. He halves the entry price before we even ask. As happy as I am to save a euro or two, I'm mildly concerned at this unsolicited reduction in price. It smacks of a grocery store owner putting a half-price sticker on an expired item.

Not surprisingly, the meagre ruins are a disappointment – particularly in the wake of the Valley of the Temples with its columns blocking out the sun. The onsite museum is especially lame – just a few unadorned chunks of stone accompanied by 1950s-style placards estimating what century they're from: 'VII c. BC', 'IV c. BC', 'VI c. BC'. It's really not very exciting.

'And I thought the Vulcanelli were good,' says one of my friends.

'*Buongiorno!*' squeals another.

The situation is partially redeemed when we climb over a padlocked fence and walk to a headland to take in some impressive coastal views. Standing on the bleached limestone cliffs of Capo Bianco (White Cape), we peer over the edge at a rugged beach lined by pine trees.

Finally we return to the car – and when I say 'finally', I mean ten minutes after arriving. The fellow in the ticket booth gives an embarrassed half-wave as we depart.

I glance in the rear-view mirror at the passengers in the back seat. They seem very quiet. Most of them are stifling yawns. One has dug out a novel. Another chews gum and stares out the window.

Things aren't going to plan.

Sciacca

We stop at Sciacca for some lunch. Despite the winter cold, this part of Sicily feels decidedly North African. The various towns take on a whitewashed look; the surrounding hills are arid. In Sciacca's expansive main square, Piazza Scandaliato, stalls sell semolina for couscous and long strands of intensely red chillies. The town derives its name from the Arabic word *xacca*, meaning water, and in midsummer when a scorching sirocco blows across from Libya, I reckon you'd need about ten litres a day.

We eat lunch of toasted *panini* in a restaurant-bar. Richo enjoys his first *arancino* of the trip – it's one of the especially delicious *ragù* variety. By the look on his face I can tell what he's thinking: 'I've wasted every second of my life up to this point by never eating one of these things before.'

Sciacca is home to the Bongiovi family, whose son, John, tinkered with the spelling of his names and forged a career playing hard-rock dross in America.

Good enough reason for us to leave.

Selinunte

'Hey, Trip Nazi,' says one of my companions from the back seat of the car. 'What's next on the itinerary?'

'Erm . . . a place called Selinunte.'

'Okay. And what's Selinunte all about?'

'It's . . . it's a beach. A really nice beach.'

But they're onto me.

'It says here,' says Kirsty, reading from a guidebook, 'that Selinunte is a major archaeological site.'

The entire back seat groans in unison and various items of collected refuse are hurled at my head.

'More ancient shite,' says someone, possibly my wife.

But here's the thing. Selinunte turns out to be *brilliant*. We all love it.

Selinunte takes its name from a variety of wild parsley (*selinos* in ancient Greek). It's a sprawling mess of pillars and pediments occupying a kilometre of prime beach real estate. In my opinion, it's one of the great archaeological sites in the entire Mediterranean.

What I like about the place is that it's not weighed down by its own history. It's more adventure playground than classroom. Even the nine massive temples are simply referred to as Temples A, B, C, D, E, F, G, M and O. So much for Concordia, Asclepius, Heracles and those other mouthfuls. Some of the temples are standing almost perfectly; others are just a tumbled pile of column sections, as though someone sneezed too loudly and they collapsed in on themselves. In fact, earthquakes did the bulk of the damage. There's not a single rope or barrier, so the six of us scramble everywhere, splitting into random groups, finding ourselves alone between a pair of stone pillars of the most astounding dimensions, and racing down to the windswept beach and its raggedy dunes.

To top off the whole experience, I manage to witness a couple of living, breathing dogs. They're lazing on the grass in front of a temple, hind legs cocked, licking their balls. In view of my brother's recollections of southern Sicily, it's a nice touch. Not the balls so much, but the fact that the dogs are alive rather than roadkill.

Scopello

The sun is now low in the sky. There are no hotels at Selinunte, so we leave the south coast of Sicily and cross to the north. The island tapers here at its western end, so the drive takes just thirty minutes. Yet the two coasts couldn't be more different. At Selinunte, flat plains slope down to shrubby dunes and beaches with a distinct Tunisian feel. By way of contrast, the town of Castellammare del Golfo, where the road from Selinunte meets the north coast, is ringed by steep mountains. The sea is rocky here, with jagged outcrops called *faraglioni* (literally 'stacks') thrusting up from the surface like shark's fins.

Castellammare is a town of fourteen thousand people an hour or so west of Palermo. It's a troubled soul. For a time, there were more murders per capita here than anywhere else on the island.

Our destination is mellower by far: Scopello, population forty. Half an hour's drive along a winding coastal road west from Castellammare, Scopello is just a handful of alleys set around a ramshackle piazza overlooking the sea.

By the time our car pulls up, only the palest crescent of dusk remains of the day. A wind is brewing. In the middle of the piazza, a villager fills a plastic barrel from a fountain. Over the back wall of the square is a shadowy citrus grove; beyond it, a pitch-black peak almost invisible against the darkening sky.

Despite the tiny population, Scopello has plenty of accommodation options, thanks to its status as a summer retreat for Palermitans. In the dead of winter, though, most of the guesthouses are locked and bolted.

The only place we find open is a mid-priced *albergo* called La Tranchetta. The woman at the front desk quotes sixty euros for a room. But one of my mates – okay, it's Simmo – has been reading about off-season discounts in the car. So he argues for forty-five euros. Rather insistently.

The ploy backfires. The woman sticks to her guns; so does Simmo. Things get heated. Eventually she refuses our business altogether and we end up on the cobbled lane outside. It's now well and truly dark, with some spots of rain adding to the wind swirling up from the sea.

Just when it looks like we'll have to backtrack to Castellammare, a chap named Vito Mazzara comes to the rescue. He's the stout owner of a similarly stout inn of chunky stone a few hundred metres from Scopello's square. It has one double room left. Thankfully a friend of his can also rent us a *casetta* (little house) on the hill behind the village.

We draw lots. Gill and I pull the 'Vito' ticket out of the hat. The other four are forced to hobble up the hill to the *casetta*. It's a tiny leaky joint with a suspect bathroom and only a foldout bed for the second couple.

'That'll teach 'em to grumble about Greek and Roman ruins!' I say to myself.

While the others struggle up the path, Gill and I share a glass of wine with a delightful French couple occupying one of the other rooms in the inn. The male half looks like the chiselled and dreamy young diver from *The Big Blue* – or so Gill tells me – but is actually a scientist working on the distinctly undreamy job of developing long-lasting seafood products in tins and tubes. His partner is devastatingly attractive – or so I tell Gill after she makes the *Big Blue* comment – and can work on whatever she wants as far as I'm concerned.

Our friends return, seemingly content with the *casetta*, and we head for the only restaurant in town that's open. The food is excellent. After antipasti, we're served platters of whole calamari, lightly floured and grilled. There's also *pasta con le sarde* – hollow spaghetti (*bucatini*) with sardines, fennel and raisins – and a risotto rich with fish, squid, prawns and clams. Outside, the night lengthens and resilient Scopello faces the brunt of some wicked winter weather.

Later, my joy at drawing the hotel room out of the hat turns sour. The heating system seems stuck on the 'cremation' setting and there's a non-stop creaking noise in the roof, not to mention dogs howling outside. Gill just bungs in her earplugs and nods off immediately.

The wind has disappeared by morning, so our group visits the abandoned *tonnara* (tuna station) a few hundred metres below Scopello's promontory. It sits right on the beach in a narrow and secluded bay of perfect azure water.

Dwindling tuna numbers forced the closure of the *tonnara* in the 1980s – another victim of the overfished Mediterannean – but what a place it must have been to work at when it was fully operational.

We meander through the ruins in silence, running our hands over rusted anchors, peering in at the shadowy outline of boats through the windows of a locked shed, and skimming shells across the glass-like water. It's glorious, even in the cold. So glorious, we decide to stay another night. Rather than pack our bags again, we'll take an afternoon drive to Erice, forty kilometres away to the west, then purchase some supplies, return to Scopello, and try a home-cooked dinner in the *casetta*.

Erice

Erice is a medieval marvel. It looks like the town that stared at the Gorgon and was frozen in stone for eternity.

To get there, we drive up some queasy hairpins through a thickly wooded slope. The road levels out at a modest car park outside the town gate, seven hundred and fifty metres above sea level. A break in the weather allows us to see southwest to Trapani and the salt pans of Mozia and Marsala. Beyond lies the ocean, patchworked by squares of sunlight that have prised their way through the murky sky. It lasts three minutes before a thick fog rolls in, obliterating visibility for the remainder of the afternoon.

Still, Erice in fog bestows a significant benefit: it makes the town look smaller and quainter than it really is. The population is thirty thousand; today it feels like three hundred.

Erice's castle was formerly a temple to Astarte under the Carthaginians, to Aphrodite under the Greeks and finally to Venus under the Romans. All three were goddesses of love and fertility – the temples likely doubled as sacred brothels. Then the boring old Normans turned the site into a fortification in the twelfth century.

Gill and I leave our four friends to explore the town while we walk up a stone rampart, through an archway and into the remaining tower of the castle. Inside, a young man sits silently at a table. A sign on the table says '*Offerta*'. We hand over a donation and the fellow immediately starts mumbling the history of the place. Seems he's coin-operated.

There's nothing particularly memorable about his spiel. It's given in fidgety, frequently inaudible Italian. 'They made cheese here after the war,' he says at one point.

'What kind of cheese?' I ask.

A nervous laugh. '*Cheese!*'

Here, it seems, is an ancient whorehouse, manned by a tour guide who happens to be the most celibate man in Christendom.

We wander into the empty square at the heart of the castle. I turn to my reading materials to flesh out some details of the place. According to the haughtier of my two guidebooks, one feature of the castle is its 'Ghibelline castellation'. It sounds like a sub-Saharan method of male birth control.

To be honest, this particular guidebook is beginning to grate. Time and time again in Sicily I've stood before a church façade or a Greek temple looking for a simple, readable description of the major architectural features before me, only to be faced with phrases such as 'alternating metopes and triglyphs', 'mullioned windows', 'rhomboidal white stone inlay' and 'trilobated arches'. Who do they think I am, Frank Lloyd Wright?

Erice's castle at one time or another incorporated a prison, a graveyard, a bathhouse, a well and a council chamber. Now, though, the chunks of crumbling brick are indistinguishable. Only the prison looks prison-like: a *Silence of the Lambs*–style pit of mossy rocks and trickling water. It's covered with an iron grille, to stop people falling in and suffering a Ghibelline castellation.

The fog thickens. Gill and I scramble for extra layers, including hoods and scarves, then shuffle back down to the silent town.

Erice's paths are paved with deep-rooted stones, scuffed by clip-clopping horses. Vapours cool and condense then drip from a drain's underbelly of moss. Wrought-iron lanterns cling to a wall. This is the very epitome of medieval – even the rubbish bins look like they've been forged by a smithy. If someone walked past in chainmail armour I wouldn't raise an eyebrow.

Nobody does walk past, except one elderly fellow in full tweed suit, waistcoat, cane, porkpie hat and handkerchief. Where's he going? Why's he dressed to the nines? If I lived in dank Erice, I'd probably slink around in Ugg boots.

Our final stop is for restorative coffees and cakes at a pink-painted *pasticceria* run by famous pastry chef Maria Grammatico. Gill orders a hot chocolate and gets exactly that, melted chocolate in a glass. She swoons.

Some of the others buy pieces of marzipan fruit, those incredibly accurate and dainty replicas of strawberries, blood oranges and prickly pears for which Erice is renowned. They look nice, though they're ghastly to eat – like biting down on a handful of slightly dissolved sugar cubes.

Back in Scopello, the wind blows even harder on night two. We lock ourselves away in the *casetta* with plates of antipasto and bottles of red wine, and cook *penne all'arrabbiata* with an extra tablespoon of chilli, then a grilled coil of speckled pork-and-fennel sausages, and a tray of roasted vegetables.

The foul weather persists in the morning. Unfortunately, this means a visit to the nearby Zingaro Nature Reserve is pointless. I was hoping we could hike in the Reserve – it's known for its plant and bird life, not to mention six of Sicily's best and most secluded beaches. But late December is beach weather in Bondi, not here.

We drive to the Reserve entrance anyway – it's only ten minutes north of Scopello. Another empty car park. With the engine off, the only sound we hear is heavy rain on the roof and the rubbery metronome of the windscreen wipers: *vvvtt, vvvtt, vvvtt, vvvtt . . .*

Thirty seconds pass.

'What now, Trip Nazi?'

After another pause to think, I order an immediate and unconditional evacuation of the area. 'Let's go to Cefalù.'

Cefalù

There's something distinctly phallic about Cefalù, halfway along Sicily's northern coastline. I'm guessing it's the rod-shaped mountain called La Rocca that thrusts up from the water, circled at sea level by a compact brim of ochre-red roof tiles.

Erections and Cefalù go hand in hand, so to speak. At least, they did for one of the town's most notorious residents, Aleister Crowley. The British occultist moved to Cefalù in 1920 and got up to all kinds of scandalous misbehaviour until Mussolini expelled him in 1923.

I'm familiar with Crowley, mainly as one of the cardboard cut-outs on the cover of *Sgt. Pepper's Lonely Hearts Club Band*. Led Zeppelin's Jimmy Page was supposedly a fan of his teachings. But I didn't know of a Sicilian connection until this trip.

Crowley chose Cefalù as a retreat based on his consultion of the Chinese classic text, the *I Ching*, as an oracle. Once there, he transformed his house into a college of the bizarre. He called it the 'Abbey of Thelema'. It's still in Cefalù today, hidden away in a suburb. The place is said to be in a state of ruin, boarded up, with smashed tiles, and shrubs growing through the floor. Some of Crowley's demonic frescoes remain on the walls. There are snippets of his poetry, too, which was almost unfathomably X-rated for the time. Read 'Leah Sublime' and you'll get the idea.

Other stories about Crowley: his disciples called him 'Beast'; he thought his wife was a bat and forced her to sleep upside down in a closet; he was a drug addict (hashish and opiates were apparently consumed in vast quantities at the Abbey of Thelema); he was an experienced mountain climber with various Himalayan summit attempts under his belt; he sharpened his fangs like a vampire; he urged a fellow Brit to drink the blood of a sacrificed cat, resulting in the man contracting acute enteritis; he finished his written signature with a little picture of a penis and testicles (one can only imagine the embarrassment this would've caused down at the bank).

I mention the Crowley details simply as a way of introducing Cefalù in a more interesting manner than merely describing it, like so many guidebooks and pamphlets do, as Sicily's second most popular beach resort after Taormina. Which, admittedly, it is.

One final story about Aleister Crowley. He was apparently prone to evacuating his bowels on the carpets of luxury hotels.

I doubt he'd have bothered to unbuckle his pants and straddle a rug at La Giara, the unexceptional two-star joint that we find ourselves in at Cefalù. It's hardly posh. However, it does have nice views of La Rocca from the rooms and a pleasant rooftop terrace, just an olive's throw from the ocean. Doubles are sixty euros, the same sum we squabbled over in Scopello. This time we don't risk asking for a discount.

Cefalù's best feature is its delightful little port, where a sagging row of medieval terraces and stone arches – the fishermen's quarter – sits flush against a wintry beach. After checking in at our hotel, we walk down there and brace ourselves in a rugged breeze, dodging the spray from waves crashing against the pier.

'You could almost surf that,' says Simmo with envy, watching these same waves peel into the bay and morph into a modest right-hander.

Cefalù is actually one of Sicily's dozen or more recognised surf spots. Another, called 'Kamikaze' by locals, is three kilometres to the east. Not exactly Bells Beach, but it'll do at a pinch.

On holiday with close friends, beer o'clock tends to toll rather earlier in the day than usual. Such is the case on this particular day. I also blame the bleak weather, which drives us into the bars by mid-afternoon.

Drunkenness ensues. I only remember a few snippets from the rest of the day and night: a little deli-cum-bar called Le Petit Tonneau (The Little Tuna) with a balcony overlooking the foamy sea; several bottles of wine in rapid succession at Bar Duomo; dinner at Al Porticciolo, where we garner raised eyebrows by using the complimentary *grissini* as drumsticks on the edge of the table.

Normally I keep decent notes while travelling. Those from the eight hours of this particular bender, however, are scrawled illegibly on the back of a stained brochure for our hotel. The few sentences I can read the following day make very little sense: 'western end Cefalù very seventies'; 'check tall tuna things on boats'; 'green olives = apples!'.

I wake ridiculously early the next morning. Some people sleep forever when they're drunk, but I'm the opposite. Alcohol is like a liquid alarm clock in my system. The day is stupendous. Everything has blown over during the night. It's a perfect morning for sweating out my toxins on the slopes of La Rocca.

After a quick pick-me-up coffee (a double), I labour up a fiercely vertical set of steps in the cliff face. Twenty minutes later, I'm three hundred metres above Cefalù, staring down at all those ruddy rooftops.

Like many of the historic sites of Sicily, the ruins on La Rocca tell the story of the island's constant occupation and reoccupation: there are Byzantine walls, the remnants of a Greek temple and a few chunks of a Norman castle. The vista from the top is as spectacular as the one at Taormina. Plus there's no Mount Etna to be seen, which makes a nice change.

I wander through a thin copse of firs, open a rusted gate that leads into a stone hut, stroll along the molar-like remnants of a crenellated wall, and take photos of the occasional boat out on the flat, sunlit sea. The low light of the morning sun makes each boat and its wake look like a comet fizzing against the blue.

Then it hits me: an unwelcome sense of isolation. I'm the only soul on this entire towering boulder. I begin to receive weird vibes from the rocky landscape, like the characters in *Picnic at Hanging Rock*. If someone were to creep up behind me and play a few notes on a pan flute, I'd tumble down the cliff in fright. Maybe the Aleister Crowley nonsense is giving me the heebie-jeebies. Or maybe it's just the double-shot macchiato. As much as I love caffeine, it has a tendency to shatter my nerves.

Back down in Cefalù, I seek sanctuary in the town's twelfth-century cathedral. This is one of Sicily's most important Norman monuments and one of the great churches of southern Europe. From the outside it looks more like a fortress than a religious building. There's none of the curly, florid façades of Sicily's countless Baroque churches.

I love it. But not everyone is so pleased. A guestbook in the cathedral's foyer includes this recent comment by a woman from New Zealand: 'Next time you choose to illuminate something, could it be the apse and not the modern art display? Because that's what we've travelled halfway across the world to see.'

My view? If you've travelled halfway across the world with the sole intention of seeing the apse of one church in a tiny Sicilian town, then you've either got too much money for your own good, or you're a criminal bore.

Having said that, she does have a point. It's extremely gloomy inside. In particular, the central apse with its huge and famous mosaic of Christ can barely be seen for shadow. Almost mockingly, the piece of scripture accompanying the mosaic comes from John 8:12 – 'I am the light of the world; he who follows me shall not walk in darkness.'

At the hotel, my hungover friends are in various stages of checking out. Gill and I get chatting with the girl at reception. She's a cheerful soul, eager to practise English with us. She says there are several English-language colleges in town and suggests we move to Cefalù to teach.

'Forget about Catania!' she says in a sprightly tone.

'Oh, don't worry,' I assure her. 'We do.'

Cefalù marks the endpoint of our loop of Sicily. The others have to make their way up the Italian mainland to Rome so they can catch a flight back to London.

Gill and I talk briefly about coming along with them for part of the way – it's the day before New Year's Eve, after all, and it would be nice to celebrate together. But our wallets are thinning fast and probably wouldn't cover the extra travel and accommodation. We'd need to cut down on our wine consumption, too. ('We?' says Gill, giving me a look.)

Not only that, but our friends are indecisive about their plans. A couple are keen to stay in the resort town of Matera in Calabria, the province that makes up Italy's toe, but when Gill and I phone ahead to enquire about vacancies at hotels, every place is booked out for New Year's Eve parties. Another couple likes the idea of the Amalfi Coast but prefers not to drive so far in the hire car. I suggest they all get the ferry from Palermo to Naples – it leaves twice daily and would bring them out near Amalfi, Capri and Pompeii, and not far from Rome. But someone says, 'I'm not getting on a wobbly old boat!' (Said boat comes with a casino, bars, a cinema and well-appointed two-person cabins with ensuites.)

In the end, Gill and I decide to leave them to their own devices. It just goes to show, sometimes with group travel the best solution is to have a dictatorial Fascist at the helm.

10. A trip to the Aeolian Islands

> My wife and I, we like to ride where there's not much traffic.
>
> – Evel Knievel

Learning Italian is a cinch. Just take any English word you know and add a vowel at the end to form the Italian equivalent (*atomica bomba*, *gastro-intestinale*, *botulismo*). It doesn't matter which vowel you use, though avoid 'u' as it's generally reserved for the tricky Sicilian dialect. Occasionally you have to change vowels rather than add them (*ombrello*); other times, you needn't do a thing (*weekend*, *tennis*, *nightclub*). It's effortless.

There is the occasional thorn in the side. 'Aeolian Islands' is one. It's hard enough in English. In Italian, though, it's Isole Eolie, a devilish succession of open syllables: *EE-so-leh ey-OH-lee-yeh*.

No matter. Following our visit to the islands, neither Gill nor I are likely to utter the name ever again.

Day 1
After Cefalù, we say farewell to our four friends at the coastal town of Milazzo. We've decided to spend New Year's Eve on

Lipari, the largest of seven islands that make up the Aeolians, a volcanic archipelago off Sicily's northern coastline. We circle a cheap hotel in our guidebook and ring to make a booking.

The forty-four-kilometre ferry trip from Milazzo is turbulent but invigorating. I stagger un-seamanlike to the stern deck and stare back at our wake as the mainland disappears. An oversized Italian flag flutters wildly on a pole.

At Marina Corta, Lipari's pretty port, a much larger crowd of people meets the ferry than I expect. It's the dead heart of winter – the Aeolian Islands should be ghostly quiet.

Among those waiting (some of whom, I notice, appear strangely anxious) is a woman in her fifties, distinctly non-Italian-looking, with white, short-cropped hair. She clutches a folder to her chest. Spying Gill and me, she wanders over and introduces herself in a South African accent. Her name is Diana Brown and, if we're interested, she can undercut the price of our booked hotel by ten euros. We're interested.

Diana moved to Lipari from South Africa in the 1970s. The *pensione* she operates is a two-star delight, and the thirty-euro price tag she offers us is a steal. We promptly ring the hotel holding our initial booking and cancel the reservation on account of a tragic accident involving a family pet back in Australia.

Gill and I check in, then head down to the waterfront again for a drink. A bar called Alta Marea (High Seas) is done up – rather predictably – in a nautical theme. It has comfy couches and doors open to the port. I order a beer for myself and a Campari for Gill. We chat with two Italian backpackers at the bar. They've got wide eyes and grubby black sand on their clothes. When we ask why, they tell us their story.

A couple of hours earlier, they'd been sitting in their hotel room on Stromboli, another of the Aeolian Islands, when it started to rain. The rain, they noticed, was black. Then it became heavier. Drops turned into chunks. Then they twigged: the island's volcano was erupting.

Stromboli erupts every twenty minutes – it's one of the most active volcanos in the world. But those eruptions, which now lend their name to a general pattern of volcanic behaviour known as 'Strombolian activity', are consistently minor. This one – which would appear on worldwide news bulletins the next day – was different. First, it caused five million cubic metres of volcanic rock to break off and tumble into the sea. The resulting splash triggered a pair of tsunamis several metres high; these caused boats to overturn on Stromboli, injuring six people, one of them seriously. It explains why the anxious-looking crowd had gathered at the port when we arrived. They were waiting on friends, family or further news about the eruption.

Here's the weird thing, though. The waves made it all the way to Milazzo – where Gill and I caught the ferry from the mainland – and they even caused minor damage there. It seems our boat passed directly over them in the open water between the coast and Lipari. We hadn't noticed.

With a feisty volcano to deal with, it's no wonder so many Strombolians migrated to Australia ('the eighth Aeolian Island') a century or so ago. Extreme poverty was an additional impetus. Many who made the long journey wound up in Melbourne and Geelong. If you run into a Mr or Mrs Sidoti, Ristuccia, Virgona or Pittorina in Melbourne (try one of the fruit shops), there's a good chance they or their ancestors hail from Stromboli.

Apparently a number of Italo–Australians have returned and resettled in the Aeolians, in particular on the small island of Filicudi. The main village even sells XXXX beer. If we had more time, and if the ferries weren't cancelled because of the eruption, I'd happily go to Filicudi to say g'day to my countrymen (and to propose that they start selling a real beer instead of dishwater).

While every Aeolian Island has boasted an active volcano in the past, apart from Stromboli only one has any fizzle of energy left: Vulcano – etymologically speaking, the first volcano in the world. Today it sounds like a ghastly place to visit. The main attraction is the Laghetto di Fanghi, a lake of mud that fills with hordes of near-naked tourists who come to wallow in egg-smelling goo on account of its 'health-giving' properties. For centuries, the mud has been renowned for relieving skin disorders.

I repeat: skin disorders. No matter how much sympathy I have for people with this kind of medical concern – and it's a lot, I promise – it doesn't mean I'm champing at the bit to roll around in the same gloop they've smeared on their afflictions since the time of the bubonic plague.

On Lipari, we're safe from full-scale eruptions and tepid mud-baths of flaking skin. This is the major service centre for the Aeolians. It's where most of the ferries arrive. Lipari also houses the bulk of the archipelago's population – eleven thousand out of a total of fifteen thousand.

At ten kilometres long, Lipari is also the biggest of the islands. A single main road winds around for twenty-five kilometres, passing through five towns, including Lipari itself where Gill and I are staying.

After a second and third drink (to steel ourselves against further Strombolian activity), we set off from Alta Marea to explore the town before dinner. Lipari is dominated by a walled citadel sitting on a bulge of land that separates two arcs of waterfront. The town sprawling around the citadel isn't particularly attractive: it feels distinctly like a place where people lucky enough to live in the more secluded corners of the Aeolians come to stock up on petrol or groceries.

The citadel, accessible via a set of mossy steps called Via del Concordato, is only two hundred metres across, but boasts several centuries-old churches. Neolithic, Greek and Roman remains have also been dug up here. These include terracotta masks worn by actors during theatre performances in ancient Greek times. The comedic masks are my favourite: two of them bear a striking resemblance to Statler and Waldorf, the two old men from *The Muppet Show*.

There weren't too many laughs in Lipari's later history. From the age of the Romans (whose emperors would often exile their political enemies to the island), the town was variously conquered, ransacked, reconquered, evacuated, slaughtered, abandoned and repopulated. The sturdy walls erected by the Spanish in 1556 – the ones that still surround the citadel today – went a long way to guaranteeing safety for the populace. But it wasn't until the final decline of Mediterranean piracy in the twentieth century that Lipari could be considered a haven of any sort. Only then did the summer tourists start rolling in. In 1950, there were as few as fifty beds for guests in the whole of the islands; a decade later, five hundred. Now? Countless thousands.

When night falls, we hit the town again to find some dinner. Not easy. Now that the Stromboli eruption has lost its fizz, Lipari is in winter hibernation again. Plus it's a Monday night – the worst night of the week for restaurant dining, according to Anthony Bourdain. Eventually we find an open *panificio* and snack on a couple of chewy bakery items. There's a wine bar on the main drag, too, so we stop for a nightcap.

It has been a bit of a dismal day of food. But this being Italy, glorious culinary treats are surely just around the corner.

Day 2

I expect the sky to be heavy with Stromboli's sulphurous ash the next morning, but we wake to bright sunshine and a canopy of royal blue.

'Maybe we should hire a couple of Vespas,' I suggest to Gill. 'Explore the nooks and crannies of this island.'

'Sounds fun!'

First, though, breakfast. The only place open is a seventy-year-old *pasticceria*, Café Subba. It's something of an institution in Lipari. Unfortunately, it only has *dolci* on offer.

I find it hard to face rolled wafers of chocolate and sweetened ricotta at eight am, so I settle for a coffee. Anyway, I tell myself, I have a full day to gorge at my leisure.

Having drained our heart-starters, we wander down to a scooter hire place and pay a typically hefty deposit for two bikes. Since we're Vespa virgins, a school-aged girl (Italian children are handed scooter licences in the womb) shows us to a small courtyard and provides a driving lesson – of sorts. It's barely helpful. After a wobbly five minutes, we tell the girl we're ready to go. No point wasting time.

Off we ride. Turning into Via F. Crispi, effectively the island's one 'highway', our bikes are immediately engulfed in a convoy of trucks from the port, legions of young Italians on zippy scooters, three-wheeled vegetable carts and the occasional donkey. It's quite a baptism, and I'm happy enough when three minutes later we pull into the nearest Agip service station to fill up the tanks, as per the instructions of the rental company.

Gill already has some trouble with her bike. 'It's not idling properly,' she says, and I take her word for it. A spotty young Agip employee tells us it's a simple issue and demonstrates how to get around it. He stands next to the bike, kicking the pedal repeatedly and pulling the throttle, before jumping on and zooming away for a few metres. Looks easy enough.

Not far after the petrol stop, we plunge into a short tunnel that cuts under the Monte Rosa promontory. It brings us out at the beachside village of Canneto, a one-kilometre seaside road of shops and *pensioni*.

Canneto has a 'leisurely air', according to one of the guidebooks. It seems true enough. Gill and I park at the end of the *lungomare* promenade and walk out to the beach. Mushroom-coloured pebbles shwoosh softly as they're lapped by the sea. I snap a photo of Gill basking in the glorious morning sun, her oversized motorbike helmet tucked under one arm like a bowling ball. It'll be her last smiling photo for a while.

Returning to the scooters, I study the Lipari map. Our next stop is the island's famous pumice-stone quarry another few kilometres along the road.

'Shall we go?' I ask, folding the map and putting it into my backpack.

Gill doesn't answer – she's having trouble with her machine again. I watch as she follows the instructions given by the young man at the petrol station ten minutes earlier. First she kicks the pedal and revs the engine simultaneously. Next she rocks the bike off its stand and lifts a leg to jump on. But at the same time as the stand folds down, Gill impulsively pulls on the throttle. The bike is already in gear. There's a loud roar, then the machine does a brief Knievel-esque wheelie. It lurches from Gill's hands, dumps her unceremoniously in the middle of the paved road and continues in a fast, straight line for about twenty metres, like a racehorse without a jockey. Finally it crunches into a telegraph pole with an almighty splintering of plastic, metal and glass.

The impact seems to occur almost in slow motion. It reminds me of stock footage of a crash-test dummy in a collision. Shaking myself back into the moment, I bolt over to the prone scooter. The engine is still howling and the back wheel spins violently. I reach in and turn the key to the off position. An ugly silence descends.

I run back to Gill to see if she's okay. There's blood on her hands and knees, and some on her chin. But they're flesh wounds – no problem with bones or organs, as far as I can see.

'What day is it?' I ask, looking into her eyes for signs of concussion.

'*The worst fucking day of my life*,' she replies, not without venom.

I'm relieved. It's a spirited riposte considering she's just been dragged viciously along the ground like Hector from the back of a chariot.

The scooter hasn't fared as well. Various bits and pieces are smashed and lying on the concrete. The two long poles that go up from the wheel to the handlebars – I find out later that these are called 'forks' – are badly bent. Other scraggly things seem to be sprouting from the engine at odd angles. In short, my encyclopaedic knowledge of motor vehicles leads me to conclude that Gill's scooter is pretty much fucked.

Having helped her over to a bench on the footpath facing the sea, I retrieve our phone from the backpack and ring the rental place. They seem unsurprised to hear that we've had an accident, almost like it's the expected thing.

'Where are you?'

'Canneto.'

'Okay. There in five minutes.'

Five minutes. That's the measly road time we covered before crashing. Embarrassing. As we wait, I think of all my friends who've had amazing experiences riding motorbikes over hills and dales in various locations around the world. Two hours after touching down in Thailand and – *vroom!* – they're humming around on a scooter. Travel writers pen entire books on the subject of Vespa journeys. Gill and I, on the other hand, have managed to stay upright for the time it takes to boil an egg.

And it's not Gill's fault. I'm clearly to blame. Any other husband or boyfriend would have put his hand up at the Agip service station and offered to ride the dodgy scooter. But I let Gill persist because I was secretly worried about my own lack of ability with vehicles. I am chillingly incompetent (not to mention passionately uninterested) when it comes to cars, bikes, boats – anything with an engine. This is my retribution.

The rental people arrive in minutes – a young punk and his girlfriend in a yellow sports car. They scream towards us at top speed, as if to confirm the oceans of difference in our respective driving abilities. Climbing out of his hotrod, the punk takes one look at the scooter and raises a bemused eyebrow. 'How did it happen?'

'You rented us a piece-of-shit bike!'

That's what I want to say, but I don't. I decide that a cool head is best. So I explain step by step in broken Italian about the faulty scooter and Gill's attempt to get it started.

He makes a closer examination of the wreck then says, 'I'll arrange to have this one taken back. You two drive the other one for the rest of the day and we'll go through the details when you're finished.'

Here we are, ashen-faced and upset, my wife with blood oozing from chin and knee, gravel scrapes up her arms, and this guy thinks we might like to hop onto one of his dodgy scooters for eight more hours of sightseeing.

'No. I think we're finished.'

'Okay,' he says. 'You drive your wife back to town on your bike, and we'll meet you at the garage.' Again, a slight lack of comprehension about our state of mind.

'We're finished with the bikes. Completely finished. *Basta!*' ('Enough!')

He shrugs and motions for us to get into his car. The trip to Lipari takes mere minutes, but it's enough time for the driver to receive a very thorough all-over groping from his girlfriend. Gill and I stare coldly as they writhe.

Back at the scooter shop, the three ringleaders of the rental circus listen with impassive faces to our story. But they've got us over a barrel. I may as well have walked backwards into the shop with my pants around my ankles and a sign saying 'GO YOUR HARDEST'.

'Faulty idle?' says one of them. 'What faulty idle? The bike was perfect when it left the garage.' How can we refute it?

The sum of each broken part is tallied up. The final figure is ruinous. Four hundred and eighty-six euros – more than we have to live on for a month in Catania.

'I feel sick to the stomach,' Gill whispers, reminding me of my hunger.

The storeowners insist that we pay the money immediately – perhaps they want the cash before a local news team commences an investigation into scooter scams on tourists. From this point on, the day becomes a succession of solemn trudges between the garage, our *pensione*, an ATM and several banks as we try to sort out payment.

I only have a few euros in my wallet so I go back to our room for the rest. There aren't enough notes stashed in my travel folder so I dig out some US dollars and bring them back to the shop. They say they need them changed into euros. I change them at a tourist information place where I get ripped off so badly on the exchange rate that I need to get even more euros. I go to the bank. It's closed. I go to another bank. *All* banks are closed. I get more euros out with my credit card. And on and on it goes.

Meanwhile, our friends who we farewelled after Cefalù call us from the Amalfi Coast and leave a message on our mobile: they've found a brilliant – and cheap! – hotel in Sorrento, they're about to crack their first bottle of New Year's Eve champagne, and they hope we're having a good time back in Sicily, too.

Aren't we just.

Back in our hotel room, I apply various bandaids and salves to Gill's wounds. What to do with the balance of this depressing day? Even the weather has changed. A bank of cloud begins to swell on the horizon. But rain seems a few hours away yet.

'We could go and get drunk,' I suggest.

'No thanks.'

'Okay, *I* could go and get drunk, while you watch.'

Gill has a bit of a laugh. I hadn't really intended it as a joke, but it's good to see the mood lightening nonetheless.

Downstairs, I ask Diana Brown for directions to Lipari's nicest beach. She gives me a quizzical look – it's December, after all.

'There's a decent spot called Valle Muria,' says Diana, 'a few kilometres out of town. Take one of the orange buses from the main street.'

The trip through elevated farmland is thoroughly pleasant. We should have stuck with public transport from the get-go. The friendly driver, barely out of his teens, gets out of the bus at one point to help an elderly passenger with her shopping bags. You don't see that in Catania.

At the village of Quattrocchi, he makes a special detour in order to drop us right at the top of the path to the beach. 'Valle Muria!' he says, like a game-show host unveiling a new car.

From the road, it's a longer-than-imagined hike down a muddy winding track to the beach. If the rain comes it'll be a difficult proposition getting back up. After ten minutes, the track hits dunes and we walk past the flotsam and jetsam of the previous summer. Prostrate in the salty grass are broken wooden signs advertising items for hire, from beach umbrellas to pedal boats and canoes (*singole o doppie* – singles or doubles).

The beach itself is secluded, with not a soul to be seen. It's also dramatic – a tiny arc hemmed in by cliffs whose walls are threaded with seams of volcanic rock of different colours: mustard, ochre and olive.

While Gill sits on a towel and grabs a ray of the disappearing sunshine, I hobble across a shoreline of baseball-sized stones and into the water. It's choppy and frigid. Usually I enjoy a bit of masochistic invigoration in an arctic ocean, but this isn't much fun. It's not the temperature that bothers me (though it's cold enough to vasectomise), nor the painful boulders underfoot, but the thin meniscus of oil on the water. Later I hear that the previous day's eruption and tsunami resulted in two fuel boats overturning and spilling oil into the sea. Seems I've swum right through the slick.

On my return, Gill is still sitting on the beach reading a tattered yellow paperback with the title *Déjà Dead*.

'What's the book about?' I ask, towelling tanker fuel from my body.

'Murder,' she replies in a detached tone.

'Nice one,' I say. 'That's bound to lift the spirits!'

'Surprisingly enough, it is.'

Twenty minutes later, the sky is almost completely shrouded in cloud.

'Might be some rain soon,' I say. 'We'd better not miss that bus.'

'Okay,' says Gill. 'When does it leave?'

Good question. I'd forgotten to check the schedule.

'Shortly,' I reply, figuring it's best to tell a white lie with Gill in a delicate frame of mind.

We pack our things and walk with some difficulty up the half-kilometre path back to the road.

So begins a horrible seventy-minute wait for a bus. After ten minutes, the heavens open. The bus stop has no shelter – it's just a sign on the shoulder of the narrow road. We can't walk back to Lipari because Gill has a gammy leg from the crash. There's no passing traffic, so no chance of hitchhiking. And we have no *ombrello*. All we can do is stand under a tree and grimace for an hour. Gill could justifiably rip me apart for lack of planning, but she's oddly silent – caught, perhaps, in the eye of her own personal storm. And me? I'm nauseous from starvation.

Just when Sicily really has you by the balls, though, it contrives to take your breath away. Towards the end of our long wet wait, the clouds suddenly break open in a couple of places near the horizon and the valley below us fills with a soup of afternoon sun. The Lipari citadel glows like a distant golden beacon. In the other direction is an expanse of ocean, with the gently smoking island of Vulcano a few kilometres beyond that.

It's quite an astonishing view. Locals joke that the name of the nearby village, Quattrocchi – it means 'four eyes' – refers to newly married couples who come up here and pose together for photos, with a backdrop of Aeolian glory behind them. (As opposed to newly married couples who come up here to get rained on while contemplating a road accident and the loss of all their savings.)

While possibly not in the mood to link arms and belt out a rendition of 'Auld Lang Syne', Gill and I are still eager to make something of New Year's Eve. Back at Diana Brown's, we dry off, warm up, scrape together our coins and hit the streets.

Far from running into a town full of happy revellers, we discover that Lipari is desolate. We creep along Via Vittorio Emanuele looking for the tiniest sliver of light from a window or laughter from behind a door. Nothing. In the main square, I watch a plastic bag gusting up and down in the air for several minutes. It's my *American Beauty* moment.

The wind has been strengthening all afternoon. No great surprise. The Aeolian Islands, after all, take their name from Aeolus, the god of the winds. December and January are when they blow the hardest. Homer tells how Odysseus stopped at the islands on his voyage home and was given an ox-hide bag by Aeolus. The bag, bound with a silver thread, contained all the winds that might otherwise impede Odysseus's ship as it sailed. Only the favourable Zephyr, the west wind, was free to blow. But ten days later as the boat neared the hero's homeland of Ithaca, his crewmembers opened the bag, jealously believing it to contain gold and silver. They were promptly blown all the way back to the Aeolian Islands. Poor bastards.

It's the last day of the year on Lipari and someone has opened the bag of winds. Now if only they would open the restaurants. Everything is shut – every bar, restaurant, café and kiosk; so much for a New Year's Eve countdown. We tuck our hands into our armpits and march into the bracing wind for ten minutes but don't find a thing.

There's nothing for it but to slink back to Diana Brown's, where we can at least finish the packet of chocolate biscuits that we bought from a *tabaccheria* earlier in the evening. I make a cup of tea. Gill stares blank-faced at the TV. After a period of time I look at my watch as it flicks over to midnight.

'Well, happy New Year then,' I say, before walking across to give Gill a kiss.

She half smiles. 'Yeah, happy New Year.'

Then we both surprise each other with gifts: a pair of romantic red underpants each. This is an Italian New Year's Eve custom. The windows of Catania's boutiques started filling with red lacy lingerie and g-strings from early in December. I guess the idea is to guarantee a sexy start to the year.

Quite frankly, we'd be more aroused if someone handed us a plate of cooked food, the promise of three consecutive days of sunny weather, and a cheque for four hundred and eighty-six euros.

Day 3

A good lie-in can solve any number of ailments – particularly on the first day of the year. Less therapeutic is the thunderous tolling of church bells at six am. Gill and I shoot up from our beds instantly. We have a small laugh when we recognise the tune of the bells – 'Silent Night'. The laugh becomes even smaller as the bells continue to ring, non-stop, for much of the morning.

There's nothing to do but spring into action. Anyway, I've eaten so little in the past thirty-six hours that my stomach has developed a Strombolian grumble loud enough to confuse local volcanologists. I leave Gill to block out the bells with a pillow while I hit the main street of Lipari to find breakfast. A whole spit-roasted *porchetta* would be ideal, though anything will do.

Lipari remains deserted. Thankfully there's a café open along the waterfront. The place boasts Dustin Hoffman, Kevin Costner and Prince Harry as previous customers. Today it's just me. I buy takeaway cappuccinos and the only available snacks, *pizzette* (mini-pizzas). The coffees do the trick but the pizzas are tragic – arguably the worst I've sampled in Sicily. I can only hope that Kevin Costner bought dozens of them.

A soul-cleansing stroll in the country seems in order after the tribulations of the previous day. Gill is having none of it, particularly in the wake of our drenching at the Quattrocchi bus stop. Her bruises have ripened overnight, too, so she understandably opts to lounge on the hotel bed for the day. There is *Déjà Dead* to finish, after all.

I hike up Monte Rosa, the headland separating Lipari from Canneto. Among the wet weeds and abandoned shepherds' huts are a number of blackened stumps suggesting a recent fire. Later I discover that blazes are common on the Aeolian Islands: hunters light them deliberately so rabbits can't use the foliage to escape. What a strategy. Burn those fields, hunters! Slay those bunnies!

At the Monte Rosa summit, I find a ten-foot upright crucifix fashioned from metal bars and lined with neon bulbs. Presumably the whole thing lights up for religious festivals, with the glowing cross visible from the main town below.

And speaking of bunnies, on the ground is the skeleton of one that seems to have mistaken the power cable at the back of the crucifix for a snack. Its little buck teeth, set inside a toasted skull, remain firmly clamped around an electrical wire. Where's David Lynch with a video camera when you need him?

Out towards the horizon are two more Aeolian Islands – the tiny celebrity hideaway of Panarea, and the steep and perfect cone of Stromboli, still fuming from its flare-up a couple of days earlier. Back down to my right is the bay of Lipari. I choose not to look in the direction of Canneto, the scene of our recent expensive mishap.

Still, I feel much better for my half-day hike. So does my wallet.

That night we emerge from the hotel to hunt for food again. A small restaurant called La Piazzetta is already filled with Lipari's entire contingent of winter tourists. The manager asks us to come back in half an hour. We do so. Then he tells us to come back in another forty-five minutes. We do that as well. When we come back a third time, he looks at us and says, 'Sorry, no tables.'

Under normal circumstances, Gill would give this guy both barrels of a verbal spray (while I hid to one side, nodding in nervous agreement). Here in Lipari, neither of us can be bothered raising a fuss.

As we stand there contemplating what the next disappointment might be, a woman walks past with a pile of takeaway pizzas tucked into the crook of her arm. The smell is delectable – the pizzas, I mean, not the crook.

'How about takeaway pizza?' I ask the manager.

'Finished for the night.'

Gill quietly leans her forehead against my shoulder.

It's after ten pm. We walk down to the port to check ferry times for the following day – we need to make absolutely certain that escape is possible lest we starve to death. Malnutrition is not a word synonymous with holidaying in Italy, but for us it's becoming a distinct threat. Fortunately, there's a boat back to the Sicilian mainland at midday.

Along the waterfront, gleaming like a rescue beacon, is an open restaurant. It specialises in organic salads. Under normal circumstances, I'd rather eat a computer mousepad. But I'm too hungry to care. We place an order and soon a bowl of leaves arrives which we chew methodically like giraffes, extracting all the necessary nutrients for survival.

Day 4

The wind gets up again during the night. Occasionally I wake to the sporadic bang of a slamming door or the stop-start tinkle of a bottle rolling in a gutter. When the day dawns, though, all is silent – even the bells give us a break. It's a perfect day, too. The weather has been blown to oblivion by Aeolus.

Gill wants nothing more than to laze around the sunny waterfront until the ferry arrives, but I'm fidgety as ever. I jump on a tiny electric bus for the village of Acquacalda at the northern end of Lipari. The twenty-minute trip takes me past pumice quarries that have been gouged into the chalky cliffs. Apparently, in summer there's a party atmosphere here, with dozens of yachts moored off the coast, and brown-bodied children sliding down pumice chutes into the cerulean sea.

Despite the closure of many old workshops, pumice mining continues on Lipari. The stone is used in everything from pencil erasers to exfoliates. I vaguely remember having my hands scrubbed – and possibly my mouth washed out – with grey pumice soap as a child. It's even in toothpaste. There's only one downside. Someone discovered that pumice could be used to fade denim in all manner of garish patterns. Blame Lipari, then, for Italy's ongoing obsession with stonewashed jeans.

Minutes later, the bus reaches Acquacalda. The name means 'hot water', from the thermal springs that once flourished in the area. More recently, the village served as the original port for pumice: the odd wooden jetty remains, gnarled from disuse, like the bony spine of a dead fish.

I wander into a place advertised as a café but which looks more like the front room of someone's house. A family lolls about in pyjamas eating breakfast. Apologising, I turn to walk out, but they call me back in. It *is* a café after all. Lovely people, too. They make me a macchiato and suggest I walk to the far end of town and up the hill for fantastic views of another Aeolian Island, Salina. I do just that.

They're right about the views – astonishing. Salina, where Michael Radford's *Il Postino* was filmed, boasts one of the most perfectly shaped mountain cones on the planet,

Monte dei Porri. It's a joy to behold from afar, especially with tiny tufts of passing cloud using the side of the mountain as a projection screen for their shadows.

In my eyes, the Aeolians have just about redeemed themselves.

Gill has also had a delightful morning. Yet it's not enough to convert her. 'Let us never speak of the islands again,' she says, as our ferry churns through the ocean back to Milazzo.

11. Praying

St Agatha's girdle, when brought forth, is said to have
arrested the fiery stream pouring down from Mount
Etna on the city below!
— T. L. Kington, *History of Frederick the Second,
Emperor of the Romans*, 1862

January in Catania is relentlessly cold and wet – a Ground-
hog Day of miserable winter.

'*Dreich*,' says my friend Dave when I comment on the
appalling weather one day.

Dave and his partner Kate, a pair of Scottish vegans in
their late twenties, have recently arrived in Catania after a
stint in Naples. It seems they're attracted to cities with high
crime rates.

Kate's working with Gill at the Giga school. Dave's a
stay-at-home writer, specialising in vegan poetry (not to be
confused with Vogon poetry). He wears sandals, Bob Marley t-shirts and dreadlocks. Because he's prematurely balding,
the dreads barely cling to his head; instead they look like
tufts of ropey grass at the edge of an eroding dune.

Dave's writing, like mine, is yet to attract JK Rowling-
esque attention. But everyone has to start somewhere. And

that's precisely what the two of us have done; by hooking up with women who seem happy enough to support our folly.

Then again, maybe it *isn't* folly. I've just received some happy news via email: an editor at Canada's leading national newspaper, *The Globe and Mail*, is interested in buying a China travel story that I pitched to him about climbing Yellow Mountain. Could this be the start of something big? Let's hope so, especially as my motivation levels for completing the biography of Caracalla are at their lowest ebb. So much for finding my Roman-history mojo in Sicily.

Listening to Dave and Kate talk can be like trying to decipher an Irvine Welsh novel.

'Sorry, Dave, what did you say?'

'The weather – it's *dreich*.'

My face remains blank.

'*Dreich*, man! Miserable, gloomy, depressing. Likely to *pish doon*.'

Sicily isn't easy for a vegan. The markets are particularly confronting and meaty, with tables full of horseflesh, skinned rabbits and castrated goats. Some of the *mortadella* sausages are a metre long and thirty centimetres thick, studded with golf-ball-sized chunks of fat.

Fortunately for our Scottish friends, Catania has a small imported-food store called Cristaldi. Here you can buy sacks of spice from the subcontinent, pulses and rice, tins of 'mock duck meat', oolong tea and Thai fish sauce. Italians avoid the place like the plague. Gill and I go there occasionally – me to buy curry pastes, Gill to buy a rare treat of Scandinavian muesli priced at several euros per oat. For Dave and Kate, though, it's a second home.

The Scots are champion cooks, too. We enjoy several boozy dinners in their fourth-floor apartment on Via Crociferi, the most heavily churched street in the city. While it's a more salubrious area than ours, next to the central shopping boulevard of Via Etnea, their apartment is just as rundown; during one unpleasant stretch, they have no running water for five days. It does boast a sliver of an ocean view, though. The dinner menu is usually Indian: onion pakoras, vegetable curries, naan breads – all cooked in vegan ghee. Another night, Dave makes a mean polenta cake with a blow-your-head-off chilli dip. We wash it down with cheap bottles of Splügen, the only Italian beer named after a German sex act.

Later, after lots of drinks, Dave commandeers the stereo and plays songs by vegan rap and reggae artists, turning up the volume whenever they start ranting about meat-eating scum like me. If he's especially *pished*, he'll perform his poetry. My favourite poem of Dave's is 'To a Vegetarian Haggis', an animal-friendly version of Robbie Burns' famous ode. The poem is a plea for people to eat meatless haggises full of 'tatties, neeps, caulie and kale'.

If nobody feels like listening to music or poetry, we just drink beers and take the collective piss out of the Poms instead.

Dave (singing): 'Scotland the bold and mighty, England the wee and shitey!'

Perhaps the rain god is English. In fact, I'm sure he is. The weather deteriorates.

All of Europe is suffering. Newspapers begin to report on the coldest winter in decades. Russia is worst hit – well over two hundred Muscovites have perished since October ('There is no war, but people are still dying,' says one spokesperson). In a single province of Finland, fifty-five people lose parts of their arms or legs to frostbite. Germany records eight deaths; France, four. People are even expiring from the cold in *India*.

There are fatalities in Italy, too – and not just people. A zoo in Calabria is forced to close when Arabian camels and exotic parrots start keeling over in their enclosures.

I'm not unaccustomed to extreme winters. After all, I'd spent the previous year living in northeast China, not far from Vladivostok, where temperatures in January dipped below minus thirty degrees Celsius and poor families used chopsticks to chip the ice from their living-room walls. I taught in a classroom where you could see your breath. Catania's chilliest days (maximums of five or six degrees *above*) seem almost tropical by comparison.

For whatever reason, though, the cold snap in Sicily feels harder to deal with than the outright brutality of the Sino–Siberian border. At least up there I knew what was coming – like in that Far Side cartoon where the Eskimo climbs out of his igloo, surveys the day, and pronounces that it's cold again. Here in Catania, Gill and I are poorly equipped. We have no quilt or doona on our bed – just an unzipped sleeping bag stretched across both sides. A single fan-heater serves to warm the entire apartment, though it only works if I unplug my laptop. There seems no point spending money to alleviate the problem when our finances are so tight and when the worst of the cold weather will only last a few weeks. Instead, we eat breakfast in bed, fully clothed, with jumpers, jackets and beanies.

Compounding the misery is Mount Etna and her relentless plume of filthy ash. The eruption has continued unabated for well over two months now. Our courtyard is filled with bulging bags of volcanic detritus. They look like military sandbags, especially against the backdrop of our age-ing *palazzo*, whose stucco is pocked with bullet holes from World War II.

Exacerbating the dishevelled look is a steady stream of dog shit speckled about the square courtesy of Minnie and Maggie, the Maltese terriers from next door. Thankfully it never stays on the ground for long. The dogs have come to a reciprocal arrangement: 'You eat mine, I'll eat yours.'

Again, though, it's the ash from Etna that most gets on the nerves. 'Can't someone shove a giant cork in that thing?' I say, staring wistfully in the direction of the volcano. But Gill has gone inside again, temporarily escaping her moaning husband and the neighbours' shit-eating dogs.

Then, suddenly, it stops. Three months and a couple of days after Catania's sky first turned black, the volcano falls silent.

No doubt there's a detailed scientific explanation for the dramatic cessation of volcanic activity. Any local I speak to, though, has only one answer for it: 'Saint Agatha.' End of conversation.

As I've mentioned, Saint Agatha ('Sant'Agata' in Italian) is Catania's patron saint. She was born here in the third century AD and lived a modest and unexceptional life until the Roman governor of Sicily fell in love with her. When she chastely rejected his advances, Agatha was tried, imprisoned and then tortured in a style reminiscent of a *Saw* film. Her breasts were pulled off with pincers, holes were poked in her sides with hot irons, and she was encased in a limestone kiln where she roasted on sizzling coals. It took her two days to die. She was fifteen. Terrific race, the Romans.

Rather than haunt Catania for eternity, as I might have done, the beatified Agatha generously set about protecting the city whenever Mount Etna threatened its destruction. In the centuries following her martyrdom, Agatha's name was frequently invoked when the volcano roared into life. Waving the saint's veil – or, indeed, her girdle – at a lava flow was said to be enough to make it stop.

Superstitious codswallop? Surely. Then again, there's something uncanny about this most recent end to Etna's violence. After so many months, the volcano has fallen silent with just forty-eight hours left before the start of the biggest event on Catania's calendar: a four-day festival in honour of . . . guess who?

Festival of Saint Agatha: Day 1

Until now, the nearest thing I've seen to a fervent religious parade was held in my hometown of Byron Bay in the 1980s. Every Christmas, a hundred or more Hare Krishnas would band together in orange robes to pull a teetering, pyramid-shaped shrine along the beach. I'm still not entirely sure what it all meant but it made for an enjoyable spectacle when I was a kid. There was a bonus, too: the Hare Krishnas served excellent curries from a big tent they set up as their headquarters. Not only was the food free, but once you'd finished you could clean your hands using the promotional literature they'd foisted on you earlier.

The Festival of Saint Agatha in Catania promises more than a free plate of palak paneer. Held from 3 to 6 February each year, it's said to be one of the largest religious processions in the world, rivalled only by Holy Week in Seville, Spain, and the Corpus Domini festivities in Cuzco, Peru.

Despite this, I find the opening day a bit of a yawn. An interminable street parade called 'The Offering of the Wax' edges its way along Catania's main boulevard, Via Etnea. The city's various religious, civil and military groups march by, looking like the cast of an Elizabethan period drama. I see breeches, cassocks, capes and smocks – even some puffy shirts.

I'm more intrigued by a nearby Tunisian balloon vendor, whose bouquet of helium Teletubbies, Tweety Birds, Pokemons and Pinocchios is so immense it's a wonder he doesn't float up into the sky and across the Mediterranean back to his homeland.

Things get more interesting with the arrival of the *candelore*. These towers, five metres tall and weighing up to a ton each, look like giant candelabras of ornately carved and gilded timber. They are among the iconic elements of the Festival of Saint Agatha. There are eleven *candelore*, each one representing a particular city guild – butchers, bakers, fishermen, florists, pasta-makers and others. Over the coming days, teams of eight to twelve men from the respective industries will be assigned to each tower, hoisting it onto their shoulders to carry it for dozens of kilometres through Catania on a predetermined route. It's an arduous task. Already at the opening procession, one of the teams is labouring under the weight of their tower. (I'm guessing it's the florists.)

On closer inspection, each tower is decorated with miniature theatre boxes cut into its side, like puppet-show stages. On these stages, tiny terracotta figures act out the Saint Agatha legend in gory detail: Agatha being led away by Romans and stripped naked; Agatha bound to a pole, awaiting her fate; a snivelling man opening a pair of metal pincers around one of Agatha's breasts; Agatha with both breasts ripped away and circles of bleeding flesh on her chest; Agatha being dragged over blazing coals; and – for a happy change – Agatha's ascent to heaven in the arms of angels.

Later that evening, Gill and I brave frigid temperatures and walk down to Piazza Duomo for the *pirotecnico spettacolo* – a fireworks display which serves as the festival's official launch. In contrast to the midday procession, Via Etnea is now jammed with people.

After a ten-minute prelude by the city's orchestra, the lights in the main square blink off. A few preliminary fireworks shoot into the sky with a soft pop. Another batch follows. Fountains start firing up from the ground. The explosions get higher, louder and more frequent. Soon the whole night sky is ablaze. This is more like it. For thirty uninterrupted minutes, Catania quakes under an onslaught of light and colour. Even the *cupole* of centuries-old churches are rigged with rings of pink fireworks.

'Wow,' I say to a young man beside me. 'Cool festival.'

'*Non hai visto ancora niente*,' he replies. You ain't seen nothin' yet.

Festival of Saint Agatha: Day 2

The next day is colder still. 'Catania the Refrigerator', proclaims the front page of *La Sicilia*, as minimums drop below zero.

Despite the cold, I'm out of the apartment by five thirty am, trudging towards Piazza Duomo once again. The famous Messa dell'Aurora (Dawn Mass) is due to start in the cathedral at six. Afterwards, Saint Agatha herself will make an appearance.

Gill, on the other hand, will *not* make an appearance. Not at five thirty in this weather. She remains cocooned in bed. Fair enough, too. As I crunch down the road with my woollen scarf wrapped around my head like a mummy and an ache in my toes from the cold, I think to myself, *I bet I'm the only one there*. But I'm wrong. Locals begin to appear out of alleyways and side streets, all of them making a beeline for the heart of town. Appropriately, a good proportion of them are dressed like they've escaped from a madhouse. They're wearing knee-length tunics of white linen, with matching white gloves and jaunty black velvet hats. They each carry a pleated white handkerchief in one hand. By the time I reach the piazza, I'm surrounded by swarms of characters in Renaissance garb. These are the *devoti* (devotees). Over the next forty-eight hours of the festival, they'll have a special role to play. The vast majority are aged between fifteen and thirty, with a smattering of older participants. Nearly all are men. Until recently, women were forbidden from this particular aspect of the Festival of Saint Agatha.

Not everyone is in costume. Thousands more Catanese join the throng outside the cathedral. The church itself is jam-packed. Onlookers perch on tiptoes in the hope of glimpsing the city's patron saint. The wall of people in Piazza Duomo is virtually impenetrable, but by easing my elbows into the faces of grandmothers and small children, I'm able to manoeuvre myself to a decent view.

At seven am, after an icy wait while mass is performed in the church, the whisper goes through the crowd that Agatha is on her way outside. Beside me, a mother in a full face of makeup bends down to her baby and says, '*Alleluia!*'

Finally the saint appears, having been hauled up from a double-locked vault beneath the cathedral then carried from the church on the shoulders of dozens of white-smocked devotees. A puff of smoke is released into the sky.

Of course, it isn't Agatha in person – she's been dead for almost two thousand years and there wasn't much of her left in the first place (not by the time the Romans had finished). Today, the saint is represented by a life-sized wooden effigy of the top half of her body. On her head she wears a one-kilogram crown encrusted in precious stones – a gift from Richard the Lionheart in the twelfth century. Her robe also glitters with valuable jewels, including emeralds the size of eyeballs. The effigy is exquisitely painted, with locks of golden hair tumbling down beneath a glittering crown. With her faintly blushing cheeks, Agatha seems from different angles to emanate a raft of characteristics: courage, benevolence, determination and sorrow.

Suddenly one of the devotees near the church doors turns to the crowd in the piazza and screams at the top of his lungs, '*Cittadini! Cittadini!*' ('Citizens!')

In unison, everyone in a white tunic and black cap bellows a reply: '*Viva Sant'Agata! Viva Sant'Agata!*' ('Long live Saint Agatha!')

The fellow up the front yells once more, '*Siamo tutti devoti tutti?*' ('Are we all devoted? All of us?')

The crowd responds: '*Certo! Certo!*' ('Yes! We are!')

This is the first airing of the Saint Agatha war cry, a call-and-response that I will hear ad nauseam for the next two days. The rules are simple. Any devotee can start the chant at any time. It's then up to the remainder to respond as one – like an ecclesiastical version of 'Aussie Aussie Aussie! Oi Oi Oi!' (Torture by pincers and hot coals would be too kind for whoever came up with the latter.)

As each devotee yells a response, he waves his pleated hanky in the air. Considering the machismo of your average Sicilian man, it's a very effeminate look. Not everyone appears comfortable – particularly some of the teenage boys in eyeshot of pretty girls. This makes me smugly content.

Next, Agatha is transferred from the shoulders of the devotees onto her enormous silver carriage, currently parked at the entrance to the church. This four-metre-high carriage (called the *fercolo*) looks like a Greek temple on wheels. Two rows of columns hold up an ornate silver roof of tiny carved skulls. The saint rides inside the temple, surrounded by sacred objects, pink flowers, yellow candles and other bits and pieces. Around the outside of the columns is a skirting board. Here, six experienced devotees in costume stand above the crowd, tending to the saint and directing proceedings. There's a man hidden inside the carriage, too, to operate the steering and brakes.

Fireworks ring out, loud but invisible against the wan morning sky. They mark the start of the festival's main event – Agatha's annual procession on the *fercolo*. Over the next two days (equal to the length of time of her martyrdom), she will be transported along the streets of Catania, first in a huge loop around the outskirts, then through the historical heart of the city, passing the key areas where her imprisonment, torture and death are believed to have taken place.

Thousands of devotees, onlookers and tourists will accompany the procession. Many will get no sleep at all. Some may even end up in hospital – maimed by fireworks, overcome by exhaustion or crushed by the crowd.

The *fercolo* travels very slowly on its wheels, only a few metres every minute – it weighs eighteen tons, after all. In front, two long lines of devotees stretch for over a hundred metres. Their white gloves are wrapped around a pair of ropes as fat as anacondas, each one attached to Agatha's carriage. This is how the saint makes her epic journey around the city, pulled by hand.

More fireworks explode. These will go off almost continuously for the next two days, in random locations and at random times, in darkness and in full daylight. As I soon learn, time becomes irrelevant during the Festival of Saint Agatha. All that matters is the slow, relentless procession of the *fercolo*, surrounded by devotees yelling their call and response.

'*Cittadini! Cittadini!*'
'*Viva Sant'Agata! Viva Sant'Agata!*'
'*Siamo tutti devoti tutti?*'
'*Certo! Certo!*'

I follow the parade for most of the day. It's an extraordinary experience. Everywhere along the route, Catanese spill out of their homes and businesses to watch the saint go marching by. The whole city has a carnival atmosphere, with piazzas and footpaths filled with stalls. Onlookers surround the silver carriage to offer candles, flowers and even handfuls of cash to Agatha, accompanying the offerings with prayers for ailing family members or friends. In particular, because Agatha's torture included the removal of her breasts, she is the patron saint of breast cancer sufferers. But people pray for all kinds of things. Healthy locals whisper a plea that Agatha might continue to protect the city from Etna's eruptions.

Then things get a little out of hand. A designated spot on the route has been set aside for the blessing of children. Dozens of parents crowd the *fercolo*, holding their infants in outstretched arms. The officials hoist them one by one onto the carriage, face them towards Saint Agatha's bust, say a quick prayer, and pass them back to Mum or Dad. I watch at least a hundred babies and young children get shown to the saint. Several, I notice, are blind; others have cerebral palsy. Nearly all of them are bawling out of sheer terror at the bedlam around them. People are starting to yell and shove, as more fireworks boom overhead. There's a hint of desperation in some parents' eyes. The *fercolo* is set upon like a UN food truck in a war-torn African village.

It's tough work for the guys on the carriage. Not only do they have to control the crowd, they also have to lift all these kids. Imagine snatching a ten-kilogram weight a hundred times and you get the idea. Nobody is working harder than Alfio Rao, the man selected as the *capofercolo* (leader of the *fercolo*) for this year's festival. Doubtless he feels honoured by such a position of responsibility, but it must require the strength of a weightlifter and the stamina of a long-distance runner.

Finally it's clear that the men aboard the *fercolo* are utterly spent. 'NO MORE BABIES!' yells someone in the crowd, like my brother after he and his wife had their third boy in a row.

Alfio Rao wipes the sweat from his brow and rings the little bell hanging from the roof of the *fercolo* – a signal for the devotees to pull the long ropes and move the carriage onwards again.

In the evening, Gill and I throw a small 'Agatha party'. No, it's not one where you stand in a circle and yank each other's breasts with hot pincers. We happen to be the only couple among our friends whose apartment lies directly on the processional route of the *fercolo*. The plan, therefore, is to have some drinks and cheer Agatha from our courtyard whenever she happens to pass. Our neighbour Angela tells us that the saint will enter Via Garibaldi shortly after midnight.

Brock comes armed with *cedri* – citron fruits. These are traditionally sold on Catania street corners around the time of the festival. If you've not seen a citron, it's basically a big ugly lemon covered in rough bumps – the Elephant Man of fruits. Sicilians sprinkle segments of citron with salt and eat them raw, so that's what we do, too. We cheat a little by adding our own ingredient: shots of tequila.

Outside, Via Garibaldi is filling with onlookers, so we don our heavy winter gear, grab some beers and move the party onto the street. A roadside barbeque is selling millimetre-thin steaks of horsemeat in crusty rolls. This neighbourhood is the horsemeat capital of Catania – it seems that every third shop is a *macelleria equina* (horse butcher).

'I'm so hungry I could eat a horse,' I say to Gill, motioning towards the stand with the neck of my beer bottle.

'Don't you dare!' she says.

'Why not?'

'That's disgusting.'

'What's wrong with eating horse?'

'What's right with it?'

'Don't be a *neigh*-sayer.'

'Very funny.'

Now seems as good a time as any to confess something to Gill. 'Um, I don't quite know how to tell you this . . .' I ask her to cast her mind back to the previous weekend, when our neighbour Carmelo made one of his regular appearances at our door with offerings of barbequed food – on this occasion, a plastic plate of four steaks. They'd been marinated in oil and vinegar, and quickly seared on a grill. We thanked him for his kind gesture and tucked into the lunch without a second thought.

Gill can already see where I'm heading with this. 'That was *horse*?' she says with a look of horror.

'Yeah. I bumped into Carmelo later and he asked me if we'd enjoyed the *carne di cavallo*.'

There is silence as Gill struggles to comprehend what she's done. Doubtless she's thinking about every pretty pony she ever rode as a child in Brisbane. 'I can't believe I've eaten a poor *horse*,' she says finally.

I almost reply, 'And you'll be saddled with it for the rest of your life,' but decide to refrain.

It starts to rain. The drops sizzle as they hit the hot grill. Still contemplating her culinary crime, Gill trudges back to the apartment to get a waterproof jacket.

While she's gone (and while the vegan vigilantes, Dave and Kate, have their backs turned), I quickly order myself a steak and glug it down with a beer chaser. Carmelo's lunch was one of the tastiest I've had: I'm not about to miss out on seconds.

In the end, the *fercolo* doesn't come past until 2.45 am. We are three sheets to the wind by then, and I've even gone back to the grill for a second helping of horse. (I avoid a third – don't want the trots.) Everyone buys long candles and tries to light them in the frigid drizzle. Even little Erminia is still awake: she runs out onto the road and squeezes in between a couple of devotees so she can put her hand on one of the fat ropes that drag the *fercolo*. The crowd surges as Saint Agatha passes, then falls away again as her carriage maintains its grand procession through the streets of cold Catania.

Festival of Saint Agatha: Day 3

While the devotees continue to follow the *fercolo* around the city, Gill and I enjoy a morning of recuperation. Gill recuperates by staying in bed until noon; I recuperate with three aspirins and a fry-up breakfast.

Italians don't do bacon and eggs for breakfast. By extension, they have no such thing as a bacon-and-egg roll with barbeque sauce. Surely this throws into serious doubt the oft-repeated claim that Italy's cuisine is the best in the world.

Our downtime is short. By mid-afternoon, Gill and I are setting out once more for Piazza Duomo. There, preparations are afoot for 'the River of Fire' – part of the bizarre, night-long antics that bring the Festival of Saint Agatha to a close.

Devotees are milling around the square. Their white cloaks and velvet caps look ragged. After two nights without sleep, exhaustion has set in. From time to time, someone raises a cupped hand to cracked lips and gives a shout: '*Cittadini, cittadini . . .*'

Hundreds of tired accomplices attempt a reply: '*Viva Sant'Agata . . .*'

It sounds like a tracheotomy symposium.

The devotees, we notice, are huddled around special oversized candles, unlit for the moment. By oversized, I mean gigantic – they're like wax menhirs, up to two metres tall and weighing as much as a man. Seven ropey wicks sprout from the top of each one. Over the course of the evening, the giant candles will be lit and then lugged by small teams – or individuals if strong enough – all the way up Via Etnea to Piazza Borgo in the city's northern suburbs, then back again. They will accompany the *fercolo* and the eleven *candelore*, the towers representing Catania's various guilds.

It's now four pm. We have an hour before the ritual lighting of the candles. Gill soon finds a way of passing the time.

If such a career existed, my wife should get a job as a Chocolate Diviner. Sweet-toothed people in need of a fix could go to her for help. Set her loose in any city and, with just a couple of Pocky sticks as divining rods, she'll quickly find the primary source of chocolate or chocolate-related products.

In this case, it's a stand selling hot crepes smeared with Nutella – not the same thing as chocolate, admittedly, but close enough to ease the cravings. Handing a crepe across to Gill, the stall-owner says, 'Happy World Nutella Day!'

I assume this is a joke until later when I Google it. He's right. The fifth of February is indeed World Nutella Day. Why this particular date? I'm not sure. Perhaps it celebrates the day when some marketing genius came up with the idea of pitching Nutella (whose main ingredient is sugar) as a 'nutritional breakfast spread'.

At five pm, as the sky begins to darken, the candles are lit. It's an arduous process getting seven thick wicks to stay alight in the bitter breeze. Finally the flames take hold. Beneath a sky tattooed with fireworks, each devotee heaves his enormous waxy burden onto one shoulder, like Christ and the cross, and begins the uncomfortable trudge up Via Etnea. Anyone flying over Catania right now would mistake the thousand blazing candles as a lava flow from the volcano itself.

The only downside of the spectacle is the amount of liquid wax spilling from the candles onto the road. A layer of sawdust has been dumped on the ground overnight and it helps, but in the following days teams of workers will still be shovelling slippery gunk off the street. Apparently the rate of car accidents in Catania – already high – shoots up stratospherically after the festival.

The procession marches on. Midnight approaches. More celebrations – 'an amazing phantasmagoria of fireworks' (in the words of the festival guide) – are scheduled for when the saint reaches Piazza Borgo at the top of town.

'I don't think I'll stay to the end,' says Gill as midnight passes.

'But honey, *siamo tutti devoti tutti!* We're all devoted, right?'

'I'm devoted to getting some sleep and avoiding a cold.'

She has a point. Word on the street is that the *fercolo* won't arrive back to the bottom of Via Etnea until five am.

After walking Gill home, I return one last time to the heart of the procession. The hours tick by. Finally, everything is in readiness for the *salita* – the climb. This is the showpiece of the festival, but also its most dangerous moment. As the *fercolo* approaches our end of Via Etnea again, just a couple of hours shy of dawn, it turns right into Via Antonino di Sangiuliano, a street with a short but steep ascent to a higher tier of the city.

Thousands of devotees close in around the two long ropes in front of Agatha's carriage. The idea is to sprint up Sangiuliano, towing the massive vehicle two hundred metres to the crest of the hill. Performing the feat in a single motion means favourable auspices for the coming year. (This tradition comes from the fact that Catania's official New Year's Day, with all its legal and contractual implications, used to coincide with the Festival of Saint Agatha.)

I've already seen the *fercolo* get pulled up a shorter incline the day before – the so-called *salita dei Cappuccini*. It was dramatic enough. First a surge of devotees, eight men across, came ploughing through the cheering crowd; next, the *fercolo*. Its attendants clung tightly to the carriage's columns so they wouldn't fall off.

But the *salita di San Giuliano* is much longer and steeper.

I jostle into position at the top of the hill and wait. Five o'clock drifts out to six am, then six thirty. The sky begins to lighten. Perhaps I should've stayed home with Gill, caught a few hours of sleep, then come back for the finale. On the other hand, the crowd is now immense – as thick as I've seen it all festival. It would be impossible to wend my way to where I stand now, in the middle of the action.

At ten past seven, a commotion sounds from the bottom of the slope. Then a wall of white tunics approaches up the hill at considerable speed, like an avalanche going the wrong way. The climb has begun! In no time at all, the devotees have reached my position. They rush past in a blur, yelping through tattered vocal chords. The *fercolo* follows. All I get is a brief glimpse of Alfio Rao, the *capofercolo*, hanging from one of the columns of the carriage, swinging his arm like a jockey wielding a whip, urging everyone to keep running.

Pamplona couldn't be any more dangerous than the *salita*. People get injured all the time. The streets are covered in candle wax, remember, and when you combine that fact with a mass of overly tired, uncomfortably dressed characters dashing as fast as possible up an incline, it spells trouble. The *fercolo* weighs as much as a tank. The following year, a twenty-two-year-old devotee is crushed to death on the Sangiuliano ascent.

For the moment, there is one final theatrical flourish left in proceedings. (The Festival of Saint Agatha is like a Hollywood action film – one big ending after another.) When the *salita* finishes in a whirlwind of white motion, the thousands of spectators plunge down narrow Via Crociferi towards the Church of St Benedict and its adjoining Benedictine monastery. I am literally carried by the crowd, pinioned between the shoulders of people around me. So tight is the crush that the safety officials – a team of men wearing fluorescent yellow overalls so they can be recognised among all the white tunics – have to barge through the crowd from time to time and haul someone out when they faint.

We stop in front of the church. I have a prime position for what is to follow. Behind me, people strive for vantage points, scaling statues and hanging from balconies. It's like Test Match cricket in India.

Just before eight am, the *fercolo* squeezes through the masses (amid more ragged shouts of '*Cittadini! Cittadini!*'), parking just metres away from my position. The sky above has turned intensely blue but the air is still freezing.

A dozen nuns emerge from the doors of the convent. Suddenly an incredible silence descends. There must be fifty thousand people in this little laneway alone, and not one of them breathes a sound. Then, as they face the *fercolo* and the smiling bust of Agatha, the nuns break into a short Latin hymn, sung *a cappella*, in honour of the saint.

Eroina del cielo. Agata bella:
deh! splendi al mio morir,
al mio morir, propizia stella!
O eroina del cielo.

It's an extraordinarily emotional moment. There are tears in every eye. Even *I* get misty – something that's only happened twice before in my life: once during my wedding vows and once when Steve Waugh cracked a boundary off the last ball of the day's play at the SCG to bring up a career-saving century.

And so the Festival of Saint Agatha comes to an end. The *fercolo* still needs to be pulled back to Piazza Duomo, where three different keys held by three different people will lock

Agatha away for another twelve months. But most of the crowd disappears after the nuns have sung their song.

It's funny to watch the devotees resuming their normal lives. As I walk home (where I will sleep from midday through to the next morning), I see one of them waiting at a bus stop in his dirty, waxy outfit, carrying his black velvet hat and white gloves. Another goes by pushing his baby in a pram. Two more drive past in their car – the passenger doesn't realise he's caught the bottom end of his tunic in the door.

It's not just Catania where Agatha is revered. She's the patron saint of as many as forty-four Italian towns – a third of those carry her name in their title. She's also worshipped throughout Spain, including in Zamarramal, where, on 5 February, the women of the town act as masters for the day. ('Unlike all the *other* days,' I can hear the menfolk mutter.) Agatha plays an important role, too, in various municipalities in Portugal, Germany, France and Greece. Even in India there is said to be a cult of Saint Agatha.

Yet in none of these places does the worship remotely reach the fervency witnessed in Catania. The men, in particular, seem to treat Agatha almost as they would a new girlfriend. They're not only besotted with the saint but fiercely protective of her. They would do just about anything to express their devotion.

Especially the bakers. While a bunch of them are lugging one of the *candelore* around the streets of Catania for four days, the rest are busy in the kitchen preparing the *minni di virgini*, or 'breasts of the Virgin'. These cupcakes are baked in honour of Agatha, and shaped exactly as their name might suggest, with a maraschino cherry for a nipple. Buying them is an odd experience; eating them, even odder. It honestly feels like you're cheating on your wife before her very eyes.

'How's your cake?' I ask Gill, as we're midway through the nice pair of *minni* I've brought home from our local *panificio*.

'Not bad,' she says. 'More to the point, how's *yours*?' And there I am, suckling the better part of an entire bosom, crunching through an areola of marzipan to get to the ducts of sweet ricotta inside.

Aside from tasting pretty good, these little cakes represent everything fascinating about the Festival of Saint Agatha: tradition and dedication on one hand, irreverence and eccentricity on the other; and always an earthy joie de vivre.

When there's a religious celebration to be had, the Sicilians certainly milk it for all it's worth.

12. Stealing

Statistics may or may not support the view, but I am
inclined to attribute the general impression that Sicily is more dangerous than other countries, less to the
frequency of crime there than to the operatic manner
in which it is committed.

– Henry Festing Jones, *Diversions in Sicily*, 1909

On my way back from the Pescheria one afternoon in March,
I walk past Turi, the local pizza maker. He's standing outside
his takeaway restaurant near our apartment. We exchange
pleasantries. (That's if one can call Turi's acknowledgement
a 'pleasantry' – he may just be clearing phlegm from his
throat.)

It's like every other afternoon in Catania, except that Turi
is covered head to toe in what appears to be shaving foam.

'Odd,' I think as I continue up the street.

Maybe Turi has been interrupted while preparing for a
full-body shave. No denying he needs one – the guy's a bear.
But it doesn't explain why there's foam on his clothes and
through his hair.

Perhaps it's whipped cream. Was Turi trialling a new dessert when something went horribly wrong in the kitchen?

Or has his lover kicked him out into the street in the middle of their kinky, food-themed foreplay? Surely Turi doesn't get involved in those kinds of shenanigans; if he does, I'm finding a new pizzeria.

The plot thickens when I arrive at the entrance of our courtyard. Reaching up to buzz the *citofono*, I find the entire intercom system has also been caked in fresh foam. Rather than push a finger into the goo, I yell through the iron gate to our apartment. Gill hears me across the courtyard and presses the button to let me in.

'We're under attack,' I say, once I'm inside.

'What do you mean?' answers Gill from our tiny box of a kitchen.

'Someone's spraying white slime all over the place. It's like a bad science-fiction film.'

'I think you'll find it's Carnevale.'

'Doesn't look like a carnival to me. Looks like a schoolboy prank.'

'No, *Carnevale*.'

'What, gay blokes on Harleys?'

'No, that's Mardi Gras in Sydney. Carnevale. You know, like Carnaval in Rio de Janeiro.'

'Oh, hot chicks in bikinis.'

'Something like that,' says Gill, trying to remember why she ever married me.

I soon discover that Carnevale in Sicily is much more G-rated than I've envisaged. In fact, it seems mostly aimed at the kids. This has been the case since the sixteenth century, when the five-day period leading up to Lent was marked by sack races, tug of war, and play-fighting with rotten eggs. Five hundred years later, it's shaving cream, confetti and liquid string. Pizza-maker Turi has been caught unawares by a troop of passing adolescents armed with cans of Gillette foam.

Fancy dress is also a big part of Carnevale in Catania: children dress as fairies, superheroes, jungle animals or *Star Wars* characters. In the tougher area near our apartment, commando gear is popular. Imagine, if you can, a bunch of four-year-olds in full army attire with bullet belts and Guevara-style beards drawn onto their faces with black marker pens. It's like a preschool production of *Rambo*.

One night, Desi, Gaetano and little Erminia (wearing a pink princess dress by Barbie with matching plastic tiara) invite us to the coastal town of Acireale for '*il più bel Carnevale di Sicilia*' – the most beautiful Carnevale in Sicily. We pile into Gaetano's car and set off up the coastal highway.

Acireale is thirty minutes north of Catania, directly under the eastern slope of Mount Etna. Gaetano parks in a dimly lit back alley strewn with ash. Before we get out, he opens a cheap-looking packet of novelty contact lenses and starts prodding them onto his eyeballs. It looks painful – he's clearly never worn contacts in his life. He squirms, groans and blinks. Tears stream down his face. He tries again and again to position the lenses correctly, only to abort the procedure. Finally persistence pays off. Gaetano turns his face into the beam of the car's cabin light to reveal a pair of fake cat's eyes: bright yellow with thin horizontal slits instead of pupils. Next, he wiggles a pair of white plastic fangs over his own teeth. These look painful, too, like the edge of the plastic might be cutting into his gums. With his costume done, Gaetano spins around and hisses at the girls in the back seat. Erminia squeals and leaps out.

'Cool!' I say to Gaetano. 'Where'd you get that stuff?'

'Same place I got this,' he replies, opening the glove box to reveal an authentic red rubber Whoopee Cushion. The instructions read: 'When anyone sits down, it emits a REAL Bronx cheer!'

So, Gaetano, in his late twenties, has come armed with cat's-eye contact lenses, vampire-style teeth and a fake farting device. Maybe I was wrong when I implied that Carnevale is only for kids.

We follow Erminia out of the car. Gaetano doesn't even bother locking the doors. Instead, he pops the hood then reaches into the darkness and removes a chunk of the motor. Wrapping it up in a cloth and shoving it in the pocket of his jacket, he flashes his feline eyes and says, 'Let's go!'

As an automobile owner in Sicily, you have two choices. Either you walk around with a greasy piece of carburettor in your jacket pocket, or you leave your vehicle at the mercy of the island's car thieves. And what thief could resist stealing a car with a Whoopee Cushion in the glove box?

Acireale's Carnevale celebrations are fun, if a little migraine-inducing. Festivalgoers who aren't carrying cans of foam are swinging enormous inflatable hammers instead. I get donged on the head a thousand times by complete strangers. Gill gets doused with liquid string – one long stream of the stuff ends up inside her mouth.

'What's it taste like?' I ask.

'Chemicals,' she replies, spitting out bits of coloured gunk.

We see music, fireworks, food stalls, samba dancers and puppets – even a group of majorettes from Slovakia. We buy *zucchero filato* (fairy floss) for Erminia. Gaetano isn't the only adult who has embraced the youthful spirit of Carnevale: there are grown men dressed as court jesters, cowboys and ducks. As I watch this crowd of carefree Sicilians, I wonder how many of them are carrying a piece of car engine in their pocket as a precaution against thieves.

By ten pm we've had enough. Gaetano's car is sitting where we left it – his cunning plan of dismantling the engine has worked. Either that or the crooks are hiding away, waiting until everyone is asleep to commit their crimes.

The bonus for a criminal in Sicily is that people sleep *twice* in a twenty-four-hour period rather than once. So, if you can't pull off your heist in the wee hours of the morning, then you can always have another crack during siesta.

Before living in Catania, I thought people who took siestas (namely, Spanish speakers and Australian council workers) took them lying on park benches or reclining in car seats. In my mind, a siesta was a very public exhibition of lethargy. For this misleading view, I blame *Looney Tunes* cartoons – in particular, an animated Mexican mouse named Slowpoke Rodriguez. When I was a kid, Slowpoke tied with Foghorn Leghorn as my favourite *Looney Tunes* character. He was a friend of Speedy Gonzales, only far lazier. Slowpoke spoke in a slow Spanish drawl. 'I go take my siesta now,' he'd say, then toddle off to lean against the nearest tree for a doze, next to some equally sluggish rodents.

Shaping this notion, too, was my recent stint in northern China. Many Chinese are so keen for an afternoon kip (*wushui*) they don't bother finding a bed. They just catch forty winks wherever they sit. I can't tell you how many Chinese butchers I saw with heads buried into folded arms, snoring, on tables full of flyblown giblets. If you were valiant enough to want some of their produce, you'd first have to prod them awake with a pork hock.

In Sicily, though, I discover that the siesta is a very private affair. More than that, it's a vanishing act. At one pm, the streets of every town and city are choked with traffic as people rush home for lunch. By one thirty, everyone is locked away inside and the whole island becomes a ghost town for two hours. If you're out walking during this time, it's not uncommon to hear the clicking of your heels on the pavement echoing back across the empty street.

This can be unsettling. Suddenly what should theoretically be the safest time of the day to be outside, with the sun at its brightest, begins to feel decidedly dodgy. Narrow side roads seem more sinister than usual. The only people left on the streets are the tourists with money belts and cameras, watched by calculating eyes from shadowy corners.

Sure enough, at two thirty one afternoon – smack-bang in the middle of siesta – we get robbed. Not Gill and me specifically, but our friends Dorothy and Keith who we're with at the time.

I know Dorothy from university: she was one of my professors and then a teaching colleague. She and her husband Keith are holidaying in Sicily after spending a fortnight in Tunisia. One morning they make the three-hour journey across from the capital Palermo to visit. They manage to park reasonably close to our apartment on Via Garibaldi. This is a relief: Dorothy has a bad knee which troubles her when she walks.

We catch up on each other's news while eating Tunisian figs and sipping Sicilian wine, and Dorothy and Keith show a slideshow of photos from their two-week trip. They've recently purchased a state-of-the-art laptop computer and the images look stunning on the extra-wide screen.

After lunch, we pile into their hire car to visit Catania's historic sites. Keith drives. I'm in the passenger seat. Because of the siesta, the city is whisper quiet. Getting around is a breeze. We weave through backstreets to the ancient Roman theatre, which I figure is a worthy starting point for a tour. A parking bay is ahead on the left. I tell Keith to pull in.

Suddenly, with the vehicle still moving – at around thirty kilometres an hour – Dorothy's door gets violently yanked open. She's sitting in the seat behind Keith. Someone yells as a man's arm shoots into the car and loops around the black laptop case at her feet. Then, *yoink!* – the arm and the case disappear. There's ten seconds of noise and mayhem: a voice barking in Italian; a roaring bike engine; Dorothy's despairing shout, '*They've got the computer!*'

By 'they' she means two Catanesi thieves on a Vespa. In a millisecond, the rider has gauged the speed of the car and drawn parallel, allowing his accomplice to reach towards the door, pull it open, and grab the most valuable thing in our possession. As petty crimes go, this one is audacious, almost acrobatic.

My heart sinks. I haven't felt this aghast since the time Gill leaned across to me in the cinema, forty-five minutes into *Titanic*, and whispered, 'It goes for three hours.'

Suddenly we lurch forward. It's Keith: he wants his laptop back. He slams the car into gear and presses his foot to the accelerator. We shoot off down a narrow stone alley – not quite with the élan of Jason Bourne – through a couple of tight intersections, missing oncoming cars by the width of a linguine strand. A gap opens up and for a few seconds we spot an escaping bike. But already it's hundreds of metres ahead of us. With their local knowledge of back lanes and one-way streets, the men are soon long gone. The chase is over just moments after it begins.

It's an almost silent drive to the police station. There are no parking spaces nearby, so we're forced to walk the last few hundred metres. Dorothy insists her knee is fine, but I can see that it's a struggle. What's more, it's now pouring with rain. We have one small umbrella between four of us.

All Gill and I can do is apologise profusely for what has happened. We feel violated. Dorothy and Keith are ashen-faced but immensely kind, brushing it off as 'one of those things'. But the fact is we invited them to drive their shiny new hire car across Sicily and into our crime-ridden suburb, where they promptly lost a new laptop and, with it, every photographic memory of their trip to Tunisia. Welcome to Catania.

Inside, we meet with two policemen. At first, they're brusque – lots of shrugging shoulders. Eventually one of them picks up a phone to speak with a colleague about our plight. After a brief conversation, he cups his hand over the mouthpiece and says, 'Where are you from?'

'Australia,' we answer on behalf of Dorothy and Keith.

Further discussion ensues. The policeman turns to us again. 'What part of Australia?'

'Brisbane.'

More talking. Suddenly the man's face brightens. He cups the mouthpiece again and looks our way: 'My boss's cousin lives in Brisbane!' The last bit is relayed with the same kind of enthusiasm you'd expect from someone saying, 'We've just found your laptop!'

A few minutes later, the policeman from the other end of the phone bursts excitedly into the room. All discussions of recent thefts are immediately abandoned in favour of Brisbane-related anecdotes. The cousin, it turns out, owns a café in Milton. Gill and I know the one – we've had coffees there in the past. There's always a red Ferrari on the street outside for patrons to admire. It belongs to the cousin, of course.

'*Piccolo mondo!*' says the cop with a cheery grin. Small world indeed.

'So, can you help us?' I ask, getting back to the matter at hand.

The policeman looks at me like a child whose favourite toy has been taken away. He rummages around for some insurance forms for Keith, then gives me a folder of mug shots to peruse, in the hope I might recognise our assailants.

It's thicker than a Vikram Seth novel. Each page contains dozens of numbered photos of Catanese criminals. You've never seen so many low-set brows.

The task is hopeless. I only caught the thief's face for a millisecond in my side mirror. After a few minutes, I tentatively stab my finger at numbers 13, 92, 160 and 215. I have no real idea, so I choose a bunch of redheads on the off-chance that one of them gets put away for a few years.

Finally, though, I find a photo of a man I do recognise. He looks eerily identical to Nicolas Cage – who, speaking of relatives, is the nephew of *Godfather* director Francis Ford Coppola.

'I've seen this guy before,' I say.

The policemen swivel their heads my way. 'Yes?'

'He was in *Raising Arizona*.'

Tourists aren't the only targets of this kind of crime in Catania. One story tells of a prominent local surgeon who was robbed at knifepoint in an alley (during siesta, of course) only to recognise his assailant the next day – on the operating table! The perpetrator had come down with appendicitis overnight. Ever professional, the surgeon performed the necessary operation and only notified police afterwards.

If I were a doctor (of the operating sort), I wouldn't be so kind. 'I've removed the patient's appendix,' I can imagine myself saying while peeling off a pair of latex gloves. 'But I also thought his testicles were looking a little worse for wear so I've hacked those off as well.'

Crime touches everyone in Catania. It's one of the reasons the city scrapes the bottom in any poll of Italy's most liveable cities. I've even heard people from Naples talk about 'crime-ridden Catania'. Naples!

Well before the car-jacking incident with Dorothy and Keith, Gill and I get a strong sense that this city is dodgier than most. By dint of having no money, we're forced to live where the rents are lowest and the streets seediest. Our first apartment on Via Gesuiti wasn't too bad – though we did have the Ultras Ghetto on our doorstep, and a nearby overgrown park was a black spot for heroin users.

Our second home, on the corner of Via Garibaldi and Via Plebiscito, is located on the fringe of Catania's poorest suburb, San Cristoforo. Across the road from us – and within earshot – is the hardcore porn cinema Eliseo (next to a baby clothing store called 'Magic Moment Bonboniere'), as well as a place where Africans can make dirt-cheap phone calls to their families back in Ghana and Nigeria. Perhaps it's one of them who etched a message into our front gate one night: '*Sono solo un nero povero*' (I'm just a poor black man). On one of my first strolls down Via Garibaldi I saw a jewellery store with a shattered front window and police crunching around outside. Via Plebiscito, as Palmina told us, has a reputation as the city's shiftiest thoroughfare. Each night during my brisk evening walk to collect Gill from school, I pass an apartment numbered 666 Via Plebiscito. The world's most evil address?

The strong feeling of unease is exacerbated by an almost criminal neglect of infrastructure in this part of town.

Everything looks like it's about to collapse. Graffiti is rife, too, and it's all hostile:

ANARCHY
Sinn Fein
U.S.A. ASSASSINI
Catania Skins ⌘
Palermo *merda!* (Palermo is shit!)
100% HATE

Another night when I'm walking along Via Plebiscito, the red dot of a laser light appears on my shirtfront, dancing in the dark. I can't help but imagine it's a sniper, taking aim from a nearby grassy knoll (if only Catania had any grass). The quivering red light stays with me for a disconcerting minute or two then disappears again.

There's one foolproof method to combat anxiety in the backstreets of Catania: make yourself look more menacing than everyone else. I manage to do this one time, completely by accident. Brock's girlfriend is celebrating her birthday, so Gill and I head to the Fiera market (similar to the Pescheria, but for goods and knick-knacks) to buy her a gift. We decide on a CD holder. It's a narrow holder, about a metre high – the kind you stand against a wall next to your sound system. It comes in a long rectangular box that the vendor wraps in tissue paper for us.

I offer to take the gift home while Gill keeps shopping. With the wrapped CD holder tucked in an ungainly fashion under my arm, I stride up the street in the direction of

Via Garibaldi. I have a strange aversion to carrying large shopping items at the best of times: one of my pet fears is to emerge from a busy supermarket clutching a new ironing board or a set of beans for a beanbag, or – even worse – a pack of twenty-four toilet rolls. I don't know why this bothers me; perhaps because it gives strangers an insight into my personal life. They see the twenty-four toilet rolls and I know exactly what they're thinking: 'Looks like *someone*'s got a bad case of the shits.'

But I've never felt as conspicuous as this day in Catania. Here's a word of advice: if you intend to walk for kilometres through a Sicilian city, avoid carrying a long paper-wrapped package under your arm. Otherwise you'll look exactly like a guy on his way to whack someone with a shotgun. I swear that the windows of several apartments slammed shut as I passed by. Might as well have worn shiny shoes and a pin-striped suit.

Which brings me, inevitably, to the Mafia.

Think of Sicily and you think of the Mafia. Catania, though, hasn't always been associated with hardcore Cosa Nostra activity. In the first half of the twentieth century, western Sicily was more famous as a hotbed of *mafiosi* – especially Palermo and the town of Corleone.

Not that Catania was saintly by comparison. In fact, one reason the Mafia initially kept its paws off the place was because of the activity of other organised crime groups: the Cursoti, the Carcagnusi, the Malpassoti. Ugly names, ugly business.

But you can't keep a good mob down. In the 1950s, the Mafia beefed up its operations in Catania, starting with a contraband cigarette racket. Before long, nicotine had been replaced by heroin. By the 1970s, the Mafia's position in Sicily's second city was immeasurably stronger. Important, too, was the work of the so-called *Cavalieri del Lavoro* (Knights of Labour), four Catania-based construction entrepreneurs who used the Mafia to protect their costly developments around the island.

The bosses in Palermo and Corleone slowly began to cock an ear in Catania's direction. Soon enough, the spheres of influence overlapped. In 1975, the head of the Catania mob, Giuseppe 'Pippo' Calderone, became secretary of a regional Mafia commission – an organisation designed to smooth conflicts of business interest across provincial borders.

With Pippo elevated to a regional role, someone had to fill his shoes in Catania. In stepped his friend, protégé and 'underboss' Benedetto 'Nitto' Santapaola. (Pippo? Nitto? Where's Groucho?) Known as *il cacciatore* (the hunter) because of his love of game hunting, Nitto immediately began to strengthen his position by forging ties with the now-dominant Mafia in Corleone.

Trouble began to brew. By the late 1970s, the Corleonesi were thumbing their noses at any attempt by rival clans to enforce business boundaries. They strived instead for island-wide dominance; Nitto became their man-on-the-ground in Catania. When Pippo Calderone and others tried to stop what was happening, they paid the price. Pippo was murdered in September 1978 – by his old friend Nitto, of course.

The hit had been ordered by Corleone-based Totò Riina, the 'boss of all bosses' who would later be embroiled in the scandal of The Kiss. Afterwards, Riina came to the funeral and gave a heartfelt speech that allegedly had many *mafiosi* in tears, even though they knew it was him who ordered the murder.

Corleone wrested back control via a spate of killings in 1977 and 1978, though their supremacy would be challenged again in the early eighties during the so-called Second Mafia War. Nitto himself was seriously wounded in an ambush in 1981. The body count in these years was breathtaking. On one day alone, twelve men were murdered in Palermo, all in separate incidents. The Naples-based Camorra became involved, as did a raft of Milanese mobsters.

For a hint of the brutality of this period, consider the fate of imprisoned mobster Francesco 'Francis' Turatello. While exercising in the yard of his high-security prison on the island of Sardinia, he was set upon by a group of notorious hitmen, including two from Catania. One of them is said to have stabbed Turatello sixty times, before another disembowelled him, chewed on his liver (whether with or without a nice chianti, reports didn't say), and spat the dead man's offal on the ground in contempt.

In an effort to stem the carnage, Carlo Alberto Dalla Chiesa, head of the *carabinieri* in Italy, was appointed prefect of Palermo in 1982. He lasted four months. One evening, he and his wife were being driven through the city in their Lancia A112 when the car was forced off the road by men on motorbikes. As it crashed to a halt, the riders produced weapons and riddled the police chief, his wife and their driver with bullets. A black-and-white photo shows the Lancia – inconspicuous and pint-sized, like something a single mum might drive to the shops – against the side of the road, its windows shattered and a trio of bloodstained bodies slumped at lifeless angles against the seats. Once again it was Totò Riina in Corleone who'd given the order.

In an interview before his death, Dalla Chiesa had indicated that the Cosa Nostra in Catania was gaining strength and influence. So it seemed. In 1983, Giuseppe Fava, a Catania-based journalist and editor-in-chief of a new magazine called *I Siciliani*, used the launch edition of the magazine to expose links between the Mafia in Catania and the aforementioned 'Knights of Labour'. He was promptly murdered on the orders of Nitto Santapaola. (Another journalist, Mauro De Mauro, had been killed for speaking out a few years earlier.)

Amid more violence – both within the clans and against the authorities – the Catania Mafia consolidated its power. Photos from the second half of the 1980s show Nitto hobnobbing with councilmen – even embracing a member of the Antimafia Commission.

On it went. In the early 1990s, the Archbishop of Catania penned an open letter to Pope John Paul II on the occasion of a pontifical visit to the city. On the topic of organised crime he wrote: 'The open, painful and bloody plague of the Mafia remains in our social fabric and in our flesh, returning like a bitter blow with its arrogance, its tentacles and its recurrent works of death.'

The Pope duly touched upon the problem when he spoke before an enormous, enthralled audience in Catania's Piazza Duomo – the same space where I joined a similarly large crowd to watch the arrival of Saint Agatha: 'Too many times, the people of Catania have suffered the humiliation of being seen as residents of a degraded and violent city, dominated by crime. Catania, rise up again in light and justice!'

In 1993, Nitto Santapaola was captured in a farmhouse near Catania. This was part of an intense crackdown following the notorious murders of two prosecuting judges, Giovanni Falcone and Paolo Borsellino, in Palermo in 1992. Measures included the alarming introduction to Sicily of seven thousand troops from the Italian mainland.

After myriad court cases and appeals stretching over almost a decade, the head of Catania's Mafia received a string of life sentences for multiple murders, including that of the police chief Dalla Chiesa. But nothing much changed. Nitto, it seems, simply continued his day-to-day operations from his prison cell. Whether he sat around drinking red wine and smoking cigars like the Mafia prisoners in *Goodfellas*, I can't say. Probably. Meanwhile, his son Vincenzo and other 'regents' helped run affairs on the outside.

It's likely still the case today. Vincenzo has been in and out of jail ever since his old man got put away – he was busted in 1998 as part of Sicily-wide sting, then again in 2007. But doubtless there are other protagonists in play. As for Nitto, in a bizarre twist he is said to have developed lycanthropy, a psychiatric disorder where you actually believe that you're a wolf.

There are hints that Mafia strength has begun to wane in Catania and across the island. Yet some commentators say the relative quiet is only because the criminals have so successfully entrenched themselves in various levels of government and high finance that the need for overt violence has diminished.

The other impediment to Mafia domination has always been its own internal wrangling: clans fighting clans, dons killing dons. In this regard, there has been a chilling recent development. In his prison in the province of Umbria, Nitto Santapaola has apparently forged an alliance with his former sworn enemy, Leoluca Bagarella, one of Totò Riina's foot soldiers. The deal was done by ritual: the two men switched cells and each one left his gold wedding band hanging from a nail in the wall. This exchange of rings indicates that the powerful Mafia factions in Corleone and Catania have formed a coalition.

Two rings to bind them all?

As foreigners, Gill and I aren't exactly prime targets for *mafiosi*. As we go about our daily lives, we're not often reminded of their existence. Still, we do meet *one* middle-aged fellow who we're sure is connected. Among other telltale signs, he goes everywhere with his 'nephew' – a tall, strong, silent fellow in his twenties who clearly means business. And when he writes down his mobile phone number for us one day, insisting we call him the minute we run into any trouble in Catania, he adds, 'Don't ever give that number to anyone else. *Ever.* Do you understand?'

Despite what we don't see, there's no doubt that the Mafia's nefariousness surrounds us on a daily basis. For one thing, many of the small businesses in our neighbourhood are surely paying the *pizzo* (protection money). The word literally means 'beak', and comes from the Sicilian phrase *fari vagnari a pizzu*, 'to wet one's beak'. One estimate says as many as nineteen out of every twenty businesses in Sicily pay protection money to the Mafia. Extortion nets billions of dollars for the organisation – their second biggest earner after drug trafficking.

It's also very simple. One day you arrive at your bakery or your car dealership to find the keyhole of the door covered with glue. This is like an invoice: it means *pay up*.

Thankfully, Gill and I have nothing worth extorting. What can a hoodlum do with a broken television and a fridge full of lettuce? I can just imagine someone grabbing me by the collar and saying, 'For every dollar you earn, I'm gonna take half, *capisce?*' and me replying, 'Sorry, Mister, I don't work.'

There are other hints and whispers of Mafia activity in Catania. One fellow tells us of a dank subterranean tunnel that connects all the Roman remains dotted around the city. It's a dumping ground, he says, for the Mafia's murder victims. These are the so-called *lupara bianca*: victims whose bodies never turn up. (A *lupara* is a sawn-off shotgun.)

Then there are the coffins. Ten minutes' walk from our apartment is a small backstreet filled with funeral parlours selling coffins and other accoutrements of the burial business. The street is near a thirteenth-century fortress called Castello Ursino, in an area that guidebooks always advise tourists to avoid. Rumour has it that the coffins are used for stashing weapons and running them between Catania and Palermo.

Perhaps it was a gun from one of these coffins that was used in the most high-profile Mafia incident during our time in Sicily. It happens a week before Gill and I are due to leave. The headline in the local newspaper reads: 'The Mafia returns to kill again'. And how. A thirty-three-year-old man from Palermo, married with two children, is found dead in a backstreet of the Sicilian capital. Two things point to a Mafia killing. First, the fellow was the cousin of a former *mafioso* who years earlier had become a *pentito* ('informant' – literally 'one who has repented'). Second, he was shot five times in the face at point-blank range. This is apparently done to prevent the possibility of loved ones farewelling the person in an open casket at a funeral. These *guys*: they think of everything!

Living where we live, with all these stories flying about, it naturally makes us jumpier than usual. So, when the intercom lets out a shrill buzz in the middle of a noiseless night, we get quite a fright. Good thing I lugged those twenty-four toilet rolls home.

Bzzzzzzzzzzz!

Gill and I lurch up simultaneously in the darkness, hearts pounding through a fog of sleep. Somebody is down at the front gate of the courtyard, pressing our button on the *citofono.*

Bzzzzzzzzzzz!

My mind processes the possibilities. Could it be Carmelo, coming in late from fishing and accidentally pressing the wrong button? Or perhaps it's Brock, Tash or another friend, who've lost their keys during a pub crawl and come here to crash. Or is it somebody else altogether – someone we don't know . . . ?

Bzzzzzzzzzzz!

'Don't answer it!' whispers Gill. Like me, she's thinking sinister thoughts.

Our bedroom has French doors that open onto the courtyard. I lift the bolts from the floor, turn the key in the lock, and slowly pull one of the doors open a couple of centimetres. I peer through the gloom, across the open courtyard to the iron gate and the street.

A man stands there. It's dark, but I'm certain I don't recognise his features or body shape. He stands motionless, arms by his side, staring in my direction. I wonder if he saw our door swing open.

'Who is it?' whispers Gill sharply.

'Not sure. There's some guy down there, hanging around.'

'Don't let him in!'

I look through the crack again. He's disappeared.

It's 2.15 am. I lock the doors again, and Gill and I huddle together under the covers for comfort.

By breakfast we've largely forgotten about the episode during the night, dismissing it as nothing more than a simple case of mistaken addresses, perhaps. A short time later, we leave the apartment and walk out onto Via Garibaldi. There, just twenty or thirty metres down to the left, is the smoking shell of a firebombed car. It's completely gutted and stuck fast to the road by four half-melted tyres. Locals walk past without even glancing twice, but Gill and I stand and stare. Somehow I doubt a faulty cigarette lighter is to blame for the conflagration.

'I wonder if this has something to do with the man who buzzed us last night?' ponders Gill.

'I guess so,' I say. 'Maybe he was walking along when he saw the car on fire and thought he should tell someone in a nearby apartment.'

'Yeah. But why wouldn't he press any other buttons? Nobody else got buzzed. Just us.' It doesn't bear thinking about.

Firebombing is common in Catania. It's often used as a stronger message for business owners who choose to ignore the glue in their keyholes.

One month after the midnight buzzer, Gill and I walk past a second smouldering car, closer to the centre of town. On the wall behind the violent, twisted wreck of metal I notice a piece of old graffiti, *'CATANIA, IO TI AMO!'* (Catania, I love you!) Priceless.

It's not just cars. Even the main police station gets firebombed at four o'clock one morning.

For a city that faces the everyday threat of immolation from Mount Etna's lava, it's perhaps not surprising that fire is one of the more popular techniques employed by people wishing to grind an axe or make their presence felt for one reason or another.

Another midnight visitor buzzes our *citofono* a few weeks later. I follow the same routine as before, unlocking the bedroom door in the darkness while Gill watches from under the covers. I push the door open with two fingers so I can peer out.

This time, I find myself looking directly into the face of a stranger, gazing at me from just ten centimetres away. I scream like my mother did when The Beatles played Sydney in 1964 and slam the door.

'What's wrong?' Gill whispers sharply. 'What is it?'

'There's someone right outside our door! In the court-yard. A woman.'

Next comes an urgent banging on the glass. Gill gives a yelp. 'What does she *want*?'

'I don't know!'

'What does she look like?'

'*I don't know!*' I snap. I try to recall the female face that I saw for a microsecond. The only image that comes to mind is the Stephen King character Annie Wilkes, cauterising the stump of some guy's leg with an oxy-acetylene torch. 'Nobody we know,' I add.

More banging.

'I'd better see what she wants,' I say, trying to take stock of the situation.

Smoothing down my bed hair, I open the door three or four centimetres, half expecting the woman and a bunch of male associates to push through the gap, bind us to chairs and pull out a tray of dental-style tools.

She doesn't look quite as murderous as I imagined. Angry, yes. Murderous, no.

'What do you want?' Gill and I ask simultaneously.

Gill has come over to stand behind me. I'm in boxer shorts and a t-shirt; she's in long pyjama pants and a black singlet top.

The woman delivers a two-minute rant in the jabbering style of the oracle at ancient Delphi. We ascertain, finally, that she's looking for a woman in our *palazzo*. She mentions a name. We say we don't know it. (A lie.) She keeps pointing to an apartment upstairs and repeating the name, but again we claim ignorance. Eventually she dismisses us with a flick of the hand and reels away.

More is to follow. The woman begins banging on random doors in the courtyard. She's yelling now, too. Finally, someone from the apartment in question unlatches the door to the stairs. Up strides the mad lady and a fierce confrontation follows. The arguments are garbled, though I do hear: *'Basta! Basta!'* ('Enough!') Or maybe it's *'Bastardo! Bastardo!'*

A horse comes clomping up Via Garibaldi carrying a mounted policeman. I notice that many of the lights in the apartments that had come on when the disturbance started blink off almost immediately at the sound of the fuzz. Everyone has something to hide. Gill and I keep the door open a crack. We don't have television, after all, and this is like an episode of *CSI: Catania*.

Soon a cop car arrives with its blue light flashing. A policeman in a dark jacket and a white leather gun-belt speaks briefly to his colleague on the horse, then goes upstairs and brings the mad woman back down into the courtyard for a discussion. After twenty more minutes of coming, going, bawling and pointing, silence descends and the police leave. It's two am. The show is over.

In the morning, we walk past Angela as she whispers conspiratorially with another neighbour in the courtyard.

'What was all *that* about?' I ask, pointing to the apartment upstairs.

Angela rolls her eyes: *you don't want to know*. The other neighbour, however, gives me the classic 'heavy metal' gesture with her hand – index and pinky fingers extended, the other two fingers tucked under the thumb. In Italy, this particular gesture means that someone is 'wearing the horns' (*cornuto*). More simply, it refers to adultery.

Forget car-jacking, firebombing, vandalism and extramarital affairs. Forget the Mafia. The one transgression that hits me the hardest during our time in Catania is the theft of my basil plant.

It's a tiny terracotta pot of the herb that I bought for one euro at the Pescheria. Every couple of nights, I pull a few leaves off to garnish a pizza or add to a pasta sauce. With a bit of love and attention, the plant thrives. I even nurture it through the heaviest falls of ash from Etna's eruptions, brushing black grime from the leaves and digging residue away from the stem. Ready access to fresh basil for cooking gives me a real sense of satisfaction.

And some fucker steals it. Steals it, I might add, from directly outside our front door. Not only that, but I'd placed the plant at the feet of a small statue of the crucified Christ located in a niche in our outside wall. This brazen thief tip-toes away with the goods while under the very gaze of the saviour. Thou shalt not steal? Like hell.

In his Mafia crime novel *The Day of the Owl* (*Il Giorno della Civetta*, 1961), Sicilian writer Leonardo Sciascia famously described mankind as consisting of five categories. There are the men *(uomini)*, the half-men *(mezz'uomini)*, the wimps *(ominicchi)*, the suckers *(pigliainculo* – literally 'those who get it in the arse') and, finally, there are the piddling little ducks in a puddle *(quaquaraquà)*.

The guy who took my basil plant? A piddling little duck in a puddle.

13. A trip to Vizzini

Vizzini: A word, my lady. We are but poor, lost circus
performers. Is there a village nearby?
Buttercup: There is nothing nearby . . . Not for miles.
Vizzini: Then there will be no one to hear you scream.
                         – *The Princess Bride*, Rob Reiner, 1987

At eight thirty on a spotless spring morning, Gill and I board
Catania's 431 bus, which does the Via Plebiscito loop to the
train station. The plan: take an hour-long train ride to the
village of Vizzini.

First, though, the bus, which writhes with excitable teenagers. When the driver gets off to change his destination sign,
two boys commandeer his seat and tootle the horn a few
times. Cheeky. The prank elicits snorts of laughter from an
oddball line-up of friends who are mostly pale and lean, but
unfailingly pimply. No surprise about the pimples considering the amount of hair gel these kids use. Hold a match to
their heads and they'd burn like candles for hours. (There's a
thought.)

Admittedly the teenagers have good reason to be excited.
Today is 25 April, a public holiday in Italy – Giorno della
Liberazione, Liberation Day. It marks the Allied victory in

World War II and the downfall of Mussolini. Like all young people around the world enjoying the fruits of a non-school day, these boys and girls don't actually care about the significance of the event. They probably have no idea what Liberation Day even means: 'Is it . . . liberating my girlfriend from her pants?'

To be fair, Liberation Day doesn't mean much to me either. I've marked 25 April on our calendar for an entirely different reason – the Sagra della Ricotta in Vizzini.

A *sagra* is a sacred festival. Sicily is rife with them, and the majority are devoted to a particular foodstuff. If you've been to Beef Week in the New South Wales town of Casino (I once dated the Second Runner-Up in the 'Miss Beef Week' pageant), you'll be familiar with the idea. Small towns across the Sicilian hinterland choose a particular day of the year to hold colourful celebrations for their agricultural specialties. So, there's a festival for sausages in Caccamo, cherries in Chiusa Sclafani, pistachios in Bronte, capers in Salina, artichokes in Cerda, bread in Acate, couscous in San Vito Lo Capo, peaches in Bivona, onions in Giarratana, and carob in Frigintini.

I'd happily attend every one of those festivals and eat myself silly. Except the last one. Carob trees (*carrubi*) are a common sight in Sicily's southeast. They're a boring-looking tree, and the chocolate substitute they produce is evil. I know that sounds harsh but, well, I hate carob. When I was at school, the people who ran the canteen figured it would be a good idea to replace all the Mars Bars and Flakes with brown-paper bags full of flat disks of carob. How they didn't realise the stuff tastes like *arse* is anyone's guess. Enterprising mothers used to make tidy profits by sending their kids to school loaded with proper, edible chocolate to sell in the playground. Apparently the farmers in this part of Sicily feed carob to their horses. That's animal cruelty in my book.

The only interesting thing about the carob tree is that its seeds are virtually identical in size and weight. Because of this uniformity, they were used for centuries as a means of weighing precious stones. The word 'carat' comes from 'carob' – eighteen carats of gold weighs the same as eighteen carob seeds.

Nice piece of trivia, but I still think carob trees should be axed to the stump on sight.

The agricultural specialty of Vizzini, a wizened hilltop town of eight thousand people in the Iblei Mountains southwest of Catania, is ricotta. Over the course of a three-day party, the Vizzinese celebrate with music, dance, parades and the main event, a live ricotta-making competition. It sounds worth a look. I'm therefore surprised to arrive at the station and find we're the only passengers for Vizzini. Doesn't anyone care about ricotta?

'Maybe we should just go to the beach,' says Gill, not without some justification.

But we forge ahead with the plan. That's to say, *I* forge ahead, dragging Gill along with me and silently praying that things don't go pear-shaped.

Only, they do.

The train ride is sixty kilometres of pastoral pleasure. Grassy fields explode with wildflowers. The flowers are thickest along the edge of the railway tracks, like coloured confetti tossed from the train windows. Beehives shelter in the shade of an olive grove.

Then, an announcement on the speaker system. I don't catch all of it, though I do hear the crackled word 'Vizzini'.

'This must be us,' I say to Gill.

We walk along the aisle of the carriage. A couple of Syracuse-bound occupants flash us an anxious glance, as though on the verge of saying something really important.

As our feet hit the platform, an impatient whistle blows and the train speeds away like it's escaping a crime scene.

And so it is. The crime is Fraudulent Misrepresentation, and the guilty party is the tourism board back in Catania for suggesting Vizzini as a worthwhile place to visit. We are literally in the middle of nowhere. In every direction a treeless hill rolls gently away. Occasionally a sandy track leads past the ruins of a farmhouse.

When the sound of a sheep's bell blows in on the breeze, I'm reminded of the scene in *Butch Cassidy and the Sundance Kid* – the one where Robert Redford and Paul Newman find themselves at a ramshackle train station in Bolivia. 'You just keep thinkin', Butch,' says Sundance, deriding his partner's bright idea to bring them to such a desolate location. 'That's what you're good at.'

'Where's the town?' asks Gill with a similar inflection.

There isn't one. There's not a person in sight. The station, we discover, is automated, so there's not even a railway worker or stationmaster.

I spy the entrance to a waiting room and peer into the gloom, looking for fellow travellers. Instead, I see a deserted concrete shell filled with broken glass, jagged planks of timber and fading graffiti: 'Bob Marley Breakdance'; '*Vota Alleanza Nazionale!*'; 'Nothing lasts forever: remember me'. Certain corners of the abandoned space have been set aside for the depositing of faeces, much of which has desiccated in the baking heat of successive summers. And while I'd love to tell you that these are the droppings of an Etna fox or some kind of ferret, soiled tissues in the vicinity have me leaping to a sorrier conclusion.

As I stare at the detritus, I realise this is the first complete silence I've experienced in Sicily since exploring the upper reaches of Mount Etna. This time, though, it's not welcome. Why has the train even stopped here? Perhaps it *wouldn't* have stopped if Gill and I weren't on board, clutching our tickets for Vizzini. Is this what the other passengers wanted to warn us about?

Actually, I do hear *one* sound as I stand on the platform wondering what to do next. It's my wife's teeth, slowly grinding. She's glaring at me.

I almost say, 'You can't blame me for this!'

Only, she can.

There's a paved road behind the station, winding up into the surrounding hills. I walk around the building and onto this road to look for a sign pointing to a nearby village. And that's when I notice a bar in the corner of the yard outside the station. It's called La Ruota (The Wheel). Miraculously, it's open. When Gill and I walk in, a sleepy but friendly barman in his forties spins around in surprise.

'Oh, this isn't Vizzini,' he says when I quiz him.

'No?' Out of the corner of my eye I see Gill glare at me afresh, arms folded across her chest. She's probably tapping a foot as well.

'No. Vizzini doesn't have a train station – the town's too high. Anyone who *does* try to get to Vizzini by train' – and the cobwebs in the corners of his café hint that this number is small indeed – 'arrives at this place. We're halfway between Vizzini and a town called Licodia. This station is called Vizzini–Licodia.' Astonishingly, he says it with pride.

'So, how long will it take us to walk to Vizzini?' I ask.

The fellow looks up from wiping the counter. 'You mean . . . *a piedi*?'

'Right. On foot.'

It's as if I said we wanted to tunnel our way to the town using a pasta colander. He reaches behind for a nearby stool to steady himself. 'I . . . I'm not sure,' he says. There's a long pause. Finally, he waves a hand in the air in the general direction of Vizzini, averting his eyes as if to absolve himself of any responsibility for sending somebody out there to *walk*. 'Six – seven kilometres . . . maybe more. Uphill. Very steep. Long time.'

Italians are happy to stroll for hours if it means being assessed for the fashions they're wearing (consider the evening *passeggiata*), but the notion of walking as a method of getting from A to B is roundly abhorred.

Gill and I, however, have no choice. We pay for our drinks and pull our daypacks on.

Mere minutes after we begin crunching up the road in the direction of Vizzini, the barman comes puffing after us. 'It's too far!' he says, with a flat hand on the middle of his panting chest, like he's just dragged us from the wreckage of a burning plane. 'I've spoken to a friend. He can take you into town.'

It's a kind gesture – entirely unnecessary, but kind.

Before long, a car appears. It's the barman's friend. He beckons for us to get in. I perform a brief mental assessment of the driver's appearance and character (is he, for instance, the type of person who keeps strips of human flesh in a jar in his refrigerator?), after which we thank the owner of La Ruota and jump in.

The driver couldn't be chattier. He asks what we're doing in Sicily ('Well,' says Gill, '*I'm* working'), then wants to know all the places we've seen. At the mention of Taormina, he starts to swoon: '*Paradiso!*'

As for Vizzini, apparently one of the social clubs in town has a sister organisation back in Australia. The driver knows this because his cousin lives in a place called Werribee near Melbourne and is a member.

The back seat of the car is filled with dozens of rolled-up sheets of paper. 'I was putting some posters up in the station,' he says when I ask about them.

I wonder for a moment what kind of poster could possibly be of any use hanging in the Vizzini–Licodia train station – maybe 'NO SHITTING'?

We get to Vizzini in no time. The generous stranger lets

us out in the main square, Piazza Umberto. Crisis averted. This isn't the last time in the day that Gill and I will encounter spontaneous and friendly assistance from the good folk in and around Vizzini. And it isn't the last time in the day that we'll meet someone with a relative in Werribee.

Vizzini is a sleepy place. Not even an annual ricotta festival can rouse it from its slumber. Outside a *tabaccheria* in the main piazza, two elderly suited gentlemen with pitch-black sunglasses and walking canes sit statuesquely on stools, watched by a nonchalant cat. The nearby Mini Market has its corrugated shutters pulled firmly shut.

Leaving the piazza we begin a slow, steamy climb to the highest point of town to take in the views. Halfway up one flight of weathered stairs, we pass a woman sweeping her courtyard. Her voluminous red hair offsets a red pencil skirt, white knit top and matching red-and-white apron. An impeccable outfit for housework. When we walk past she leans on her broom for a chat.

'Lots of Vizzinese live in Australia,' she tells us. 'Especially in Werribee.'

She wants to know our favourite parts of Sicily. We list the usual suspects.

'It's beautiful, Sicily,' she says proudly. 'So clean!'

Gill and I give a quiet nod while simultaneously stealing a glance at one another. On the train, we've just read today's edition of *La Sicilia*, whose front-page story concerned the alarming number of malformed babies born in the nearby city of Augusta, and the possible connection with pollution from the local petrochemical industry.

One after another, smartly dressed residents of Vizzini pause in their daily tasks to welcome us, talk about Sicily, and rattle off the names of their Australia-based relatives. Quite a few of them also bring up the topic of Giovanni Verga.

Verga (1840–1922) is Vizzini's favourite son. If the name doesn't strike a chord with you (it hadn't with me), this might help. In the final scene of *The Godfather III*, Michael Corleone (Al Pacino) watches his son Anthony performing an opera in Palermo. Scenes of murder – Michael's foot soldiers assassinating his enemies – are interspersed with members of the opera troupe singing arias on stage. Those arias are from *Cavalleria Rusticana* by Pietro Mascagni, based on a short story of the same name by Giovanni Verga.

Cavalleria Rusticana is one of the most regularly performed operas in the world. On its debut in 1890, it received thirty curtain calls. (Perhaps the pulley was broken.) Within two years, it had opened in sixteen cities. Its ongoing popularity is evident in the *Godfather* connection. Franco Zeffirelli made a film version in 1982 with Plácido Domingo in the lead.

Verga went on to become a celebrated writer of stories reflecting the trials and passions of peasant life in rural Sicily. He's also known as one of the earliest people to describe malaria in writing, in a short story of the same name. It boasts some wonderfully colourful passages, such as this one: 'After it had eaten up his brain and the calves of his legs, and had got into his belly till it was swollen like a water bag, [the malaria] had left him as happy as an Easter Day, singing in the sun better than a cricket.'

Vizzini was the backdrop for several of these earthy, sometimes violent tales, and it's still possible to visit the places mentioned in the books. One is the old *palazzo* where parts of Verga's last major work, *Mastro-don Gesualdo* (1888), are set. Gill and I head there for a look. The *palazzo* appears abandoned. Its walls sprout weeds and wildflowers, as if someone has deliberately fed seeds into the cracks at eye level then watered the stonework. An old marble plaque describing the Verga connection is nailed to the wall with iron pins that bleed with corrosion. If the composer's writing is best described as rustic, then the monuments to his work capture that feeling perfectly.

Hay, earth, leather and lunch: the aromas of Vizzini. It smells like a shepherd's hut during a noonday meal. Near the top of town, we come across two young boys taking turns riding a mule with a plaited yellow mane. They're wearing woollen jumpers and tracksuit tops. How is this possible? I'm in a t-shirt and I'm sweating profusely. Is this just my personal thermostat issue (Gill calls me 'The Human Heat-Bead') or do these kids have way too many layers on?

At the summit of Vizzini we find a crescent-moon-shaped piazza where we sit to catch our breath. Hilltowns in Sicily provide opportunities for excellent cardio workouts. So how can all the elderly residents be so plump? I suppose they start by holding a sacred festival in honour of ricotta.

The vista is a delight. The gentle Iblei Mountains stretch back to the horizon in layers of stubbly, sandy green. An occasional spread of prickly pears is almost the only inter-ruption, with one or two palm trees to give the place a whiff of North Africa. Here and there a mule path winds up and over a rise. There's nothing anywhere in our line of vision that gives any indication that this is the twenty-first century.

Beside us on the ledge, warming itself in the sun, is a gecko. The creature is black with stripes of vivid green. I watch a little spot on its neck pulsing in and out as my own heart rate, pounding from the steep climb, slows to normal.

Next we explore a famous historical quarter of Vizzini known as the Cunziria. (Careful with that pronunciation, folks.) The Cunziria surrounds a derelict tannery, hundreds of years old, and is famous as the setting for a duel between Alfio and Turiddu, the two protagonists in Verga's *Cavalleria Rusticana*. Their fight is prompted by – what else? – love, lust and adultery. It's initiated by means of the customary 'Sicilian embrace', in which two men hug and one ends up with half his ear bitten off. This ear-biting is intended as a challenge: 'We will fight to the death.' Colloquially the custom is known as *il Mike Tyson*. Or it should be.

Another scene from *The Godfather III* springs to mind: Sonny's son Vincent (Andy Garcia) challenging Joey Zasa to a duel by biting his ear.

'I would bite Andy Garcia's ear,' says Gill when I remind her of the scene.

'What, *off*?'

'No, just some gentle nibbling.'

There isn't much to the Cunziria, just a collection of abandoned farmhouses – the type that can be seen everywhere across the Sicilan interior, only here they are lumped together like a commune. My notes from our visit include the words 'listless', 'flyblown' and 'snaky'. It's very warm, too. We're still three months from midsummer; July must be hot enough to melt thermometers – even papal ones.

The Cunziria might be uncomfortable, but it's also atmospheric. Film directors love it as a location. The provincial government in Catania even allocated three million euros for its restoration as a centre of the arts. Unfortunately, the scheme fell apart. No prizes for guessing in whose hands the money ended up.

Nearby is a hotel that has tried to cash in on the Cunziria's potential. It offers the *agriturismo* experience, with everything from mountain-bike tours to cooking classes using local produce. I poke my head into the hotel restaurant. The décor is what you might call 'faux cave'. Surprisingly, a large group is sitting down to lunch. I notice that some of the diners are wearing those puffy jackets that you usually see on people at ski fields. After seeing the overdressed boys on the mule, this is too much. I feel like shaking their shoulders and yelling, 'IT'S TOO HOT FOR THESE PUFFY JACKETS! TAKE THEM OFF!'

Not that they would budge if I did. Italians dress themselves by the calendar, not by what the weatherman says – and certainly not by what an uncouth, unfashionable Australian male says.

Despite the decent crowd for lunch, the place looks tired. The swimming pool is clean enough, but around the side of the main building I find a deserted parking lot with an abandoned hotel bus. The side has been painted sky blue with a poorly rendered *Flintstones* motif: Fred and Wilma stand in a field of prickly pears, alongside a large boulder that reads 'CUNZIRIA'. Two tyres are missing from the bus, and rocks have been thrown through every window. Yabba dabba do.

Back in Vizzini's *centro*, the time has arrived for the highlight of the festival. People are milling around a temporary timber-and-brick shed that houses a dozen copper cauldrons. The huge pots are over a metre high and black from years of use.

Each cauldron is manned by an all-male team of four *ricuttari* (ricotta makers) – forty-eight burly chaps in total. Judging from what we hear of their bellowed conversations, you mightn't enlist them as your 'phone a friend' option on *Who Wants to Be a Millionaire*, but they do look like they know their way around a steaming cauldron of liquid cheese. Gill and I watch as they sweat and heave, stacking logs and stoking the fires beneath their pots.

Next, a silver tanker rounds a corner and lurches to a stop. A hose is unwound from the truck and passed between the twelve teams, each one filling its cauldron with a five-minute gush of pale liquid.

'Milk?' I ask a villager.

He shakes his head. 'Whey.'

Technically, ricotta isn't cheese. Cheese is made from milk; ricotta is made by recooking the liquid that forms during the cheese-making process ('ricotta' means 'recooked'). When whey is reheated almost to boiling point and cooled, new curds begin to appear, like puffs of cotton floating in a yellowish broth. The next step is to scoop out the curds or strain the liquid through a cloth bag or sieve. What's left is

ricotta. The method has ancient origins. The Roman states-
man Cato the Elder referred to it in his writings. Since then,
Italians have developed myriad ways of eating the stuff, in
cannoli, ravioli, lasagne – most of them expressly designed
to be irresistible but incredibly fattening.

Slowly the whey in the cauldrons begins to heat. The
robust *ricuttari* stir their concoctions – hundreds of litres
each – with long poles of bamboo. More locals gather,
attracted by the aroma, speculating over whether or not this
year's ricotta will top last year's.

When the brew is ready, each team of four men supports
their cauldron on horizontal poles on their shoulders, before
pouring the whey through an enormous sieve. The captured
curds are then dumped into a waist-high metal trough. A
wiry gentleman with pen and folder circumnavigates each
team's trough, judging the contents.

Now that the ricotta has been analysed, the feast can
begin. I join a queue of expectant onlookers at one trough.
Reaching the front of the line, I copy what I've seen others do
and hold out my hands. A gluggy pile of hot curds is dumped
directly into my cupped palms. Then I return to the piazza
where Gill is waiting.

Everywhere, people are eating. An old woman in a
matronly scarf, black blazer and sensible shoes has neatened
her handful of ricotta into a ball and is gobbling down large
pieces of it. A father manning one of the cauldrons leans over
the safety fence (presumably erected to stop kiddies dipping
inquisitive fingers directly into the bubbling whey) and gives
a wobbly mound of ricotta to his young daughter. I suddenly

hope that the people of Vizzini are all in the habit of washing their hands.

The Sagra della Ricotta at Vizzini proves to be a fascinating eating experience. I've dabbled with 'weird food' during my travels in Asia; my rap sheet includes eating a deer's penis in Manchuria – 'Good for virility,' said the Chinese fellow in the seat next to me. By way of instruction, he fellated his own piece of animal member in and out of his mouth, yelling, '*Chi! Chi! Chi!*' (Eat! Eat! Eat!) But slurping up a handful of hot ricotta is different. It's not about novelty or taboo. It's more about a primordial connection to the land and folklore of southern Sicily – food from fire to mouth.

It's also *horrible*. Watery and bland. Not as bad as dick, but bad enough. Cheese gains flavour by ageing; what I've just eaten is twenty seconds old. I agree with Gill's suggestion that Vizzini, instead of holding a 'Sacred Festival of Ricotta', should hold a 'Sacred Festival of Delicious Ricotta-based Products like Lasagne and Tortellini, not to mention Chocolate Cannoli'.

Time to return to Catania. Rather than hike two hours down to Vizzini–Licodia station and hope a train turns up, we opt for a bus. In the *tabaccheria*, we're told there's one leaving from the main piazza at four pm. We stand at the stop. The bus doesn't show. We wait for thirty minutes beyond the designated time – still nothing.

At least we're kept entertained. Members of a local folk group, Sikelia, stroll into the piazza playing accordions, guitars and drums. The men are dressed in black velvet trousers and red silk cummerbunds, the women in flouncy sky-blue skirts. Their music has a sprightly 'Hey Nonny Nonny' ring to it. It's transporting – unlike our bus, which still refuses to show up.

As we've almost come to expect in Vizzini, someone comes to our rescue. This time it's Mariella Sapienza, an artist from Catania. She's in Vizzini for the *sagra*, showing her paintings and charcoal portraits in an exhibition. Mariella was hoping to put her mother on the same bus that we intended to catch. We start chatting. When she asks what I do, I say I'm a 'writer'. (I don't know the Italian for 'unemployed house husband'.)

'A-*ha*, a fellow artist!'

It's a nice way of putting it, even if the only 'art' in my writing comes when I switch fonts.

Mariella says she might be able to solve our transport crisis. We follow her to where her exhibition is being held. It's the headquarters of the Vizzini chapter of the *DonnEuropee Federcasalinghe* – European Housewives. (Maybe they'll know the Italian for 'unemployed house husband'?)

As Mariella ducks off to find help, we peruse her excellent artworks – sepia-toned nudes and details from the old balconies of Sicilian *palazzi*. We also chat with an elderly Italian gentleman in a perfectly groomed suit and tweed hat. He's presumably on the hunt for a European housewife to keep him company in his dotage.

The fellow tells us that his entire family lives in Australia. ('Werribee?' I ask.) He's been to visit them several times. 'But

I still don't speak any English,' he says. 'In fact, I only know one English word.'

'What's that?' I ask.

'*Work*,' he replies, in English.

Mariella returns with welcome news. Remarkably, there's a train leaving from Vizzini–Licodia station at five thirty pm and a helpful villager is willing to drive us there. Perfect. What's more, if we get down to the station with a few minutes to spare, I'll even have time to take a crap on the waiting-room floor.

After relying so heavily on the kindness of strangers in Vizzini, it's almost a shock for Gill and me to board the train and find ourselves sitting opposite an unpleasant drunkard from the southern Sicilian town of Gela.

'I *hate* Catania,' he sneers after hearing where we live. 'Watch your money in that place,' he adds, then pulls down on one cheek with his finger and whispers, '*Occhio!*' It means 'keep your eyes open'. Not that we need more warnings about thieves in Catania.

As the train rattles on and our companion pulls the ring tab on a succession of beers, he becomes more and more fiery. There are lots of cupped-hand-on-bicep and fist-in-the-air gestures ('*vaffanculo!*'). He tosses me a beer without warning and I pluck it from the air just a millisecond before it crunches into my septum. Who says alcohol slows the reflexes?

'At least Catania is close to Taormina,' I say, thinking that even this boozy cynic will soften at the mention of Sicily's most stunning town.

'*Pah!*' he spits. 'I *hate* Taormina.'

So, he hates Catania, hates Taormina. Is there any Sicilian city he likes?

'Gela, my hometown.'

From what I've read, Gela (pronounced 'jailer') is the very *worst* of Sicily – shrouded in pollution and a stench from nearby industrial plants, beset by hideous architecture, and rife with its own branch of Mafia called 'La Stidda', who specialise in money laundering and drug trafficking. Gela's only distinction is said to be its world-class archaeological museum, though to me it reads like a yawn-inducing collection of ancient vases. At any rate, even the museum has failed to escape the town's predilection towards vice. In 1976, a hoard of a thousand ancient coins was stolen from one of its rooms, probably by a Stidda hoodlum.

The town's only other claim to fame is being the place where the Greek playwright Aeschylus died, in the fifth century BC. I've mentioned his death already – he was the one who allegedly got hit on the head by a tortoise, dropped by an eagle flying overhead. I imagine it's a slow death, death by tortoise.

The man pulls the train window open and lobs an empty beer can outside. If he weren't now stridently drunk and, I notice, liberally scarred with knife wounds, I'd launch into a tirade about littering. (Or quietly ask Gill if she might do so on my behalf.)

Despite the many violent encounters he appears to have found himself in, he's ironically petrified of travelling anywhere in the world outside Italy. Asia worries him the most

('Diseased!'). He loathes Japanese people, for no real reason he can elucidate: 'Bastards! The only good thing about them is that they make fast trains. I wish we had some of those here in Sicily.'

So do I. With our 'friend' in full cry, we can't reach Catania soon enough. And that's saying something. Why else would we want to rush back to Via Garibaldi, to be woken by domestic disputes and contend with *scippatori* (bag snatchers)? After a rocky start, it's been a thoroughly pleasant day in Vizzini; Sicily at its best. Even now, out the window of the train, the glories of an early evening sunset are revealing themselves – powdery pinks and blues, and the last light of day dancing sprite-like in furrows of shadowed grass.

14. A trip to Roman Sicily

> The sun, which was still far from its blazing zenith on that morning of the thirteenth of May, showed itself to be the true ruler of Sicily; the crude, brash sun, the drugging sun, which annulled every will, kept all things in servile immobility, cradled in violence as arbitrary as dreams.
>
> – Giuseppe di Lampedusa, *The Leopard*, 1957

Being on a tight budget is never pleasant. Sometimes it's downright dangerous. Consider my decision to save money on a barber by asking Gill to cut my hair. It's nerve-racking. Instead of standing behind me and holding the scissors parallel to my scalp, salon-style, Gill approaches from the front, clutching the scissors in two hands, with the pointy end aimed directly at my skull. It's like she intends to perform a trepanning.

'Hang on,' I say. 'What are you doing?'

'What do you mean, *what am I doing?*'

'Why are you doing it like that?'

'Like *what?*'

In the end, I escape without injury and with a perfectly reasonable cut – one which will certainly enable me to venture into society, though which, on closer inspection, resembles the short, jagged look favoured by drug addicts when they start a methadone program. In fact, with my new hairstyle and unkempt beard, all I need is a cold sore on the lip and I could approach local film directors for work as an extra: 'Crackhead in gutter'.

The other disconcerting thing about Gill cutting my hair is the way she quizzes me about my admittedly flagging career while wafting a pair of sharp scissors above my head.

'So, how's the work coming along?' *Snip.*

'Fine.'

Snip. Snip-snip. 'You must be getting through a lot while I'm up at Giga for all those hours.' *Snip-snip-snip.*

'Quite a lot.'

'Yeah? Like, what sort of stuff?' *Snip.*

In fact, work isn't coming along well at all. I've had a setback with the travel writing. Just as *The Globe and Mail* in Toronto is on the cusp of publishing my China story about Yellow Mountain, an unexpected complication arises: SARS. Outside of China, where the virus has kicked off, guess which place suffers a bigger death toll than anywhere on the planet? Toronto. So, while dozens are dying in Canada's biggest city, I'm trying to sell a travel article with the message, 'People of Toronto! Visit China – it's amazing!' I receive a polite one-line email from the newspaper announcing an indefinite hiatus on all China-related travel stories.

Meanwhile, the biography of the Roman emperor has run aground. I simply couldn't be arsed. It doesn't help that my old department at the University of Queensland is suffering serious budget cuts. Missing out on the job back there mightn't have been such a bad thing after all. Funding for disciplines such as history, ancient languages and archaeology seems to disappear daily, siphoned off into the wretched commerce faculty instead. As a thirty-year-old, it's hard to be enthusiastic about a career in a field whose continued existence is uncertain.

Before turning my back on ten years of Roman studies for good, though, I figure I should see Sicily's most famous monument from that age, the mosaics at Piazza Armerina, along with the nearby remains of the Roman town of Morgantina.

I choose a bad day for an excursion. At seven o'clock on a morning in late April, Catania is shrouded in an impenetrable fog, the kind they build lighthouses for. A whiteout like this is rare here – it makes front-page news in *La Sicilia* the following day.

It also makes for a sinister wait at the empty bus stop. Every set of clicking heels on cobblestones sounds like Jack the Ripper – or 'Jack lo Squartatore' as the Italians call him. Finally a vehicle approaches, headlights like apricots in the murk. I board the bus alone. It travels west along a vapour-filled plain towards Enna for an hour, before turning south onto a much narrower road.

Ten minutes before we reach Piazza Armerina, the fog suddenly dissolves. A sky emerges, blue as a husky's eye, and sunlight emboldens the fresh spring fields of the interior.

The beauty must be distracting: I end up leaving my camera on the bus. I've walked ten minutes away from the town's busy transport centre before I notice. Sprinting back to look for it, I'm met with an armada of identical buses moving off in different directions around me. It's like that scene in *Raiders of the Lost Ark* when Indiana Jones is surrounded by a crowd of people carrying enormous baskets, only one of which contains his kidnapped girlfriend.

A comical pageant ensues – comical for onlookers, at least – with me chasing after a dozen buses, banging the side of each one with my palm, yelling for it to stop. ('*Fermate! Fermate!*') One after another, the drivers slam on their brakes, angrily open their doors, and yell, '*Che cosa vuoi?*'

By the end of it, I've got wild eyes and sweat-drenched hair, my sunglasses have fallen from my head and smashed on the ground, and the entire bus-driving fraternity of central Sicily wants me lynched. But at least I've found my camera.

Piazza Armerina looks like a very pretty place, albeit rather glary now that my sunglasses are broken. The town hosts a tournament of 'Norman–Arab jousting' on 14 August each year. This is awesome. I believe there's still a place for jousting in society – as a means of settling minor domestic disputes, for instance, or as punishment for changing lanes without indicating.

I'm here, though, not to see the town itself but a place called Villa del Casale, five kilometres away. Shuttle buses only run in summer, so I'm soon trudging along a rural road in the hope of somehow blundering upon the site. I have a map of sorts, but it's covered in warning messages: 'NOT TO SCALE'. The sky hasn't stopped getting bluer and bluer; the morning, increasingly hot.

I don't even have my thumb out, but it must be obvious that I'm walking to Villa del Casale because a car soon pulls over. It's a navy-coloured Fiat housing a middle-aged couple with toothy smiles. We don't even exchange words – they simply open a door and gesture for me to enter. Ten silent minutes later, we arrive.

Then I discover the reason for the limited conversation. The man and woman are from Poland. At least, in their possession is a guidebook which appears to be in Polish. I ask to take a look. The book is dog-eared at the Piazza Armerina page.

'Ah, Piazza Armerina,' I say. 'So, you must be jousting Poles.'

Villa del Casale houses an astonishing collection of Roman mosaics – the largest in the world – and is one of Sicily's best-known attractions. One of its busiest, too. A vast parking bay bulges with buses. German tourists spill out of an air-conditioned coach: plump, grey-haired couples with matching caps, video cameras and guidebooks titled *Sizilien*. I never realised just how many older German men wear braces to hold up their trousers; it must be four out of every five. If I ever write a book about that country, I'm calling it *Brace Yourself for Germany*.

The villa was built in the early fourth century AD as the central residence of a giant estate. It was probably owned by a senator or even a member of the Roman imperial family. Back then, workers were employed in backbreaking labour in the fields. Now they sit in tents outside the front gate, flogging postcards and Ferrari pendants.

After centuries of continuous occupation, Villa del Casale was buried under a landslide in the twelfth century. It lay abandoned beneath the mud for eight hundred years. In 1929, famous Sicilian archaeologist Paolo Orsi began digging at the site. Work has been going on ever since, yet plenty remains to be done. A whole wing of servants' quarters is apparently unexcavated.

I'm a fan of mosaics. They seem accessible to me in the way that the canvases of a master painter don't. Even with my artistic shortcomings, I feel I could have a stab at mosaic work, insofar as I could brush some glue onto a square of coloured glass and stick it next to some other squares of coloured glass – so long as someone showed me how much glue to use, and how to hold the brush.

That's not to downplay the efforts expended by the ancient mosaicists (North Africans mostly) at Villa del Casale. More than sixty rooms are decorated by a staggering three and a half thousand square metres of floor mosaics, made up of several hundred million individual pieces (*tesserae*). One single corridor contains an uninterrupted mosaic of a hunting scene that stretches for sixty-four metres. To slowly walk along the villa's floors in Roman times observing the countless scenes from history and mythology must have been the ancient equivalent of a visit to the cinema.

For an indication of how rich and comprehensive the artworks are, consider this list of animals I observe in mosaic form during my ninety minutes in the villa: antelopes, bears, boars, bulls, camels, cheetahs, cows, deer, dogs, dolphins, ducks, elephants, fish, flamingos, foxes, geese, hippopotami, horses, lions, ostriches, panthers, partridges, pigeons, rabbits, rhinoceroses, snakes, swans and tigers. Each one crafted from tiny stone pieces.

But it's the mosaics of people that linger in the memory. Seeing the sandals, hairstyles, necklaces, clothes and jewellery of these characters – not to mention their facial expressions – brings the ancient world to life much more intensely than a towering temple ever can. Justifiably the villa's biggest attraction is the Room of Ten Girls in Bikinis (Sala delle Dieci Ragazze in Bikini), whose large mosaic floor depicts Roman women in various sporting poses, from ballgames to discus-throwing. Their 'bikinis' are actually plain old undies – big grandmother bottoms and a top like a boob tube.

'Actually, it's not a boob tube,' Gill explains later when I show her my photos from Villa del Casale. 'It's a bandeau top.'

I counter that her terminology, while more accurate, has the disadvantage of not containing the word 'boob'. She parries my counter with the fresh assertion that I am a fool of a man and when will I grow up.

Elsewhere at the site, construction work is going on. A few rooms are closed. 'We are working for you', reads an English-language sign. 'We pray to play attention on the suspending cords. We thank you for the collaboration.'

By now I'm getting a little steamy under the greenhouse-like structure that covers the mosaics. Outside again, I watch a horde of tourists in orange caps – I'm guessing this lot is Dutch – moving in the direction of an onsite eatery called 'Bar Ristorante Imperial'. The sign for the eatery is written in a Roman Empire–style font on a background of faux mosaics. The aim, I think, is to evoke the era of Nero. Slightly diminishing the sign's impact is a second line that reads: '*Souvenir – Post Card's – Gelati – Sandwich – Toilette*'. I glance at the restaurant's *menù turistico*. First course? Nero's old favourite, 'Imperial Macaroni'.

The Poles are nowhere to be seen, so I'm forced to make my own way back to Piazza Armerina. It's a five-kilometre trudge under an ever-strengthening sun.

My day's not done. From the transport centre where earlier I humiliated myself by bashing on buses in a frantic search for my lost camera, I buy a ticket for the twenty-minute trip to the village of Aidone. The driver must recognise me from the morning, because he gives me the evil eye when I board his bus.

We pass through terrain that feels oddly familiar. The gentle slopes outside Piazza Armerina are covered with leafy eucalyptus trees. The only piece of Australiana that's missing is a koala in the crook of the branches, chewing on some leaves. I wonder what a Sicilian farmer would make of a koala. Probably a *ragù*.

Eucalypts are native to Australia. They were introduced to Sicily around the time of Mussolini to combat malaria. Since the trees drain an enormous amount of moisture from soil through the process of transpiration, they can clear low-lying water that might otherwise provide the perfect habitat for mosquitoes to breed. Areas of Europe, North Africa and North America also introduced eucalypts for this purpose.

We pull into Aidone, which isn't remotely Australian, just another typically crumbling Sicilian village baking in the sun. In my determination not to leave my camera on the bus again, I promptly forget about my water bottle sitting in the seat pocket in front of me. An hour later, I will rue this oversight.

As with Villa del Casale, there is no shuttle between Aidone and the isolated Roman ruins of Morgantina. It means another sweaty stroll in the open Sicilian countryside. I set out at one thirty in the afternoon.

The lane out of town descends gently towards a green valley, passing two abandoned churches turning to powdered stone before my eyes. Incredible. In any Australian city, these stunning historic buildings would be a major attraction. A team of university geeks would keep their ornate façades from disintegrating via a state-of-the-art climate-control system, while a chic boutique would open in each foyer selling t-shirts and skinny lattes. Here, in barely affluent Aidone, the churches have no future but to erode in silence.

The lane reaches the valley floor and flattens out. I march on, accompanied now by the bandsaw drone of cicadas. Occasionally, a hot path, white and sandy, spills away into the high grasses towards a farm. I see one stone building fronted by a trellis heavy with lavender and bees.

And did I mention the heat? Temperatures, I discover later, are unseasonably high for the end of April because the sirocco is blowing across from the Sahara.

A couple of kilometres along this road, a sign for the ruins appears ('Scavi Morgantina'), leading me off to the left.

The sun is now relentless and I can feel my face glowing. My toes are like ten little embers at the ends of my sneakers. But my water supplies are back on the bus. I begin to hope that the Morgantina site has a Bar Ristorante Imperial selling cold drinks and freshly churned gelati.

This new 'road' – little more than an overgrown tractor path – creeps faintly upward again. Fields close in around me. The path is occasionally interrupted by a copse of poplars whose shade I relish.

Just as I'm beginning to worry about the possibility of heat stroke and its attendant hallucinations, I climb a short rise and the ruins of Morgantina unfurl behind a barbed-wire fence to the right. The place is deserted, the modest car park empty. I do find one person – the ticket seller. He's fast asleep at a little fold-up desk in the grass, his head resting on a cash box. I'm not sure what to do. I could tiptoe past and see Morgantina for free, but I'm now desperate for water. Worryingly, there's no sign of a shop.

I clear my throat. No response.

I give a light cough. Still nothing.

Finally, after I loudly unzip my backpack a few times, the fellow stirs. I hand over a five-euro note and he rummages inside his cash pillow for change and a ticket to the site. Next I ask about the water situation.

'Aidone,' he says, pointing in the direction of the town I've just left. Then he's asleep again. There's nothing to do but lick my desert-dry lips and block out any thoughts of dehydration.

Fortunately the Morgantina ruins are entirely engrossing.

Home to a local population as early as 850 BC, the city was then occupied by a colony from Greece. Under the Romans, Morgantina retained its importance as a trade centre – Pliny the Elder raved about the region's wine. Morgantina was also the place where Eunus, leader of the first great slave rebellion against Rome, died in 133 BC (subsequent rebellions included the one led by Spartacus). Eunus was a Syrian with a knack for magic tricks and fire breathing. He also claimed to be a prophet. Up to two hundred thousand disgruntled slaves joined him in protest against the wealthy Roman estate holders. Eunus's ragtag team won a few minor battles before Rome predictably sent a much larger army and crushed the rebellion.

The next mention of Morgantina in the Roman Empire is unsettling. It dates from a hundred years later, when Strabo wrote that the city ceased to exist. He gave no explanation. Around 40 BC, it seems, the inhabitants either died en masse, or packed up and left. The place was ignored for two millennia, its location forgotten. Then, in the 1950s, an archaeological team from Princeton University found a simple six-sided wooden dice on the site with the Greek initials 'MGT'. Could this refer to Morgantina?

A flurry of digging followed until the identification could be confirmed. Headlines in *The New York Times* between 1955 and 1957 show the puzzle unravelling piece by piece: 'Ancient mystery city unearthed in Sicily'; 'Archaeologists seek clues to sudden destruction of unnamed mountain site'; 'Excavations resolve the mystery of vanished city in central Sicily'; 'Princeton archaeologists say site is that of Morgantina, which died in 40 BC'.

Despite all the excavation work, there's not much to see. Earlier in the day at Villa del Casale, the ancient world literally jumped into life before my eyes, the mosaics of Romans, animals and mythological characters parading back and forth as if they were putting on a show for my personal benefit. I saw footwear, apples, togas, daggers and feathers – even pets wearing collars.

Morgantina, though, is just a jumble of stones lying half-buried in a swathe of yellow wildflowers. But as I pick slowly over the site, wading through muggy grass up to my knees, all the elements begin to come together. It's like I've unfurled the blueprint of an ancient city in my mind – the huge two-tiered meeting place (*agora*), the string of shops along a paved street, a crumbling furnace used for baking bread, and the tiled floor of a house, occupied now by weeds and a single brown terracotta pot, cracked open like a chocolate Easter egg.

There would probably be much more to see at Morgantina – and a better idea of why, in antiquity, the town suddenly ceased to be – if not for the nefarious activities of *tombaroli* (tomb robbers) in recent decades. These criminals operate all over Italy, creeping into fields in the middle of the night to dig for historical remains, then selling them on the international market for a tidy sum.

The problem is particularly rife in Sicily and, specifically, at Morgantina. Not long before my visit, a man received a two-year jail sentence and sixteen-million-euro fine for masterminding the export of a two-and-a-half-thousand-year-old marble statue of Aphrodite plundered from the Morgantina site in 1970. The statue passed through various hands in the 1980s before ending up in the J. Paul Getty Museum in Malibu, California. The actual digging was carried out by a *tombarolo* from Aidone, a pensioner who escaped a jail sentence by assisting police with investigations. The main charge was subsequently dropped on appeal, mired in red tape – something about a 'statute of limitations'. There have also been disputes about whether or not the Aphrodite can be connected with certainty to the Morgantina site. Not to mention the broader 'Elgin Marbles' debate about where an artwork legitimately or morally belongs. While Sicilians continue to await a definitive outcome, the Aidone Archaeological Museum displays a poster of the statue at its front entrance, in the hope that the real thing might soon stand there instead.

Meanwhile, other pieces from Morgantina look like they're definitely on their way home. The Metropolitan Museum of Art in New York, the University of Virginia Art Museum and the aforementioned Getty have all agreed to return a batch of objects determined with near certainty to have been illegally excavated from Morgantina.

Morgantina, then, is full of fascination – a much-needed fillip for my dwindling affection for the Roman world. And if I wasn't thirsty enough to drink a cup of my own piss, I'd stay for longer.

I hike for a dazed hour back to Aidone. It's mid-afternoon and hotter than any sauna I've sat in. The landscape shimmers and shifts before my eyes and the cicadas burrow a hole into my head with their relentless buzz. On more than one occasion I think I spy a person on the road ahead – he wears a Roman toga and in his right hand carries a bejewelled goblet full of freshly refrigerated spring water, occasionally lifting it to his already moist lips. I quicken my pace each time he appears, but when I reach a bend in the road he's gone.

By the time I slump up the hill into town, I'm delirious. And purple. Groups of locals walk past and I swear they're whispering, '*Melanzane! Melanzane!*' ('Eggplant!') My blistered feet lead me mercifully to the nearby Bar Sport, where I order a glass of cold water and drain it in one go.

Four seconds later, I'm lying in a crumpled heap on the floor, clutching my face. Pain shoots into my right eyeball. I've given myself a case of brain freeze. Good thing I didn't order a *granita*, Sicily's famous crushed-ice drink.

Finally I recover enough to attempt a conversation with the barman. From my position on the floor, all I can see is his quizzical face, peering over the counter. He must be horrified. A Sicilian superstition says that drinking cold water can make you seriously ill – I appear to be the living proof of it.

'Why did you do it?' he asks. 'Why walk to Morgantina on a day like this?'

'Why not?' I offer, still on the floor, but now with my head propped on an elbow for comfort.

'But why *walk*?' he continues. 'Couldn't you have driven?'

'I don't have a car.'

'A motorbike then.'

'Again, don't have one.'

He shakes his head like it's a miracle.

Outside in the main square is another miracle. It's a street market selling every conceivable object and foodstuff known to man. I see toffee apples, Navajo Indian paintings, popcorn, latest-technology vacuum cleaners, sandwiches filled with German sausage, lampshades, Moroccan carpets, rubber car-mats, African wood carvings, hookahs, miniature models of Mount Etna, Sicilian folk CDs, birds in cages, fried onions. Mostly, though, it's religious knick-knackery: oval portraits of Mary, paintings of Christ with an inflamed heart in his chest, wooden hangings for the house (*benedici la mia casa e la mia famiglia*), 'confession strings' in various colours, and miniature sculptures of Padre Pio.

For all my complaining about walking in the Sicilian countryside in the heat, I've actually got off very lightly. On the same day that I limp from Morgantina back to Aidone, crowds of people of all ages are also walking to Aidone in the heat, but from the other side of the town – and they're doing so *without shoes*. It's a religious pilgrimage. It turns out that I'm in Aidone on the eve of the town's annual Festival of Saint Philip the Apostle, held on the first day of May. This is the reason for the huge market full of religious trinkets, vacuum cleaners and other things that suck. The pilgrims are known as *nuri* (barefooted ones). On the afternoon and evening of 30 April, they walk up a particular hill into Aidone in order to show their devotion. In fact, they don't all walk. Some do the pilgrimage on their *knees*, or even with chains trailing from their ankles. For twenty kilometres. The hope is that Saint Philip might provide his blessings for a successful yield of crops for the farmers.

It's instructive to observe the devotion of the towns-people to this age-old religious festival. There aren't too many Aussie friends of mine who would walk twenty kilometres barefoot through the countryside to end up in a church.

There are quite a few, on the other hand, who would walk twice that distance to end up in a Room of Ten Girls in Bikinis.

15. Healing

The trouble with eating Italian food is that five or six days later you're hungry again.

– George Miller

We're in the back seat of a white van with tinted windows, surrounded by people dressed entirely in black. It's a scene from a Tarantino film. Maybe we're part of a posse of thieves, on our way to steal some basil plants.

Not quite. We've been invited to Sunday lunch in Nicolosi, the highest village on the southern slopes of Mount Etna. It's where I stopped for beer and wild-mushroom pizza on the way up to watch the lava flow back in November. The invitation is from Giulia, one of Gill's adult students. She's twenty-seven and, like so many Sicilians in their twenties, still lives at home.

Nicolosi is an hour from Catania and we don't have a car. Hence the van. The black-clad occupants of the vehicle are Giulia, her cousin Paolo, and Paolo's wife, Francesca. Giulia's single concession to colour is a tan cardigan pulled over a black blouse.

The family is observing a period of mourning. Four weeks ago, Paolo's father (Giulia's uncle) passed away. Giulia's own father died two years earlier. As we crawl out of the city and along the scraggly, semi-urban streets of Etna's lower reaches, Gill and I hear about another uncle in the family who has Alzheimer's. Doctors have given him two years to live. He's fifty-eight. Struggling to comprehend all of this tragedy, I silently vow not to whinge the next time one of Erminia's dogs takes a shit on our doormat.

The custom of wearing black for a period of mourning might be on the wane in the northern half of Italy, but it survives in Sicily. Some women dress in black for the rest of their lives after their husbands pass away. In the Sicilian interior, in particular, Gill and I have watched countless stooped widows pegging entire wardrobes of black to their clotheslines: pants, blouses, cardigans, coats, stockings, scarves and slips. I understand that dressing in black is a mark of respect and commitment, but it must get mighty hot in the middle of summer. A tip for women in rural Sicily: avoid letting hubby die in July.

Thankfully, Nicolosi is high enough up Mount Etna's slopes to escape the savage heat that afflicts Catania for a third of every year. We feel the drop in temperature as soon as we open the van door.

Giulia lives with her mum on the bottom floor of a three-storey apricot-coloured apartment building. To the side of the building is a small square of unkempt grass and an olive tree. Giulia tells us that several of the apartments on the second and third floors are leased by American soldiers and their families who work at Sigonella.

Sigonella, eh? I'd almost forgotten about the enormous US naval airbase located just twenty kilometres from Catania.

It keeps a low profile. Occasionally Gill and I see groups of shaven-headed Americans on R&R in the city. They tend to favour the city's Irish pub, Waxy O'Connor's. One day at Waxy's, I share a beer with some friendly recruits from Mississippi, eager to teach me their recipes for alligator-tail stew. Another time, on a bus to Taormina, Gill and I over-hear some less savoury Sigonella recruits chatting. A debate breaks out among them: which soldier in the barracks smells the worst? Votes pour in for someone named Saunders.

'Yeah,' nods a nuggetty little fellow with Dolph Lundgren hair. 'Saunders smells worse than a bagful of dried assholes.' Private Lundgren nurses a warm can of Miller Lite, clearly at pains to ensure the label is facing outwards so people can admire him for drinking so early in the morning.

From further conversation – consisting mostly of vari-ations on the word 'motherfucker' – we glean that they're travelling to Taormina to let off some steam. Poor Taormina.

As many as four thousand troops are stationed at 'Sig' at any one time. Sicily is considered a vital strategic hub for military activity in the Mediterranean. People have thought as much since the Phoenicians in the eleventh century BC. Sigonella's fifteen minutes of fame came in October 1985, when a plane arrived carrying a group of escaping Palestin-ians who, three days earlier, had hijacked an Italian cruise ship, the *Achille Lauro*. Both the Italian and US authorities were eager to claim jurisdiction and make an arrest (among other things, an American citizen had been murdered on board). Tensions flared and Sigonella-based US Navy SEALs were warned that they'd be shot if they attempted to board the plane and arrest the hijackers. After a tense night, President Ronald Reagan gave the order for his troops to stand down.

On a more trivial note, Sigonella is said to have the worst driving record of any military installation in Europe. This is presumably an attempt by American troops to conform to the standards set by the maniacs in Catania.

With her decent English-language skills, Giulia has taken on the role of landlord for the Americans in the upstairs apartments.

'They mustn't be very easy tenants,' I say, remembering recent news stories in Australia of military initiations involving vacuum cleaners and testicles.

'Actually,' she insists, 'they're fine.' (In fact, more than fine. Months down the track when we've left Sicily, we learn that Giulia has fallen in love with one of the soldiers and followed him back to the States to live. We pray for her sake that it's not Saunders.)

Jumping out of the van, Gill and I and our three black-clad companions file across the car park, greet the family dog (also black, with a permanently guilty expression on his labby face) and step into the modest apartment. There's a living/dining room at the front. A couple of bedrooms are out the back somewhere, and there's a well-used kitchen to the side. Glorious aromas emanate from the latter.

The main room is a snapshot of 1970s chic: a gold-framed painting on the wall; a couch of mottled orange and green; a vase of peacock feathers in one corner; and a trophy cabinet of various underwhelming school achievements, mostly football-related (Giulia has three brothers). The television is tuned to one of Italy's interminable weekend variety shows.

Giulia's mother emerges from the kitchen. She's not in black but in a lavender knit top and grey skirt. Her hair is the same honey-orange colour as that of Angela, our neighbour in Catania; this seems to be the dye *du jour* for middle-aged Sicilian women. A white apron studded with pictures of strawberries stretches around her matronly girth.

We take our place at a long wooden table, where lunch is served almost immediately. It's preposterously generous. There's not just a *primo* and *secondo*, but a *terzo*, *quarto*, *quinto* and *sesto*, too.

First comes a hearty bowl of pasta that would on most tables around the world suffice as a complete meal. (For Sicilians, though, pasta is an *amuse-bouche*.) Giulia's mamma's version is a simple variation on a classic sauce: tomatoes, garlic, wine, fresh basil, perhaps some dissolved anchovies, and a tiny lip-buzz of chilli. I forget to ask the actual name. I think it's *spaghetti alla carrettiera* ('carter's spaghetti'), a Catanese dish favoured by the drivers of Sicily's famous hand-painted donkey-drawn carts. Regardless, it's awesome. Francesca clearly agrees. As women go, she's Rubenesque – or Botticellian, to give it an Italian context. I watch as she twists a fork in her pasta and lifts it to her mouth. Seconds later, the whole thing is gone, inhaled like a dose from an asthma puffer.

The pasta plates are cleared away and three new dishes appear: *torta di spinaci*, a quiche made of eggs, ricotta, mozzarella and spinach; *cotolette alla Milanese*, tender veal cutlets, dusted in flour and breadcrumbs and pan-fried; and *polipetti in tegame*, baby calamari sautéed in olive oil, garlic and a splash of white wine, tossed through with fresh parsley and Trapani sea salt, and served in a little metal pan.

Giulia and her cousins are fundamentalist Christians. For this reason, they're teetotallers. (Because, hey, it's not like Christ ever had a drink.) Mamma, on the other hand, looks like she's been waiting a long, long time for someone like me to walk through the door. At first she's sheepish, emerging from a hiding spot in the pantry with a single tall bottle of Birra Moretti. She tucks it behind the sparkling mineral water and the two-litre Coca-Cola on the table. 'Just in case anyone wants some,' she mumbles.

I want some. So, when the others begin pouring their white plastic cups of Coke, the old girl and I share the bottle of beer. Gill nudges her own cup in our direction as well.

The plates are cleared away again to make room for more food. I've already eaten pasta, two veal cutlets, two slices of quiche, a plate of seafood and half a basket of crusty bread. Next to arrive in the fleshy outstretched arms of Giulia's mum is a tray of veal rolls, or *falsomagri* – another local favourite. The name may relate to our words 'false' and 'meagre': the point being that a meagre piece of expensive meat (in this case, paper-thin veal) is deceptively turned into a feast thanks to a stuffing of much cheaper ingredients – boiled eggs, sausage mince, artichokes, cheese, whatever.

The bulging *falsomagri* have been trussed up with string, sautéed in olive oil, and gently braised in wine and tomatoes. They look like hand grenades because of their shape and the crisscross of string lines. Fittingly, I feel like I'm about to explode.

By now, Giulia's mother has quietly brought a bottle of red wine to the table. I watch her as she makes a discreet attempt at removing the cork from the stopper in silence. No luck: the top comes off with a loud *pop!* The other family members exchange nervous glances. Mamma pours me a glass, full to the brim. (Sicilians don't care too much for letting wine breathe.) It's a chewy red from local vineyards. The bottle itself is clear glass with no label. We sip with gusto.

Somehow, only an *insalata mista* remains on the table. Italian salads are interesting. 'Simple' doesn't do them justice: in Sicily, they border on ascetic. One time, our neighbour Carmelo knocked on our door in Catania and handed over a plate of sliced fennel. 'Salad,' he said. Similarly, the salad at Giulia's mamma's house is just a bowl of green leaves. But at least it's served with a jar of homemade Roma-style mayonnaise – oil, garlic, anchovies – which we spoon on top of the leaves like mustard.

Epitomising the simplicity of Italian cooking for me was a dish I once saw in a *trattoria* in Venice. The back-alley restaurant happened to be the place where the city's ferry drivers all met after work. I watched transfixed as six of them tackled enormous bowls of *spaghetti al burro* – not 'donkey' but 'butter'. The dish was a steaming pyramid of completely plain spaghetti with nothing but a fifty-gram cube of melting butter on top.

Back to the food at hand: what would a Sicilian lunch be without *dolci*, something sweet? Two enormous cakes are hauled out for our eating pleasure. They come courtesy of Francesca. One is *torta di mandorla* (almond cake), the other, *torta ai frutti di bosco* (wild berry cake). They're both divine in a heavy, crumbly way.

The feast ends with coffee. The cups are four decades old – a wedding present for Giulia's mother: cherry-red espresso-sized cups with dragon motifs and gold rims.

'*Cinese*,' says the mamma, aware that Gill and I lived in China for a year.

Then she does something which isn't very Chinese at all. She adds one heaped teaspoon of sugar to the two centimetres of espresso in each cup, before pointing to where the sugar jar is on the table in case we need more.

Back in Catania, inspired by the flawless lunch at Nicolosi, I resolve to add more Sicilian dishes to my kitchen repertoire.

Step one is to buy more olive oil. There's no such thing as too much olive oil in a Sicilian kitchen: Giulia's mum used the word '*olio*' more than any other when she was giving me cooking tips. One day at a seaside village north of Catania, Gill and I stop to watch a primly dressed couple eating a restaurant lunch accompanied by little glasses of olive oil – as a *drink*.

Italians, along with Greeks and other intensive users of olive oil, tend to have lower rates of heart disease than other societies. (Cold comfort for poor Giulia and her mourning family, I guess.) The fat in olive oil is much healthier than that of other oils, plus it has high levels of antioxidants. Studies suggest that the risk of heart disease can be reduced by consuming a certain volume of extra-virgin olive oil every day.

Despite this, I seem cursed by olive oil in Sicily. One day as I'm unpacking a shopping bag in our kitchen, I drop an unopened one-and-a-half-litre bottle of olive oil onto the tiled floor. From two metres. The impact shatters the glass and flings viscous oil onto the cupboards, fridge, sink and stove, and all over my legs. Every crevice in the kitchen goes gooey. It's a half-day clean-up job.

Unfathomably, one week later, I do *exactly the same thing*. How many people in the world have smashed a full bottle of olive oil at some point in their lives? Not many, surely. How many have done it twice in seven days?

'You're worse than my dad,' says Gill, and that's saying something. Tony, my father-in-law, is banned from unloading the dishwasher in the family home in Brisbane because of his inability to handle a piece of expensive bone china without accidentally dashing it to smithereens on a hard floor. It's as if the two of us have defective opposable thumbs.

As I'm bent over the tiles mopping up fruity oil for the second time in a week, I feel an ache at the top of my left arm. I pause for a moment. The ache persists. In fact, it's not just the left arm but stretches across into my chest and, well, the vicinity of my heart. Wouldn't that be devilishly ironic? To die of a heart attack while up to my elbows in a substance heralded for its role in reducing heart attacks. I can just imagine Saint Peter saying on my arrival at the Pearly Gates, 'I think the idea was to *digest* it, not scrub floors with it.'

Obviously this is a concern. The pain goes in a few minutes, but it's back again the next day. And the next. The truth is that for several weeks now I've also been having some palpitations. The latter I attributed to drinking a handful of strong coffees a day, but now I begin to fear there's a connection. Then, just to top things off, while I'm involved in all of this self-analysis I discover a grape-sized lump in the fleshy tissue of my left breast – again, right near my heart.

Fear scrambles my mind. The equation is simple: I've developed some kind of tumour which has spread (*metastasised*, even) to my heart, leaving me with months – maybe mere days – before a massive heart attack takes my life. None of which makes any medical sense at all, I'm sure.

What now? Maybe I should write a 'bucket list' of things to do before I die:

1. Find the piddling little duck in a puddle who stole our basil plant and put his goddamned eye out.
2. Remind Gill and family I love them.
3. Bungy.

I tell Gill my predicament. She's shocked. With pits in our stomachs we come up with a course of action. Being young, poor and stupid, we're entirely uninsured. So I can't just march into a local hospital and demand treatment. Instead we resolve to approach Gill's boss Palmina and ask if I can meet with her husband Salvo after work one day. Salvo is one of Catania's leading plastic surgeons, so I figure he'll know a thing or two about general health issues. If not, he can at least give me advice on my sticky-outy ears: is it worth getting them pinned?

When we meet, Salvo puts me at ease about the lump. One careful prod and he waves it aside as a small bulge of fatty tissue called a lipoma. Charming. It's something to monitor, but of no immediate concern. The pains and palpitations, though, are a different issue.

'Probably best to get that checked out,' he says, and his tone of voice implies 'soon'. It's Friday. Salvo says he can book me in for an appointment with someone at his hospital on Monday.

The weekend is horrid. Gill and I have a trip to Cefalù planned with Natasha and her sister, visiting from London. We decide not to cancel. I try to be good company for everyone, but I can't help the occasional feelings of dread. They come and go in silly surges, playing havoc with my train of thought: *Isn't it nice to be out of Catania for the weekend; this is fun, the sun is shining, the birds are – OH MY GOD, ON MONDAY I DIE.*

Still, I'm at least reminded that Cefalù is one of Sicily's best towns. I love its cluster of medieval buildings facing the sea, and the formidable crag, La Rocca, that rises behind them. A bracing bodysurf on the main beach lifts my spirits, too.

It's a brief respite. Soon we're back in Catania, and D-Day dawns. Our trip to the doctor is preceded by a visit to Signor Pull-the-Rent-in, to whom we owe a heinous chunk of rent as well as payment of an unexpectedly large electricity bill (Gill's hairdryer, I'll warrant a guess). It leaves us completely broke. If heart surgery is required, I may have to do it myself using a can opener and a spool of thread.

Gill has taken the day off from work to hold my hand – I'm not the most stout-hearted of patients. It requires two bus trips and almost ninety minutes for us to get to Ospedale Cannizzaro. The hospital is up near Aci Castello in Catania's north. The grounds are immense, so we also have to wait for a shuttle bus to drive us to the main building.

Patrolling the hospital grounds are a roving crew of vigilantes – I don't know what else to call them. They wear knee-high black leather boots, cool shades, peaked caps and gloves. They seem to act as security guards and administrative personnel at the same time.

'Can I help you?' asks one in broken English when the shuttle bus drops us off.

'Yes,' I reply, 'I'm here to see Dottore Paccione.'

'Ah, Dottore Paccione. He is a very well doctor.'

'I'm glad *he's* well,' I almost say, 'but what about *me*?'

Soon I'm led to a shabby waiting room. The reception counter is manned by another vigilante, a gnome-like fellow with a nicotine-stained beard. In his hand is a piece of paper torn from an exercise book, with a list of the day's patients written in biro. From time to time he calls a name. Occasionally someone gets up and limps through a door into the doctors' rooms beyond; more often than not, nobody answers, and the dumpy guy from the Hell's Angels shrugs his shoulders and scribbles a line through the name. It's not particularly reassuring.

I pass the time by examining a list of the resident doctors at the hospital and trying to guess their speciality based only on their names. Here's what I come up with:

- Dr Gullota – Ear, Nose and Throat
- Dr Illuminato – Radiologist
- Dr La Spina – Chiropractor
- Dr Siringo – Anaesthesiologist
- Dr Zito – Dermatologist
- Dr Achille – Podiatrist
- Dr Sorbelli, Dr Tumminelli – Gastroenterologists
- Dr Fallico, Dr Fontana, Dr Pennisi – Urologists

There are others, too. Dr Trifiletta clearly specialises in treating hypochondria. Dr Buongiorno? Probably a psychologist. But something tells me that Dr Lo Gatto – 'The Cat' – is in the wrong place.

Glancing at the long list of doctors, I decide that I don't particularly care which one of them looks after me, so long as it isn't Dr Accurso.

Eventually I'm called. On hearing my non-Italian name, everyone turns to stare. I can tell they're all playing 'guess the ailment'. I walk up a hallway and into another waiting area. Actually, it's just the dimly lit corridor outside the doctor's office. Four people are standing in a queue. Why send us here? Why not leave us in the proper waiting room until the doctor's actually ready? There are no chairs in the corridor, there's nothing to read, no plants, no water dispensers, and nothing on the walls, aside from grime. There's a used swab on the floor with a shoe's treadmarks on it. From behind a door, I hear a woman yelling in pain – just presented with her bill, perhaps.

Finally it's my turn. Dr Paccione is in his mid-fifties, entirely charming, though with a bedside manner that could best be described as lackadaisical. Salvo is here, too, having come along to lend some support and provide the doctor with a few details of my problem. It's a nice touch.

Various tests are administered, culminating in an EMG: the doctor puts electrodes on different parts of my body, then pokes and prods my skin with something that looks like an acupuncture needle. A printer chugs away, preparing one of those earthquake-style graphs.

After an hour of tests, I'm given a diagnosis as good as it gets for someone who's been contemplating life with coronary disease. My heart's fine. Instead, I have an issue with a muscle or nerve in my left or right arm, and/or neck and shoulder. (The doctor is a little vague on the details.)

'You say you're a writer,' he notes, attempting an analysis of the results.

'Sort of,' I reply.

'And you spend all day hunched over a laptop?'

'Perhaps not *all* day,' I say, glancing briefly at Gill.

'Hmm,' he ponders. 'It might be your posture. And a bad chair.'

As for the palpitations, he says they're probably caffeine-related. I'll need to take it easy on the macchiatos.

'Anything else I can do?' asks Dr Paccione.

How are you with defective opposable thumbs?

By way of treatment, I'm given a neck brace big enough for a heavyweight boxer, a sling for my arm, an anti-inflammatory gel, and a prescription for a series of injections, the purpose of which I never discover. The first of the injections is to be administered immediately. A young nurse leads me down another grubby corridor and shoves me onto a bed, face down. She yanks at my pants and applies some rubbing alcohol.

'You'd better watch this,' I hear her say to Gill.

'Why?'

'Because you're going to be doing the next five of these at home.'

I almost spin around on the bed. It's a good thing I don't – the needle might snap or, worse yet, insert itself somewhere far more painful than a fleshy buttock. Instead, I let out a feeble cry with my mouth buried in a pillow: '*Harmph!*'

It's the cry of a man whose wife has just been given carte blanche to stab him with sharp objects every day for a week.

We return home via a *farmacia* to get the prescription filled. I'm sure I detect a glint in the chemist's eye as she looks at me in my neck brace and hands the needles to Gill.

The next morning, Gill opens the box of medicine on our small table. Out tumbles a hodgepodge of sealed brown pots half-filled with freeze-dried powder, a bunch of glass vials and a set of hypodermic syringes in various segments. Already on the table are swabs of different sizes, a bottle of sterilising alcohol, some surgical tape and a pair of scissors.

'What am I supposed to do with all of this?' Gill asks.

'I thought the nurse explained everything?'

Gill gives me a cautionary look. 'The nurse showed me how to give you an injection. She didn't show me how to assemble a hypodermic needle or prepare medicine from powder.'

Stuck to the cardboard inside the box, we find a folded set of instructions. They're in Italian only. They're also complicated: '*Nicetile 500mg/4ml. L-acetilcarnitina. 5 flaconcini di liofilizzato + 5 fiale solvente per uso i.m. ed e.v.; Polvere e solvente per soluzione iniettabile IM EV, 5 flaconcini + 5 fiale solvente 4 ml.*'

My pulse quickens. Needles freak me out, so I don't want this done incorrectly. When I was twelve, a doctor took some blood from my arm. He asked if I wanted to lie down, but I said I'd be fine. As the point went in and the first curl of red filled the dropper, I blacked out almost immediately, slid off the bed where I was sitting, cracked my head on a chair on the way to the floor, and bit through my tongue when my jaw hit the marble tiles. My paranoia has some justification.

'I'll ring Palmina and see if Salvo is there,' says Gill. She opens the doors to the courtyard to get a weak bar of reception then punches the number into the mobile phone.

Salvo's not home, but Palmina offers to help instead. Gill explains the problem with the needle kit and the Italian instructions. A conversation unfolds between the two of them, though of course I can only hear Gill's responses.

Gill: 'We've got instructions but can't understand them.'
Pause.
Gill: 'Yes, I suppose I can just guess.'
Pause.
Gill: 'So, I actually snap the glass piece off the top?'
Pause.

Gill: 'And how do I mix it?'

Pause. I watch as she shakes one of the pots of medicine and plays around with a syringe.

Gill: 'Okay, I've pushed the needle through the rubber shield.'

Pause.

Gill: 'Air bubbles? Yes, a few.'

Very long pause.

Gill: 'Okay. Well, we definitely don't want *that* to happen.'

Pause.

Gill: 'But how will I know the right spot?'

Pause.

Gill: 'His bottom.'

Pause.

Gill, laughing: 'No, no, his *bottom*.'

More pausing, more laughing.

Gill: 'Okay. Thanks, Palmina, I'll do my best. *Ciao*.'

Happier now, my wife turns to face me, holding the needle with the sharp end pointing straight up, spurting medicinal liquid into the air in an almost celebratory fashion. 'Let's do this, shall we?'

I unbuckle my trousers and pull them down to my knees. Now I know how Singaporean wrongdoers feel as they line up to be caned.

'On the bed,' says Gill. I lie face down. 'Okay, here goes.'

I squeeze my eyes and clench my teeth. I continue doing so. Thirty seconds pass. I open my eyes again. Turning my head to look at Gill, I say, 'What's going on?'

Suddenly she's looking less enthusiastic. 'I'm still not sure about this. What if I can't pierce your flesh?'

'What do you mean?'

'What if I can't push it hard enough to break the skin?'

By now I just want the ordeal over. 'As I said, can't you just follow the instructions of that sexy little nurse at the hospital?'

The needle goes in quickly and easily. And, I'll add, rather deeply.

Any discomfort and embarrassment caused by Gill's administration of a week's worth of hypodermic needles is nothing compared to the euphoria I feel at being cleared of serious illness. I can also take solace from the fact that plenty of people in the country are going through the same thing as me, at the same time. You see, Italians are crazy about needles. Injections are apparently prescribed for almost every ailment under the sun. We hear this from various sources, including one of Gill's colleagues at Giga, an Irishman named Patrick. Patrick is married to a Catanese and he's scared to let out even the tiniest sneeze at home, lest the family shuffle him off to a doctor for a series of pricks.

The other medical obsession in Italy is the suppository. Why put a pill in your mouth, argue the Italians, when you can insert it into your anal passage? There's even a very bad joke related to the practice.

Q: What does 'innuendo' mean?
A: It's Italian for 'suppository'.

Gill should be thankful that I wasn't prescribed a five-pack of suppositories. Having said that, something tells me she wouldn't have stuck around to lend a helping hand (or finger). We're still on our extended honeymoon, after all. Some things are just a little too warts-and-all for newlyweds.

For the record, the injections do absolutely nothing. Not a thing. I feel no change whatsoever in my arm or chest. The pains continue to come and go until months later when they finally ebb away, never – touch wood – to resurface.

In any case, the neck brace is a bigger burden than the needles. Together with the sling for my arm, I'm supposed to wear it all day for a couple of weeks. But I think the hospital has given me the wrong size. It's huge and uncomfortable. My empathy for the coil-wearing women of Burma grows immeasurably.

As I'm in the internet café doing a few Google searches one day, typing in things like 'is it okay not to wear neck brace?' and 'neck brace alternatives', I discover that one of the terms for an orthopaedic neck support is a Minerva brace. It suddenly seems apt that this burden has been prescribed to me, an erstwhile Roman historian. Minerva, you see, was also the name of a figure from ancient Roman mythology. Among other things, she was the goddess of poetry.

In the spirit of the goddess, then, I have come up with a little poem of my own:

Italian doctors' remedies are best described as sparse,
All they do is ask your wife to jab you in the arse.

16. A trip to the southeast

I lived in Italy a lot as a child, in Florence chiefly, but
I never went to Naples and Sicily till the year after the
war ended. That awful word 'Baroque' has haunted my
footsteps ever since.
> – Sacheverell Sitwell, *The Gothick North: a study of*
> *mediaeval life, art, and thought, Volume 1*, 1929

Gill's brother Matt and his girlfriend, Nasrin, fly down
from London for a weekend in early May. We meet them at
Catania's airport, Fontanarossa, with a plan to hire a car and
do some exploring for a couple of days. I'm a bit iffy when it
comes to hire cars. This can be traced back to an incident in
my early twenties, during a driving holiday with my parents
in New Zealand.

It was my stint behind the wheel one morning as we
approached the coastal town of Raglan. In front of our hire
car, a black-leathered leviathan of a man sat upon a Harley-
Davidson motorcycle. From time to time he would weave
across the road, either on account of poor wheel alignment
or one too many Steinlagers. Probably the latter: it was only
nine am, but New Zealanders are quite frequently drunk by
then – what else is there to do?

On this occasion, the mildly erratic driving didn't bother me too much. I kept my distance, window rolled down, enjoying a rare blue-sky day in the Land of the Long White Cloud. Eventually, though, I found the chance to overtake the motorcyclist as our speed slowed and we pulled into Raglan itself.

Dad had been waiting for his moment to pounce. 'GET OFF THE ROAD, MORON!' he yelled as we went past the Harley, leaning across in front of me to add a quartet of loud horn blasts for good measure.

I have no problem with my father's actions – in theory. If people are endangering lives on the road, they should be warned. But the prerogative to complain by way of horn or verbal insult should remain with the driver (in this case, me) rather than the passenger (Dad). For one thing, the target of the protest will assume that it was the driver who beeped the horn and yelled, rather than the passenger. More crucially, when the wayward motorist is a pissed-up Kiwi, it can be useful to adopt a modicum of civility. Especially when there's a stop sign up ahead, meaning the two vehicles will be required to come to a standstill side by side, with the drivers eyeing each other from a couple of feet away.

'Bro,' said the biker as we pulled up at the sign. He raised a pair of pitch-black sunglasses revealing bloodshot eyes, painful facial tattoos and a curdled smile of gold-capped teeth. 'What the *fuck* did you just say?'

'Well,' I wanted to reply, '*I* didn't say anything. But my *dad* – he's the one sitting right here beside me – he called you – what was it again, Dad? – a MORON.'

However, I decided not to endanger the life of my father who, after all, was paying for my meals on this trip. 'Nothing. Sorry to bother you.'

The biker stared for ten seconds, presumably contemplating whether or not to reach inside the car and render me a eunuch with his leather-gloved hand. 'Say one more fuckin' word to me and you're *did*. Understand?'

I didn't. 'Did you say . . . *did*?'

'That's right, bro, *did*.' Mercifully he then sped away in pursuit of his next drink.

'Did he say *did*?' said Dad.

'Yes, Dad, he did,' I said.

With this trauma still fresh in my mind, I'm not surprised when Matt, Nasrin, Gill and I encounter dramas at the hire-car desk of Fontanarossa Airport. We've made a prior booking but it doesn't help. The place is a shambles – a bubbling stew of misconstrued languages. Some French guy is speaking pidgin English to us about his particular car woes (he seems to think we'll care); an Aussie fellow is reading Italian from a phrasebook to the flustered lady behind the counter; meanwhile, she's trying stilted German on a bunch of tourists beside us; and a group of Brits are addressing another employee in that LOUD, SLOW, RUDE voice that English-speaking people adopt in a foreign country when something has angered them and they're trying to explain it to a local. (I hear one of them say, 'Listen, love, it's *very* simple.') Meanwhile people are returning keys, or claiming to be returning keys so they can jump the queue, or returning cars with scratches and saying it's not their fault. The line of customers stretches out the airport door, leaving the people at the back standing directly under the hot May sun.

The airport's name, Fontanarossa, translates as 'red fountain'. Perhaps it commemorates a frenzied knife attack at the hire-car desk.

We manage to inch our way to second in the queue when Matt sees one anxious staff member, a bespectacled man with his hands clasped together, trying to make a sly break for the side door.

'*Oi!*' yells Matt. 'Where do you think you're going? Are you coming back?' The man mumbles, '*Si, si!*' and Matt says in his best threatening voice, 'You'd better be!'

(The man doesn't come back. In fact, he'll probably *never* come back, but leave Catania instead, for a new life and a better job on the Italian mainland.)

After two hours of nonsense, we finally have our vehicle. I won't mention what particular hire-car company we were dealing with. Let's just say the memory still hurts.

Noto

Having already wasted a chunk of their short weekend visit from London, Matt and Nasrin understandably want to make up time. Hence we break the land speed record between the airport and our destination, the town of Noto, ninety kilometres away in Sicily's southeast corner. Every Italian driver seems intent on breaking the record as well, so we fit in seamlessly.

Noto lies on a slight rise, ten kilometres in from the coast. Until 11 January 1693, however, the town was in a different location altogether. On that day, a devastating earthquake ripped through the area, leaving twenty-three towns and villages in tatters. 'The earth was rent from its bowels,' wrote someone called Di Blasi – possibly the same guy responsible for penning the Australian national anthem ('Our home is girt by sea . . .').

Things were bad enough in Catania, where two-thirds of the population perished. Noto, though, was annihilated. For two thousand years it had proudly boasted the motto *urbs numquam vi capta* (a town never captured by force). Yet when the 1693 earthquake finally stopped shuddering, nothing remained.

An architect named Giuseppe Lanza, the Duke of Camastra, was commissioned to build a new Noto. He chose an entirely different location, seven kilometres away. Lanza's aim was not just to build the town afresh but also to create a work of art. The result is unique. Today, Noto is justifiably a UNESCO World Heritage site. Most Sicilian towns are a mishmash of the styles of successive invaders – Greek, Roman, Arab, Norman, and so on. Noto, because it had to be rebuilt from scratch, is a snapshot of a single style: Baroque.

Noto is called the Giardino di Pietra (Garden of Stone), thanks to the glorious honey colour of Lanza's building material, a soft local stone called *tufa*. The whole place glows with a golden or rosy hue depending on the time of day. It's a delicate effect – the very opposite of Catania's blackness – and it helps temper the severity and anarchy of all the Baroque curls and flourishes.

At one pm, we arrive at the Porta Reale (Royal Gate), a lofty stone arch marking the entrance to the town. Matt flings the startled hire car into an impossibly narrow parking space beneath a line of dwarf palms, taking us from one hundred to zero in milliseconds. Where's that neck brace when I need it?

We emerge onto Noto's main thoroughfare, Via Vittorio Emanuele. The siesta has only just started but already the lone sound we hear is the crunch of our four sets of shoes. All the town's buildings face south towards the sweep of the sun. As we walk along, the *palazzi* on our right peer down from a terrace, like spectators watching from a grandstand.

The town swarms with churches. It reminds me of the ridiculous (but very welcome) ratio of pubs to people in Westport, Ireland. Noto must have a church every fifty metres, each a picture-perfect example of Baroque architecture, filled with notable artworks. A surprising number of them have convents attached as well – these were generally built for the daughters of Noto's noble families. I count three in the space of a minute.

'So many convents,' I say to Gill. 'Do you think anyone in this town *ever* has sex?'

She doesn't answer.

I ask, 'Do you think Italians have an equivalent expression for *Get thee to a nunnery*?'

Again, no answer.

A teetering clump of scaffolding appears on our right, bringing to mind a giant game of Jenga. Somewhere underneath lies the cathedral. It's cordoned off by an orange plastic fence. In 1996, the *cupola* of this spectacular church suddenly caved in, like the lid of an egg crunched with a spoon, then collapsed. The Baroque dome, the icon of 'new Noto' for over two hundred years, was a cloud of dust on the church floor. Imagine if one of the shells of the Sydney Opera House suddenly disappeared into the harbour.

'I wouldn't mind getting some aerial perspective on this town,' I say to Gill.

'No doubt,' she replies dryly.

I'm almost obsessive-compulsive when it comes to panoramas. As soon as I arrive in a place, I hunt for a high-rise building, a television tower or a hot-air balloon – anything that might provide some elevation. Twenty minutes after touching down in Catania from Australia, I'd broken through a locked door to the roof of our *palazzo* in order to take in my surrounds. I don't know the name of my particular affliction – perhaps 'altophilia'. (Or is that an obsession with having sex with very tall people?)

I quickly usher our group to the Chiesa del Collegio, the only church in Noto with public access to its bell tower. A narrow corkscrew of dimly lit stairs leads to the top. We stare over salt-and-pepper roof tiles and champagne-coloured stone. Looking west, we see the gentle rise of the Iblei Mountains, where Arabs cultivated mulberries for silk in the ninth century; looking east, the ocean.

There are two bells in the *campanile*. They're delightful old things – hefty chunks of aged, pear-shaped metal, rigged up to a dry timber crossbeam. Unfortunately, the bronze dongers have been removed, replaced by electronic timers and ringing devices. This is a sad development. What happened to standing atop an Italian bell tower and cheekily pulling on the ropes? Undeterred, Matt locates the hidden switch that activates the bells. They ring out over the empty streets of Noto, bringing us immense pleasure while simultaneously disrupting a few thousand siestas. They particularly disrupt the siestas of those locals with a sick relative, since we later discover that the bells are rung only when someone dies.

Out on the main drag again, we walk further west to the tree-shrouded Piazza XVI Maggio. The Baroque churches keep coming and coming. According to my map, there are three more in the next short street alone. Overlooking the piazza where we stand is yet another, the newly restored Chiesa di San Domenico (with attached convent).

I continue to bother Gill with silly questions: 'How does a person in Noto choose which church to attend? Is there a rotation system?'

'Probably,' she says, in the seasoned manner of a non-listener.

'Maybe they attend one church a year for every year of their lives. Maybe they get *assigned* a church in an annual draft, with numbered ping-pong balls dropping through a chute and live entertainment.'

'Maybe,' adds Gill, simultaneously browsing the window of a clothes shop.

We forget about churches for a minute and instead try some of Noto's famous cakes and ice creams, considered by foodies to be among the best in Sicily – and, by extension, the world.

'You're too early,' says an elderly bar owner.

'For gelato?' I say.

'Gelato, no problem. I mean you're too early to come to Noto. You should be here in a couple of weeks. For Infiorata, the flower show.' Handing over four cups of his finest icy treats, he also gives us a brochure about the event. Infiorata is an annual festival held later in May. A single street, Via Nicolaci, is set aside as an enormous canvas, then filled with a mosaic of flower petals, stems and seeds. Brightly coloured images begin to take shape – crests, flags, religious motifs, pop-culture icons and more. Over the weekend, the sides of Via Nicolaci are roped off for visitors to walk up and down and admire the *tappeto fiorito* (floral tapestry).

But I especially like the sound of the Monday. On that day, young children of Noto are unleashed and allowed to run through the artworks and destroy them. This act signifies the theme of creation by older generations, and destruction and renewal by the next. It must be brilliant fun for the youth of Noto. That's if they exist: everyone we've seen in this town is over seventy.

Vendicari

Despite the beauty of the place, there comes a point when the impact of Noto's Baroque splendour begins to diminish. By mid-afternoon we reach this point. Stumbling upon yet another ornate church, our eyes gaze slowly upward and someone says, in a perfect monotone, 'Look – more Baroque splendour.'

Then the terrible jokes begin: 'If it ain't Baroque, don't fix it!'

It's clearly time to leave. And not just on account of sightseeing fatigue either. The golden stones of Noto have begun to emanate some serious heat. No wonder the locals are inside, asleep.

We decide unanimously to head for the coast for a bit of breeze and a swim. I suggest Vendicari, a ten-kilometre beachside strip of national park that apparently receives very few visitors. We soon discover why. The signposts are all but invisible. We miss the turn twice then get it on the third go, but only by accident.

From the main road, a narrow sandy track leads for a kilometre or so through shrubby ocean grasses and the occasional towering gum tree. Like on my recent daytrip to Aidone, the scenery smacks of Australia, particularly the area around Byron Bay.

'This could be any back road near Broken Head,' I say.

'You're beginning to sound like me,' replies Gill.

At the car park of the reserve, a somewhat dishevelled man sits in a makeshift booth collecting an entrance fee. Hmm, I thought Vendicari was free. As we pay for four tickets and walk on, I suddenly wonder if we've just been the victims of a sting.

It's probably how the fellow makes his money. 'Any luck today, honey?' I imagine his wife asking in the evening.

'A bit,' he says. 'I got a handful of euros out of four stupid *Australiani* at Vendicari.'

'Fake ticket booth?'

'Works every time.'

Soon we're following a raised boardwalk built directly over marshland. It's exceptionally pretty. A shallow lagoon spreads out before us, dotted by islands of reeds. Remnants of a farmhouse rise from the water. The place isn't exactly teeming with wildlife, though apparently vast flocks of migratory birds – including flamingos, cormorants and swans – stop here to rest in autumn and winter, on their way to sunny North Africa. Others, like the black-winged stilt (the official mascot of Vendicari), nest in the thick, boggy grasses. On a good day, you might also see little terns, Kentish plovers, tufted ducks and reed warblers. It's straight out of a Beatrix Potter book.

I'm no 'twitcher', but I do like birds. And it was Italy where I first developed this fondness. Prior to visiting Rome in my early twenties, I regarded anything with feathers and wings with no feeling, except perhaps hunger, and occasionally anger. I lived for a while in an apartment block in Brisbane that was plagued by a treeful of noisy crows that started cawing at five o'clock each morning. I wasn't the only one driven mad by their cacophony. Another tenant put a sign up in the elevator: 'WANTED: 100 DEAD CROWS. WILL PAY TOP DOLLAR.'

Then, on my first night in Rome, I sat in the open window of my two-star *pensione*, bottle of Peroni in hand, and watched an immense swarm of plunging swallows shimmer across the dusk sky above the Baths of Diocletian. I thought, 'What's not to like about that?' (Aside from walking directly under it without a hat.)

Vendicari's lagoons and boardwalks end at a beach. It's pleasant, if not quite the image of a Caribbean postcard. The sand and shallows are strewn with seagrass, some of it in tendrils, the rest in naturally formed loofahs – perfect for a bath. There's an attractively rugged feel about the place and a welcome lack of deckchair attendants.

It must be thirty degrees by now, so Matt and I hit the water. It's invigorating, with a residue of winter cold. At its northern end, the beach ends in atmospheric fashion, with the stone remains of an abandoned tuna station occupying a low-lying promontory. A dramatic red-brick chimney rises from the ruins.

After my swim I wander over to the *tonnara* for a closer look. It's boarded up and derelict. A hand-painted sign warns that entry is forbidden 'on account of falling rocks'.

Beyond the *tonnara* is a headland of flat, grassy dunes. The Romans are said to have manufactured *garum* on this very spot two thousand years ago. *Garum* sounds nasty: fish intestines fermented for months in the blazing sun. In fact, it was considered a luxury and probably tasted similar to *nuoc mam*, the Asian fish sauce, or even Worcestershire. But not all Romans loved it. Writing in the first century AD, Seneca referred to *garum* as 'the costly extract of poisonous fish, burning up the stomach with its salted putrefaction'.

With my thoughts turning inexorably towards food, I wander over to join the others. They're also ready to return to civilisation and hunt down various menu items with '*frutti di mare*' in the title. So we drive forty kilometres north to Syracuse, where we introduce Matt and Nasrin to the delights of the island of Ortygia and its seafood dishes. Thankfully our meal is free from salted putrefaction, though the same can't be said of the house wine.

Pantalica

The next day is Matt and Nasrin's last in Sicily. Before returning to Catania, we decide to visit Pantalica, one of the biggest ancient necropolises in Europe. This rarely visited yet colossal 'city of the dead' lies twenty-five kilometres inland in the Iblei Mountains.

'A difficult place to reach unless you have your own transport,' says one of the guidebooks of Pantalica. It should read: 'A difficult place to reach even *with* your own transport.'

Again, signposts are our undoing. Sicily has been through four separate regimes of signposting in recent decades. The result is a bewildering array of directions and distances, often contradictory. Rural intersections are particularly bad. It's common to follow a sign at a turnoff, only to arrive a hundred metres later at a T-junction with no follow-up sign to guide you left or right. If you're driving in Sicily, keep a coin handy for flipping.

The first town we reach is Floridia.

'Sounds like something you'd go to a clinic for,' someone says.

'It used to be worse,' I add, reading from a brochure. 'The old name was Xiridia.'

Nice place, nonetheless. Floridia hosts a very cool horse race once a year (on Ascension Thursday) which goes through the heart of the town, galloping past all the old stone churches and piazzas. The race used to be held without jockeys – the horses found the finish line themselves.

Next comes Solarino, four kilometres down the road.

Saint Paul is said to have passed through Solarino in the first century AD and given a sermon ('How to Find Pantalica by Car'). A wooden bowl was unearthed at a nearby well and somehow identified as belonging to the saint. How could they tell it was his? Gill suggests that perhaps he wrote his initials ('S.P.') on the bottom.

There isn't much to the town, though I do discover a fascinating piece of trivia: people from Solarino whose birthdays fall on 25 January are said to be 'adept at handling reptiles'. At first I think this might be an Italian euphemism for sex (like 'hiding your snake in the grass') or urination ('bleeding the lizard'). I'm still not convinced it isn't.

We then find ourselves on a one-lane country road lined by a dry-rock fence on the left and olive groves on the right. We think it's the right road, but I decide to ask an approaching cyclist for confirmation.

'How far to Pantalica?' I ask, leaning out the window.

'Nine!' the woman yells back, zipping by at speed.

Nine what? we ponder. Minutes? Kilometres?

Nine minutes pass and we still aren't there. Nine kilometres tick by and again, nothing. Surely she didn't mean nine *hours*.

Then the penny drops. The cyclist didn't say 'Nine' – she said '*Nein*'. She was another of the plethora of Germans who explore Sicily by car, bike or foot. And what she meant was: 'No. This is not the way to Pantalica.'

Finally we find our way to Sortino, a hilltown with a mystical grid of one-way streets designed to take you past every single house and shop on your way through. The town doesn't have a great deal going for it, though its wild-thyme honey has been praised since Plato's day.

I can take or leave honey. I'm more interested in a fascinating feud that has troubled Sortino for a millennium and a half. The original inhabitants of this area, the Siculians or Sikels, were living here merrily for a couple of thousand years until the Byzantines arrived in the sixth century AD and disrupted the status quo. The two groups have been quarrelling ever since. Even today, the townspeople of this tiny place are divided along Siculian or Byzantine lines. As late as the 1960s, intermarriage between the different factions was strongly opposed. I find that extraordinary. It's fun to imagine an old-fashioned shoot-out at Sortino between the Siculians and Byzantines – stemming, perhaps, from someone hiding his snake in the wrong grass.

We pull over for a coffee in a bar. I can't work out if it's a Siculian or a Byzantine who serves me, but I'm not about to ask in case he takes offence. Instead, I ask for directions to Pantalica. Turns out we've nearly made it, despite our bumbling and stumbling. Fifteen minutes later, after one more country road, we're at the entrance.

The Pantalica site consists of a ten-kilometre gorge sliced by the Anapo and Calcinara rivers. The hilltowns of Sortino and Ferla sit atop either end of the gorge like crumbling sentinels. But there's no road through – you have to park your car and walk.

We do exactly that. Following a series of old mule tracks, some carved out of rock, others of ochre-coloured dust, we descend slowly into the rocky chasm. Wildflowers spread like upturned packets of hundreds and thousands. In a single square foot of grass, I spy red, white, blue, yellow and purple. The bees are in heaven.

We take our time hiking to the bottom of the gorge – about an hour. Occasionally we shelter under a poplar tree like so many Sicilian mule-drivers before us. Once at the bottom, Matt and I strip to our boxer shorts and leap from a two-metre rock into a crystal-clear pool, part of the Calcinara River.

We leap straight out again, too. Swimming at the beach at Vendicari is one thing, but diving into an icy watercourse channelling through the very depths of a gorge is another. My genitals don't re-emerge for weeks. (Judging from Gill's rolling eyes – she warned me the water would be cold – they won't be needed.)

Pantalica impresses not just for its natural beauty. It also houses the remains of five thousand tombs in the form of tiny square grottoes cut along the walls of the gorge. The effect is of a giant mouth organ. If the wind blew hard enough, this place could play a Dylan song. Many of the tombs are accessible. Most were built for one person, though there are larger caves, too, apparently once used by Christians escaping barbarian invasions.

As we dry off in the sun, Matt asks if I've got a chocolate bar in my daypack. He can feel his glucose levels dropping quickly with the energy we've expended on walking and swimming, but his insulin and other supplies are up in the car – we never expected to idle away so much time in Pantalica.

I don't have any chocolate but we get chatting to a couple of passing Brits and, being Brits, they naturally have a thermos and everything else needed for a dainty afternoon tea. (I'm sure I spy doilies as they rummage through their kit.) They kindly give up a bag of their sugar. Matt rips the top off and pours the contents down his throat.

'Sorted,' he says, crunching on sweet grains.

And so we hike up to the top of the gorge and set off in the car.

We think briefly of exploring some other town in the region before leaving for Catania. The problem, though, is the B-word. Nearby settlements include Còmiso ('plenty of Baroque buildings and churches'), Scicli ('Baroque streets') and Ragusa ('the best of the Baroque').

I'm eager to visit Mòdica, if only for the local delicacy called *pastieri* – little pastries filled with egg, cheese, and a combination of minced lamb and baby goat, seasoned with pepper. Genius!

Mòdica, though, has 'elegant Baroque structures'.

Instead, we take off for Catania, steeling ourselves for the inevitable dramas at the hire-car desk at Fontanarossa Airport.

17. Fishing

You know when I was your age, I went out to fishing
with all my brothers and my father, and everybody. And
I was, I was the only one who caught a fish. Nobody
else could catch one except me. You know how I did it?
Every time I put the line in the water I said a Hail Mary
and every time I said a Hail Mary I caught a fish. You
believe that? It's true, that's the secret. You wanna try it
when we go out on the lake?

– Fredo Corleone, *The Godfather Part II*,
Francis Ford Coppola, 1974

It's a sultry Saturday afternoon in late May. A southerly
breeze carries the breath of the Sahara, not to mention the
smell of well-charred steaks and vinegary marinades from the
horse-meat vendors on Via Plebiscito. Soon the city will shut
down for siesta.

Gill is reading at our tiny table; I'm pottering at my
laptop, trying to stop internet browsers from opening. I'm
wearing my hospital-issue neck brace. The week-long course
of needles in the backside is thankfully over. All that remains
is bruised flesh and bruised dignity.

Suddenly Carmelo pokes his head around the corner.

'Let's go.' He says it like we've been expecting him, but of course we haven't.

'Umm . . . go where?'

'Fishing.'

'Oh. Where?'

'Syracuse.'

'What, both of us?' I'm wondering if perhaps Carmelo has intended his random invitation as a chance for male bonding and is only being polite to Gill by including her with the boys.

'Yes.'

I look at my wife. She shrugs: *I'm game if you are.*

'Okay, we'll come along,' I say to Carmelo. 'When are we going?'

He winces at my stupidity. 'Now. *Pronto!*'

Fishing? I'm the worst bloody fisherman in the world – or, if not the worst, certainly the least enthusiastic. I've only dropped a line into the water three times. Caught nothing each time and got green about the gills for my trouble. And here I am, expected to mix it with a professional old salt from Catania, one of the fishing capitals of the Mediterranean.

Carmelo's proposed fishing trip will almost certainly end in disaster. I can just imagine the scene: while casting off, I inadvertently catch one of Gill's earrings in my hook and haul her into the sea; she pulls on the line and in I tumble; a passing shark sniffs the crusty blood covering the needle wounds on my bum cheeks and promptly attacks; all that remains is a soggy neck brace drifting on the Mediterranean tide.

Still, it's a good excuse to visit the glorious town of Syracuse again.

Outside on Via Garibaldi, we find Carmelo waiting with his younger brother Pasquale, who everyone calls Pasqualino. The suffix *-ino* is a diminutive, yet Pasquale is taller and plumper than his brother, with a paler, fleshier face. He looks like a stay-at-home grandfather compared to leathery Carmelo. A lifetime of fishing in the Sicilian sun has baked Carmelo like a potato jacket and lasered furrows into his brow.

We pile into an equally sun-faded station wagon. The boot is taken up with a huge pile of whiffy fishing net, crimson-red like raw tuna. I've seen this car before. It's the one Carmelo sometimes parks in our shared courtyard where he and his sons Orazio and Davide sit for hours, meticulously going over each strand of netting to check for imperfections. When Carmelo's not using the car, he'll lend it to the younger son Davide. Orazio has a family and kids, but Davide's still single. This can only mean one thing: the back seat that Gill and I are currently perched on must have seen its share of amorous activity.

People have sex in cars all around the world. But it's unlikely anyone else does it with the frequency of Italians. 'If you're young and have limited space at home, your car is a sort of bedroom on wheels,' writes author and social commentator Beppe Severgnini. 'Comfort-free romance and a hand brake in the lower back.' A few weeks before our fishing trip, a 'Love Car Park' opened in Tuscany especially for this purpose, even providing receptacles for used condoms.

I'm guessing the Pope didn't attend the launch. (It's easy to tell where a car has stopped for the purpose of shagging, by the way, because you'll find the ground strewn with sheets of newspaper. Italians use them as makeshift curtains.)

We set off, heading south out of Catania along the coast road rather than the highway. Carmelo's intentions seem clear. He's going to skirt the major route in favour of side roads and beachside alleys. This is either so he can drive at hair-raising speeds without worrying about the *carabinieri* busting him, or because he's drunk. Perhaps both. I'm used to seeing Carmelo drinking beers in the local greengrocer's at ten am – I've joined him on occasions. But Gill is less familiar with his habits. I decide not to tell her, at least while we're passengers in Carmelo's car.

Soon the two old brothers are squabbling. Mostly it's Pasqualino complaining about Carmelo's driving. And rightly so: Carmelo likes to occupy the middle of the road, wheels straddling the centre line so that he can more easily see to overtake trucks around corners. At other times, while tailgating the car in front, he'll snatch a Malboro Rossa from the crumpled pack on the dashboard, take his hands off the wheel to light it, then turn to face his brother and make small talk, as the car drifts slowly in the direction of oncoming traffic.

'What are you doing? *Pazzo!* Watch the road!'

Carmelo grins and pulls away just in time. We sit in the back, our cheeks working like bellows to blow away the smoke, as the domestic spat rages on and the car careens down the coast. Gill clutches my wrist with knuckles white as dice. I keep an eye on the speedo. As it nudges a hundred, the old black steering wheel shudders in Carmelo's hands.

'Just remember,' I whisper in an attempt to provide some comfort to Gill, 'Carmelo has done this trip every day for decades. It's second nature to him.'

'Okay,' she says. 'And he's always this drunk?'

We wind our way around the headland at Brucoli. Eucalypts line the road, leaves hanging listless in the warmth of the afternoon. To our right, the grasslands around the Simeto River are beginning to change from spring green to burnt yellow, almost before our eyes. Turning back to look through the rear windshield, I watch overtaken cars flash by and disappear towards the horizon. Even further back, in the direction of Catania, Mount Etna looms, cloaked in a grubby smear of summery haze.

Anyone for whom the word 'Mediterranean' evokes Greek Island perfection or Monaco glitz would be shocked by the next sight. After joining the main highway to Syracuse, we're beginning a gentle descent towards the Gulf of Augusta when an enormous industrial region appears before us. It's a vast province of pipes that crisscross with towering smokestacks, hugging the formerly pristine coast for more than ten kilometres. These refineries, factories and piers are operated by major companies like Esso, ERG Petroli, Sasol, Enel SpA and ISAB Energy. A massive percentage of the Sicilian workforce is employed here.

Scarily enough, there's plenty more of this heavy industry in Sicily, all of it right by the sea, including near Tèrmini Imerese on the north coast and Gela in the south. It's one of the reasons why, when people ask me, 'Is Sicily beautiful?' I tend to say, 'Mostly.'

Fair enough for Sicilians to make the most of their natural resources. Who doesn't? I'm just surprised more of an effort isn't made to hide such an environmental eyesore. Both the main railway line and the main highway between two of Sicily's biggest tourist drawcards – Taormina and Syracuse – plough straight through the belching petrochemical nightmare that is the Gulf of Augusta. It's almost like someone *wants* you to see it. Maybe they do.

Ironically enough, between all the catalytic hydro-desulfurisation units and cracking plants is one of the more significant archaeological sites on the island: the ancient colony of Megara Hyblaea, almost three thousand years old.

Megara Hyblaea was home to Epicharmus (540–450 BC), a Greek writer sometimes referred to as a 'comic poet'. Only a few fragments of his allegedly witty writing survive, including these one-liners:

'What is the nature of men? Blown-up bladders!'

'Afflictions of the testis and genital organs can be usefully treated by the application of a cabbage leaf.'

'The virtue of the right-minded woman is not to injure her husband.'

The last one's *kind* of funny, but none of them have me clutching my sides. I doubt I'd choose a book of Epicharmus' wisecracks over, say, a box set of *South Park* DVDs.

Megara Hyblaea isn't accessible via public transport, but with a car you can easily reach the remains. And, if you run out of petrol, don't worry, there's plenty around. Honestly, though, to battle through the maze of refineries just to see another indistinguishable pile of mossy old rocks would be madness. And that's coming from someone who studied and taught ancient history for almost a decade.

We're not even through all the factories when Carmelo leaves the main road and makes for the sea. When he said we'd be fishing at Syracuse, he actually meant we'd be fishing *near* Syracuse. So Gill and I won't be seeing our favourite Sicilian town after all. There goes my entire motive for coming along.

The road reaches grassy dunes and becomes narrow and unsealed. At the southern end of the gulf, Carmelo pulls up at a rocky inlet, twenty metres across. A dozen tiny boats of flaky timber are moored haphazardly in the water. The surrounding paddock is full of stray dogs and refinery refuse. If I ever had visions of Carmelo owning a gleaming white yacht in an upmarket marina, they've been dashed.

The four of us get out of the car and wander along the shallows. Carmelo leads us to a shack of tin and plywood. It's attached to a dented caravan that sits on four piles of bricks instead of wheels. Rising at an awkward angle from the roof is a faded flag supporting the national football team: 'FORZA AZZURRA. ITALIA. THE BEST!' On the outside wall of the shack, various messages are splashed in paint. One says 'Casa di Riposo' (House of Rest); another mentions '*farabutti*' (rascals); next to the open doorway, the word 'Pippo' is scrawled in big clumsy letters.

Pippo is the unofficial custodian of the inlet. He oversees the handful of old boats and the fishermen who own them. When we arrive, he's sitting on a chair on the dirt floor of his shack, smoking. The place smells of cigarettes, boat fuel and fish. It's three pm and so hot inside you could roast chickens on a spit. Despite this, Pippo wears a thick-knit woollen jumper that sags from his gaunt frame. I can't tell if he's eighty years old or an especially haggard fifty-five. Either way, he looks like someone whose life is draining away with each outgoing tide.

After a raspy dialogue between the three men, Carmelo and Pasqualino wander down to the boat. It's very basic: twenty feet long, flat, wide and open, painted the same jaunty blue as every fishing vessel in Sicily.

Gill and I stand near Pippo's shack, watching as the brothers ready the boat for sea. An argument breaks out – a problem with the engine, it seems. After some vigorous gesticulating, Carmelo clambers onto someone else's boat and removes a few pieces from the outboard motor, then returns and attaches them to his own motor. It kicks over straightaway. He gives Pasqualino a look, as if to say, 'Leave it to me, little brother.'

Next, Carmelo drags a large square of plastic tarpaulin from the floor of the boat and wraps it around his torso like a butcher's apron, tying it on with a short length of dusty rope. It's the kind of makeshift poncho that Rambo might craft for himself in a jungle ravaged by tropical rains.

He beckons us aboard. Gill is directed to sit next to the twenty-five-horsepower engine at the back. I'm told to stay up the front. Pasqualino unties us from the bank and jumps on, Carmelo pulls the anchor up, and we're away, puttering into the mild chop of the bay.

After Carmelo has directed us beyond the inlet, he swings the engine's throttle towards Gill. 'Okay, you drive.'

'Sorry?'

'You drive the boat. I need to put the net out.'

Gill gives me a concerned look, so I get up and offer to swap places. But Carmelo's having none of it.

'No, you stay there,' he says to me between lips clenched on a cigarette.

He gives Gill a thirty-second lesson on acceleration and steering, and soon we're smoothly navigating the waters. Carmelo looks quietly impressed, though he'd never say as much. I'm also impressed: I can't drive a boat to save my life.

Soon she's getting cocky. 'Hold this, will you?' she says, passing me her handbag in order to free up her arms.

That's my role for the day, then. Carmelo has ordered me and my eighty-five kilograms up the front of the boat to act as ballast, and my wife has ordered me to carry her handbag as she operates the engine. Together with the fact that I'm the world's least competent angler, it makes for an entirely mortifying fishing experience.

Not that any of us will be called upon to do any fishing as such. There's neither rod nor reel aboard the boat, only the pile of red netting from the back of Carmelo's car. After we've made our way past a long pier and into open water, Carmelo attaches an empty plastic fuel container to one end of the net and sends it splashing into the sea. Then he begins methodically feeding the lattice of rope out the back of the boat. All the time he's giving Gill directions and speeds – '*forte!*' for fast, '*piano!*' for slow. Pasqualino helps by untangling the net from the pile. I look on. Occasionally I shift Gill's handbag from one shoulder to the other.

The net is a kilometre in length and takes forever to unravel into the sea. While his hands grapple tirelessly, Carmelo chain-smokes and tells us stories of his family's fishing exploits. One time, he says, little Erminia came along in the boat. 'I caught the biggest fish of my life that day,' says Carmelo. From then on, Erminia was considered *buona fortunata* – a good luck charm.

'I hope you get lucky today,' I say. He shrugs his shoulders in a mildly dismissive though not unkind fashion.

We ask about Angela.

'My wife likes the sea,' he says. 'But she doesn't like being on the boat for too long.'

That makes two of us, I think, as the first surge of nausea comes over me.

As I've mentioned, I get seasick. It completes the dismal picture. On the one hand we have salty-dog extraordinaire Carmelo, and on the other we have me, a landlubber, an anti-angler, a piece of purse-carrying ballast, whose last thread of machismo is about to disappear over the side of the boat in a torrent of vomit.

Fortunately the queasiness passes.

Carmelo continues, 'On very hot days when Angela used to come out on the boat, she'd jump straight over the side for a swim.'

I get the feeling he's experiencing a twinge of nostalgia, sorry for the passing of time since Angela last plunged into the silky sea.

It's late afternoon now, and we edge closer towards a flat, chalky peninsula on our right. Carmelo continues to give the occasional instruction to Gill, which she follows confidently. When the first net ends, the brothers begin unravelling a second one into the sea. Now we're very close to the cliffs of the peninsula. They're twenty feet high and studded with caves. Carmelo pauses in the middle of setting the net and indicates a spot where fresh spring water tumbles over the side of a rocky shelf and into the sea. It's a pretty sight. I take some photos. We follow the cape all the way out, to the point where it hooks back around the coast towards Syracuse, three kilometres away. Near another craggy inlet, Gill spies a second flow of water splashing into the sea.

'Another spring?'

Carmelo shakes his head. '*Effluente.*'

Soon the nets are set and we're making for shore. Back at the inlet, Pippo sits in his hot shed, watching the water, smoking. We jump off, legs a little shaky. I give the handbag back to Gill.

While Carmelo is busy returning the spare parts that he borrowed from the other boats, Pasqualino signals for Gill and me to follow him into a thicket of tall grasses on the bank above the inlet. This is an odd development. Anyone with a vivid enough imagination might stop and wonder why a Sicilian would ask two strangers to follow him into chest-high vegetation along a virtually abandoned stretch of coastline. Fortunately it's not a 'hit'. Pasqualino has a different type of quarry in mind: *babbaluci*.

Babbaluci are tiny snails, no bigger than a fingernail.

They cling to the vegetation beside the sea, attaching themselves to plants to extract moisture and nutrients. On close inspection of the overgrown paddock, we see thousands of the tiny curled creatures. For reasons unclear to Gill and me, Pasqualino begins detaching the snails from the grass-blades and popping them into a plastic bag. He hands a second bag over and asks us to help. We duly join in the harvest. When the plastic bags are bulging, Pasqualino calls off the hunt.

My backside has barely touched the car seat and the *babbaluci* are escaping from the bag. Fastest snails in the business. Seeing me scrabbling around for the shelled vigilantes, Pasqualino leans over, grabs the bag and ties it off with a firm knot.

'They'll get away, you know. All of them. You have to keep this bag firmly shut.'

Carmelo comes over. He's done for the day. I show him the bag of snails and he nods. '*Babbaluci: deliziosi!*'

Ah, so you *eat* them.

Gill and I thank Carmelo for taking us on the impromptu fishing expedition.

'Don't thank me,' he says. 'You did all the work.'

A kind sentiment, albeit one that holds no water.

We wave goodbye to Pippo in his hot tin shed but he doesn't respond – busy renewing his subscription to *Vogue Living*, perhaps.

Back in the car, the brothers seem more content now that the job is done. Certainly there is less bickering. We drive a short distance to a small town near the water and into the driveway of the family's third brother, Salvatore. Salvatore isn't there, but a whole bunch of the extended family is, including Salvatore's wife, Katerina, their two sons (in their thirties) and wives, and an infant boy named Zizzo. With a name like that, I'm guessing he sleeps a lot.

The house is interesting. Surrounded by a haphazard yet verdant garden of fruit and vegetable trees, it's a jumble of terracotta bricks and concrete rendering that looks only seventy per cent complete. The place is begging for a lick of paint and a *Casa Dolce Casa* sign on the front door. Yet the family has lived here for years.

Unfinished buildings are rife in Sicily. In the suburbs of Agrigento and Palermo, the problem is especially bad. Often the Mafia is to blame. Illegal construction projects, known as *case abusive* (abusive houses), are thought to provide a means of laundering money. Whether or not the work gets finished is irrelevant once the crooks have extracted their clean bills.

Yet there's a less sinister reason for Salvatore's incomplete house. In Sicily, finished structures attract an additional type of tax. For low-income earners – so, most Sicilians – it's cheaper to pretend that construction work is ongoing.

It's also more practical. As families continue to grow, at least in rural areas, so do their houses. This is to accommodate the extra headcount. When a son gets married, an extra section is built on top of the existing house for the newlyweds to move into. Salvatore's house consists of two new sections of concrete and terracotta where the two boys now live with their wives.

'It's the opposite in Australia,' I hear Gill say to Carmelo. 'Most newlyweds try to stay as far away from their families as they possibly can.'

342

'Sad,' says Carmelo.

Pasqualino has wandered off. I find him around the side of the house raiding the family's incredible backyard. It's not so much a garden as a commercially respectable grove of fruit trees: lemons, peaches, mulberries and more. Pasqualino hands me a fruit I've not seen before.

'*Nespole*,' he says.

It's similar to an apricot, and comes from the same family as the medlar and loquat – whatever *they* are. To eat one, you peel back the light skin and spoon out the delicious flesh.

Carmelo joins us and soon he and his brother are elbow-deep in various bushes, plucking, twisting, pulling and snipping. They emerge with muscled arms full of fruit. Then they give the whole lot to Gill and me.

It's a pristine early evening as we drive back to Catania. The smear of haze across Etna's girth has slid away and the peak stands bold against a lilac horizon. We get caught in several traffic jams: families returning to the city from weekend daytrips. Carmelo is no longer impatient. He has fallen very quiet – tired, no doubt, but perhaps saying silent prayers for a netful of fish, too.

We get back to the city at around seven pm, just as the *passeggiata* is cranking up. Carmelo pulls over at a kiosk on Via Plebiscito. The place is doing a roaring trade, full of hardworking men with hands filthy from diesel or fish guts. Carmelo buys a round of *seltz al mandarino*. I somehow expected beers, but we're all salt-stained and parched, and the seltzers hit the spot. It's funny how Carmelo will tuck into a beer at ten am in a greengrocer's store but a soft drink at seven pm after work. Then again, like anyone whose livelihood is fishing, his daily routine is completely out of whack.

'When will you collect the nets?' I ask.

'Tonight,' he says.

I think of Carmelo's long midnight drive back down to the Gulf of Augusta where he'll scrabble around the inlet with a torch, trying to kickstart his old boat, before taking off on the inky sea – perhaps alone, perhaps with one of his sons – to spend hours heaving nets from the water. I just hope it's a big catch. The Mediterranean must be the most overfished body of water in the world.

The next morning, Carmelo knocks on our door. Before I can ask about his night on the boat, he pulls a hand from behind his back to reveal a fist-sized *aragosta* (lobster) with a speckled orange shell.

'Yours,' he says.

It's a magnificent-looking piece of marine life. I can't help but think it would earn a pretty penny at the Pescheria where Carmelo sells his modest hauls of seafood.

'Carmelo, you should keep this.'

'No, no. You caught it!' He's being generous. At best, you could say that I happened to be present when the net that the lobster would later swim into was dropped into the ocean.

We thank Carmelo for the offering and ask him for some cooking tips. His future son-in-law Gaetano wanders past our front door and adds his two cents' worth: 'Eat it plain, with mayonnaise on the side!'

'What about these?' I ask, holding up the bag of tiny snails that Pasqualino had helped us to harvest.

'Ah, *babbaluci*.' Gaetano's on shakier ground now. '*Boh!*' he says, employing Desi's favourite expression.

Carmelo, though, is an old hand. 'Bring a saucepan of salted water to the boil; add two slices of fresh lemon and a few slivers of garlic; a few minutes, they're done.' (Later I discover that the snails should also be purged for several days before cooking, to rid their stomachs of any toxic matter. *Pfft*, details.)

Gill shares the lobster with me but she won't go near the *babbaluci*. I eat a plate of fifty or so, prying the gooey morsels out of the shells with a toothpick and smearing them across chunks of crusty bread. We accompany the meal with a glass of chilled white wine from Sicily's northwest. I could get used to this fishing caper.

Later that afternoon, I run into Carmelo and his sons at the seafood market. Their stall is empty but for a beaten-up polystyrene box containing a handful of listless eels that they're selling for a pittance.

'Where are all the fish from the two nets?' I ask. 'Sold them already?'

Carmelo, cigarette in lips, gives me a detached shrug. '*Niente.*' Nothing.

'What do you mean, *nothing*?'

'The nets were empty. We didn't catch anything.'

'Nothing at all?'

'One lobster.'

18. A trip to Palermo

'Southwards we sailed again at last,' continued the Sea
Rat, 'coasting down the Italian shore, till finally we
made Palermo, and there I quitted for a long, happy
spell on shore.'

– Kenneth Grahame, *The Wind in the Willows*, 1908

There are many reasons why a person would want to visit
the splendidly decrepit city of Palermo. My reason? To eat
spleen.

This surprises even me. Offal has never been my thing.
When I was a kid, my dad would set aside one day each summer to ruin a perfectly good beach holiday by cooking a dish
that my siblings and I referred to as Red Death. The main
ingredients were kidneys. In fact, I think they were the only
ingredients.

Red Death took forever to make. It would sit in a big old
saucepan on the stove for hours. Our little beach house in
Byron Bay would slowly become steeped in the distinctive,
gamey stench of offal – a greasy mix of piss and blood. I can't
even remember what he did with the kidneys after he prepared them in his evil pot. Maybe they went in a pie. Maybe
a stew. I never hung around to find out.

As bad as kidneys looked to someone as young and fussy as me, and as bad as the pervasive smell got, it wasn't so much the dish itself that diminished my desire to eat innards for the rest of my life. It was the fact of my father's profession. He was a urological surgeon. A kidney doctor. Think about that for a minute.

Palermo's culinary specialty is *pane con la milza*, the spleen sandwich, and it gets rave reviews across the board. I make it my mission to try the stuff. It probably helps that I'm unsure what spleen actually is or does – I only know it as something my wife vents at me from time to time, especially when I forget to take the rubbish out.

Admittedly I've been keen to explore the capital, and all of western Sicily, from day one. As a househusband, though, I can't just up and leave any time I get the urge. There are responsibilities to consider. I'm needed at nine pm each night, you'll recall, to collect Gill from school and lead her home through Catania's seedy backstreets. I also do the grocery shopping, cook most of the dinners, and take our dirty linen to a laundromat across town. What's more, I should really be writing in my spare time, not striving to tick all the boxes on my Sicilian 'must see' list.

That's the theory, in any case. But my sense of adventure gets the better of me. I devise a travel route: Catania, Palermo, Monreale, Mazara del Vallo, Marsala, Trapani, the Egadi Islands and back to Catania – six hundred kilometres. In all, I'll take seven buses, four trains, two ferries and a bicycle. I'll traipse dozens of kilometres through the various towns. And I'll have just three days and two nights to do it all. Sounds manageable, until you recall that Sicily's public transport system lacks the Swiss efficiency of much of Europe. Remember: it took me almost thirty minutes to travel by bus from the hilltown of Enna to Calascibetta, *two kilometres* away. It'd be nice to have more time, of course. But I've got my hard-working wife to think about.

'So, what you're saying,' she says when I broach the idea of the trip, 'is that you want to go off and explore western Sicily for half a week?'

'Yes.'

'Alone. While I stay in Catania and teach at the school?'

'Right.'

'Okay.'

God bless her. Now I feel guilty for my jibe about venting spleen.

When Scottish travel writer Patrick Brydone visited Palermo in the late eighteenth century, he described his innkeeper as 'fat as a pig' and 'ugly as the devil'.

I have only positive things to say about the receptionist of the Hotel Sicilia, my chosen lodgings for the night, especially as he charges me only twenty euros for my room. He doesn't even flinch when glancing at my passport photo, which is part Charles Manson and part Zebedee from *The Magic Roundabout*.

The room is basic, but it boasts a cute wrought-iron balcony overlooking Via Maqueda, one of the city's best-known streets. My only concern is the miniscule shower cubicle. It seems designed to accommodate a wayfaring hobbit at best, or the actor from *Webster*. With a bit of manoeuvring, I find that I can fit my head plus one arm in there at one time, or a single leg plus the foot of my other leg. It's a simple matter of turning the taps on, undressing, and doing the Hokey Pokey and I'll be clean in no time.

But the shower can wait. I have animal organs to eat.

Palermitans adore their spleen sandwiches. The snack is thought to have first gained popularity among the city's Jewish community. Now it's everywhere. In the area around Piazza San Francesco, a small but atmospheric square near my hotel, it takes me less than two minutes to find a vendor whipping up *pane con la milza* in a café.

Here's how it works. The man, who stands before an enormous two-handled vat of bubbling offal (triggering a flashback to Dad's Red Death), takes a bread roll and tears an opening in one side. He stirs his vat for a minute – an all-important process, apparently – then grabs a fork, scoops up a generous hunk of the chocolate-brown strands of spleen, and plops them into the cavity in the bread. Next, he smears fresh ricotta onto the hot offal where it starts melting immediately. Then he sprinkles the whole thing liberally with *caciocavallo* – poor man's *parmigiano*. Finally, and mildly alarmingly, he squeezes the *panino* over a bucket to get rid of its excess juice. I've never had someone wring out my sandwich before. Wrapping the tight warm bun in a serviette, he hands it across to me with a glimmer of a smile.

'And a beer,' he says. It's an order, not a question. He passes me a cold Moretti. It's ten thirty in the morning – I've

349

arrived in Palermo on the seven am bus from Catania. I can't help but think of my neighbour Carmelo, and raise the bottle in his honour. I give the *milza* man €2.50 for my barbarous breakfast and lean against the golden-coloured stone of a *palazzo* to eat.

I'm happy to report that, in the face of deep mental scarring from my father's annual kidney-fest, the *pane con la milza* is velvety perfection. One of the best things I've eaten in Sicily, in fact.

And so, with lymphoid juices running down to my elbows, I begin my tour of the city.

For a time, Palermo was the grandest metropolis in all of Europe: 'The capital is endowed with two gifts, splendour and wealth. It contains all the real and imagined beauty that anyone could wish . . . The eye is dazzled by all this splendour.' These are the words of the famous Muslim traveller Ibn Jubayr, writing in the twelfth century. Palermo was at its peak back then, thanks to two hundred years of reformist Arab rule and another century or so under the Normans.

The Greek and Roman ruins that dominate the eastern cities of Taormina, Catania and Syracuse are nowhere to be found in Palermo. Instead, its architectural highlights are referred to as 'Arab–Norman'. Yet how can something be Arab *and* Norman? One evokes sandy deserts and camel trains, the other, chainmail and Viking ancestry. Surely it's an untenable partnership, like fire and ice.

The fusion was largely due to the adaptability and tolerance of the Norman rulers of Sicily. After landing on the island in the 1060s and taking various Saracen strongholds by force, they wisely didn't eliminate the local Arab rulers. Rather, they used them in their own administration. Arab architects and engineers were employed throughout the capital. The results survive today.

I get my first taste of this Arab–Norman legacy just north of my hotel, at the Quattro Canti (Four Corners). This is the famous intersection of the city's two busiest roads – the heart of historical Palermo. Churches line the sky, some with red Arabic domes, others with Norman-style battlements and bell towers; several have both. I take the opportunity to duck into one of the churches and wash my spleeny hands in the holy water. It's the perfect fingerbowl!

I'm joking, of course. I do go into La Martorana, however, to check out the famous interior of this twelfth-century church. It's a dazzling spectacle of marble, gold mosaic and lapis lazuli. When I emerge, a local fellow accosts me with a porno mag, thrusting one of the pages towards my face for a look.

What do you say to someone like that? 'No thanks, I've got my own'? 'Sorry, I'm gay'? In the end I settle for 'Nice porn!' – with thumbs up for good measure. My pocket phrasebook is no help at all, filled as it is with the kind of manufactured sentences that are never uttered in real life:

Arancione, per favore. Deve essere larga. The orange one, please. And it has to be large.

Com'è il conteggio del polline? What's the pollen count?

Vorrei un secchiello e una paletta per una bambina di cinque anni. I'd like a pail and shovel (bucket and spade) for a five-year-old girl.

Next I walk north to Palermo's renowned produce market, La Vucciria. It's a disappointment, especially after the authentic madness of Catania's Pescheria. Tourism reigns here; local shoppers have left in their droves. Nothing remains of the dark energy captured by Renato Guttuso, one of Italy's major twentieth-century artists, in his famous painting of the market from 1974.

I buy a single apple (that would *never* happen in Catania: 'One apple? Are you kidding me? I'll give you a dozen!'), before stopping briefly to watch a man carve a small tuna into pieces. I take some photos, pretending that I'm interested in the fish. What he doesn't know is that I'm actually photographing his faded old t-shirt. Its slogan reads: 'AUSTRALIA. GET INTO THE MAGIC'.

Near the market exit, I watch a tattered old dog, miraculously pregnant, emerge from a garage, her muddle of greying teats swaying from side to side. Two more hounds slink out of nowhere to join her. They dig their noses into a ceramic bowl of cold, cooked pasta that's been left out for them. Catania is a city of cats; Palermo, dogs.

There are horses, too – primly decorated horses with braided manes and white cloth tips on their ears, ferrying tourists around the streets in painted carriages.

Palermo's cathedral is a riveting yet schizophrenic mishmash of history and architectural styles: ninth-century Arab, twelfth-century Norman, fifteenth-century Gothic, eighteenth-century Neo-classical, twenty-first-century Scaffold. One of the classical columns in the entranceway is inscribed with a passage from the Koran.

Inside, I slyly attach myself to a group of retirement-aged Americans so I can listen to their tour guide's blurb about the cathedral. From their name tags and leathery tans I can tell the Americans are on a Mediterranean cruise. The men wear light-coloured slacks and brogues, and polo shirts with pastel-coloured jumpers tied around their necks. The women sag under jewellery. After I slink away again, I occasionally hear their voices echoing along the apse. 'Did you say this thing is a *thousand* years old?' 'Phyllis is demanding to see the tomb of Frederick the Second!' 'Are we back on the boat for lunch today?'

By way of contrast, a German group stands silently in a neat row in front of a guide who whispers into a discreet headset. The tourists look like Kraftwerk in concert, listening through wireless headphone sets with adjustable volume and nodding occasionally.

The Catacombs of the Capuchin Monastery, a long walk west of the city centre, are commonly described as Palermo's most grotesque sight. By the time I arrive, sweaty and ragged, I'm vying for the title. To make matters worse, the crotchety monk at the ticket counter tells me he's closing the doors – it's just turning midday – and he won't be back until three pm.

Wait three hours? Never! I won't divulge exactly what happens between this monk and me over the next few minutes to make him change his mind. It involves neither violent threats nor sexual favours, I promise. In any case, I am granted a ten-minute reprieve to explore the Catacombs. Down I go into the darkness. Because it's closing time, I'm alone in the entire complex. Alone, that is, apart from the corpses of eight thousand eminent Sicilians lining the walls of the tunnels.

Between 1599 and the early twentieth century, the Capuchin Monastery served as the headquarters for a large-scale embalming experiment. Priests, painters, well-to-do Palermitans and monks themselves would sign up to have their bodies mummified after death, clothed in finery, and stored in the passageways of the Catacombs. The experiment hasn't been entirely successful. A few of the bodies look superbly preserved – most famously, two-year-old Rosalia Lombardo, who died in 1920 and still seems almost huggable, with her delicate features and an apricot-coloured bow in her hair. It's a near-perfect pickling. The majority of the stiffs, though, are just skeletons covered by a thin film of moth-eaten skin. Some look heinously contorted, with caved-in skulls and jawbones collapsing to one side, like they died in bashing incidents outside nightclubs. Others have their limbs held up by pins and wire. The expensive clothing, while interesting from a historical perspective, now looks clownish. Over a set of skeletal fingers, a once-dapper velvet glove seems enormous, like one of those oversized foam hands you buy at a football ground. Here and there, a baggy hat sits lopsided over hollow eye sockets.

It's not surprising they're falling apart. The embalming process reads more like a recipe for preserving fish: remove the guts, sprinkle bodies liberally with salt, strain for eight months in a colander, clean with vinegar, pat dry and place on a well-ventilated platform. Add 'serve with toast' and you've got a Scandinavian breakfast.

(At least the monks have done a better job than the Chinese. Chairman Mao has only been gone a few decades and his bits are tumbling off already. They're forever closing the Mao mausoleum in Beijing so they can glue his nose back on.)

So, as creepy as it is to have the Catacombs to myself and sneak along the corridors past rows of misshapen corpses, there's something almost comedic about the scene that lessens the overall effect. What if the old monk at the entrance forgets about me, locks the door and wanders off for his three-hour siesta? Meh.

I'm not even deterred when my mind begins uncontrollably running through some of the scariest film scenes in cinema history – the 'spider walk' from *The Exorcist*, the drowned girl emerging from the television set in *The Ring*, and that bit where everyone sings 'I Say a Little Prayer (for You)' in *My Best Friend's Wedding*.

By the time I stumble from the gloom of the catacombs, the dazzling daylight is almost too much.

Nobody evokes the heat of Palermo like Giuseppe di Lampedusa in his famous twentieth-century novel, *Il Gattopardo* (*The Leopard*): 'It was midday on a Monday at the end of July, and away in front of him spread the sea of Palermo, compact, oily, inert, improbably motionless, crouching like a dog trying to make itself invisible at its master's threats; but up there the static perpendicular sun was straddling it and lashing it pitilessly. The silence was absolute.' And to think I'm here at the tail end of May. July must be torture.

Fortifying myself with a cold Aranciata (Italy's version of Fanta), I push on. Extra motivation comes in the form of a quote I've read by the previously mentioned Ibn Jubayr, taken from his travel diary: 'The king's palaces surround Palermo like jewels adorning the necks of maidens with swelling breasts.' This is what I want to see, Palermo's jewel-like palaces. And swelling breasts, if it can be arranged.

Ibn Jubayr was referring to two Arab–Norman castles, La Zisa (named after the Arabic term *al-Aziz* meaning 'magnificent') and La Cuba (named after a Ricky Martin album). Both are in the vicinity of the Catacombs, though to get to them I need to cut through a succession of twisting back alleys. It doesn't feel especially safe. The sinister lull of siesta is beginning, and even the most upbeat of my guidebooks calls this 'an ugly fringe area of Palermo'. At one point I walk past a congealing puddle of beetroot-coloured blood on the ground. Foolishly, I take a photo as a reminder of what I've seen.

Paranoia sets in immediately. Did a shutter in the apartment above me just draw closed? Has someone been peering down from a dark crack in the window? One tends to let one's imagination run a fraction wild under these circumstances. (Particularly when one has, fifteen minutes earlier, found oneself alone in a crypt full of dead people, most with their heads caved in.) Soon I'm imagining a whispered phone call to the village of Corleone: 'There's some new guy here, sniffing around in that spot we talked about. He's got a camera and a notebook.' Long pause on the other end of the phone, then a voice says, 'Take care of it.'

I break into a jog, glancing from time to time over my shoulder for a shadowy figure with a scarred cheek beneath a priest's hood.

Later in the afternoon, having survived siesta and Cosa Nostra in the western suburbs, I make my way to Teatro Massimo in the city centre. The staircase leading up to the famous opera house is where Sofia Coppola's character gets gunned down in the final frames of *The Godfather III*.

Inside, preparations for a season of *Macbeth* are underway. Considering the demeanour of the all-female staff I encounter, a season of *The Taming of the Shrew* might be more appropriate. They have me scrambling for all the Shakespearean insults I can remember.

First I encounter the unsmiling power-suited woman at the ticket booth ('*pale, hard-hearted wench!*'). When I say, 'One adult, please,' she responds with a series of robotic decrees: 'You must pay three euros. You cannot enter until three thirty. You cannot see the stage today. It's being prepared for *Macbeth*. You must still pay three euros.'

I reply: 'I will pay three euros. I will not enter until three thirty. Disappointing about the stage. Who is this *Macbeth*? And any chance of a discount?'

Twenty minutes later, at 3.20 pm, a second woman ('*poisonous bunch-backed toad!*') marches up to me. She snaps, 'Are you with the next group?'

I have no idea what she's talking about. 'Uh . . . I was told to wait until three thirty.'

'Do you have a ticket?'

'Yes.' I hold it up dutifully.

The woman looks exasperated. 'You must go inside immediately!'

'Oh,' I say. 'Okay. So, where do I go?'

Shaking her head in a manner that says 'troublemaker!', the woman leads me to a flight of stairs, then points to them and barks, '*Up!*'

From the top of the stairs a maze of corridors unfolds, with a series of locked doors leading to the box seats along the balcony. I see no sign of any tour group. I do, however, find a single open door. It leads to a specially prepared box that has been sealed by perspex on all sides. This is to allow tourists a view of the theatre's interior, by pressing their noses up against the see-through walls. Seems a rough deal to me – to pay three euros and only see the performance space through a pane of thick plastic.

I lean both hands against the wall and peer through into the darkness. Mostly I see roadies on the stage, testing microphones. There is a glimpse, too, of the theatre's ornate golden boxes and velvet curtains. I push my camera against the perspex and take a few shots.

A sharp voice sends a chill up my spine: 'No photos of the stage!'

Standing out in the corridor is a third woman ('*wife of small wit!*') in another severe blue suit. She points down to the floor near her feet, like ordering a dog to heel. It means: *Come here this instant.* I slink over.

'Where is your group?' barks the fishwife.

'Um, I don't have a group.'

She laughs with derision. 'Absurd!'

'I was sent in here alone.'

'Do you have a ticket?'

I pull out my ticket once more.

'If you have a ticket then you must have a group.'

'But I told you, I was sent–'

'*This way!*' The woman leads me quickly through a series of plush antechambers of marble, mirrors and chandeliers. At one point we walk past a tour group of Aussies. A fellow glances over and says, 'Looks like you're in trouble, mate.'

Finally we arrive at my designated group. It consists of fifty chattering schoolchildren in yellow caps. Leading the group is a woman of even more ogrish disposition than the previous three ('*you witch, you hag, you baggage, you polecat, you ronyon!*'). This new piece of work throws me an icy look then addresses the group: 'We are finished looking at the waiting rooms. Now we will go to the balcony and look at the stage.' She shuffles everyone from the room. Most of the schoolchildren laugh at me as they pass.

I hang back for a minute to take some photos of the exquisite décor. As I'm putting my camera back in its case, the new tour leader returns and shouts, 'It is forbidden to take pictures!'

'I thought it was only the stage that I couldn't photograph?'

'Everything!' she snarls. 'And you must stay with the group at all times!'

My patience has gone. 'Listen, lady. I've just missed out on this whole section. And now you want to take me to the crappy plastic box that I've already seen. I spent three euros. I want to see the rest of this place.'

'*No!* You will *stay* with the group!'

The tyrant spins on her heel and marches back to the schoolchildren, who are lined up in front of the perspex. But I've had enough rudeness for one day. Now it's time to be cavalier. I wander off, taking photos at will, exploring rooms, turning switches on and off, leaving taps running in washrooms, and sliding across the marble floors in my socks like Tom Cruise. But it's risky business. Twice the woman runs back and yells at me, virtually dragging me by the ear to rejoin the group, threatening my expulsion from the tour.

I return to the perspex room to see if the lighting has improved for a better view of the interior. But with fifty sets of grubby kids' palms now smeared against the plastic wall, not to mention clouds of condensation from their breathing, I'd rather walk into a spinning helicopter blade.

In the final minute of the arduous tour, I receive yet another lecture about taking photos, at which point the other Aussie walks past again and says with a laugh, 'Still causing trouble, mate?'

Then, finally, I'm outside on the street, gulping air like a resurfaced diver. I grab a much-needed cold beer at the nearest kiosk.

All's well that ends well.

Further wanderings take me past a couple of parks: Giardino Garibaldi, full of giant fig trees and surrounded by a wrought-iron fence sculpted with miniature boars' snouts, and the less appealing Giardino Inglese (the English Garden), allegedly awash with heroin addicts.

I find myself in a church called La Gancia where a wedding is in full cry. A singer is making a bit of a mess of 'Ave Maria'. At the entrance, a silver tray of wheat stalks, bread and olive oil in glass dispensers indicate the couple's wish for a fertile marriage. They might have wished for a better singer.

On the way out, a gypsy woman sitting on the church steps with her baby daughter shakes an empty plate at me. I give her my loose change and advise her not to take the guided tour of Teatro Massimo, should that be what she's saving up for.

Next I arrive at the most squalid square of Palermo's toughest neighbourhood, La Kalsa. It looks freshly bombed, as if the war ended only yesterday. Six children run feverishly among the rubble with a soccer ball. When a couple of the taller boys see me, they whisper to each other behind their hands, prompting one of them to sprint away down a shadowy archway. I suspect the idea is to summon an older and more violent brother to come along and appropriate my every belonging, possibly at knife point. Time to make a retreat.

Back in my hotel room, I attempt to unscrew the plastic panels from the shower so I can wash my whole body simultaneously rather than one limb at a time. No luck.

I give Gill a call in Catania. Everything's fine there. She asks me for the highlight of my trip so far. I jokingly say, 'The women of Teatro Massimo.' But Gill replies, 'What women? Where? What do you mean, *women*?' And I realise I've dug a hole that there's no getting out of.

At nine pm, I head outside in search of innumerable cold beverages. I walk north through the Quattro Canti intersection, dark and ominous at night, and then to narrow Via Candelai, one of Palermo's few hotspots for live music and drinks.

Despite being twice as big as Catania, Palermo (Italy's fifth-biggest city) comes a distinct second in terms of evening entertainment. Catania is a bigger student town, hence the reputation for livelier bars. Also, in Catania – near our apartment, at least – you can stand around and toast marshmallows over a firebombed car.

Indeed, Via Candelai is dead. At one point I hear the mellifluous trills of a saxophone, but it's just a young guy standing outside his apartment door, practising by lamplight. Two bars are open but empty. I have a beer in each because I feel bad for the owners.

Perhaps I'm out too early – in typical southern Mediterranean fashion, Sicilian nightlife is liveliest after midnight. I'm momentarily tempted to wait around for a local Pink Floyd tribute band whose flyer I picked up earlier, but the prospect of searching for a venue in the city's dim back alleys is unsettling. I've read about Palermitan thieves who lean from their apartment windows at night and drop heavy objects onto tourists, knocking them over so they can steal their stuff. As a method of assault, it sounds unduly complicated (why not just walk straight up with a knife and say, 'Wallet'?), yet best to avoid nonetheless.

Instead, I buy a pistacchio *connolo* and hit the hay. I need to be at Monreale Cathedral first thing in the morning anyway, before continuing my tour of western Sicily. I had originally planned to see the cathedral today, until the tourism office in Palermo informed me it was 'closed for disinfection'. Infected with what, I wonder. Cruise-boat passengers?

The next morning, I check out of the Hotel Sicilia and board a bus for the half-hour trip to Monreale. The town that lends the cathedral its name is like any modest settlement in Sicily. Old men sit on benches in the sun; workers dash into bars for one-minute espressos; and young people are noticeable by their absence, having all left for better opportunities in the big smoke.

The town's twelfth-century church, however, constitutes the breathtaking pinnacle of Arab–Norman art and architecture. The interior is decorated with six and a half thousand square metres of mosaic stones, most of them painted with gold leaf. As the morning sun rises in the sky, it passes by one window after another, allowing different sections of the golden walls to dazzle into life. Monreale Cathedral is like the Liberace of churches.

The detail of the mosaic is stunning, too. Among dozens of biblical scenes is one depicting Jesus' confrontation with a group of moneylenders in the temple, complete with tiny mosaic coins flying through the air as he overturns their tables in anger.

After drinking it all in, I climb to the top of the cathedral, where the reward is an expansive view across a flat valley known as the Conco d'Oro (Golden Shell) to Palermo and the ocean beyond.

Finally, there is the famous Cloister, part of a Benedictine abbey that once abutted Monreale Cathedral. It's almost as renowned as the church itself, and with good reason. I'm in awe as I wander along the flamboyant walkways, whose arches are propped up by more than two hundred Greek-style columns decorated with geometric mosaics. Glittering lines of colour wrap around each column like the spiral pole of the world's most expensive barbershop. Sicilians say: '*Cui va 'n Palermu e 'un vidi Murriali, si nni parti sceccu e torna armali.*' ('Whoever goes to Palermo and doesn't see Monreale, goes there a jackass.') Now I understand why.

Here's a tip, though. If you want to see all of this and truly appreciate it, get to Monreale as early as possible – say, seven thirty in the morning. This is one of Sicily's most heavily touristed sites, and not even a good disinfecting can keep the swarms at bay.

19. A trip to the west

> I left Palermo, attended by the following suite: a litter
> with two mules; another mule carrying a driver and
> half a load; and a third with a whole load, namely, my
> bed, kitchen furniture, and many other articles. Also,
> two other mules, for servants.
>
> – Sir Richard Colt Hoare, *A Classical Tour through
> Italy and Sicily*, 1819

The second leg of my odyssey to the other side of Sicily has
begun. I'm on the three-hour mid-morning train to Mazara
del Vallo, a town at the bottom of the very western tip of the
island.

Twenty minutes into the trip, a monument flits past the
window. Erected beside the A29 *autostrada*, it marks the lives
and deeds of two famous Sicilians I've mentioned briefly
before, Giovanni Falcone and Paolo Borsellino – the same
men who lend their names to Palermo's Falcone–Borsellino
Airport. In the 1980s, these men, both prosecuting judges,
blew the lid wide open on organised crime in Sicily. They were
instrumental in facilitating a six-year 'Maxi Trial' in Palermo
that led to the jailing of three hundred and fifty *mafiosi* for a
combined total of two thousand six hundred years.

Born in the Sicilian capital (in 1939 and 1940, respectively), Falcone and Borsellino grew up in a relatively poor district of the city. They knew Cosa Nostra culture. This would later prove essential in their work, enabling them to extract crucial Mafia secrets from Tommaso Buscetta. Buscetta was one of the first members of the organisation to break the *omertà* (code of silence) and become a *pentito* (informant).

Unfortunately, you don't simply put three hundred and fifty *mafiosi* in jail and then go about your daily business. There are ramifications. At around six pm on 23 May 1992, Falcone flew into Palermo's airport from Rome, where he had been posted the previous year and from where he had continued to instigate wider anti-Mafia measures. As Falcone drove along the A29, past the point where the monument now stands, a considerable stretch of freeway suddenly rose into the air, launched by five hundred kilograms of plastic explosives hidden in a tunnel beneath the road. The explosives were detonated by Giovanni Brusca who, together with other Mafia men, had staked out the highway for five days from a nearby hill. DNA tests taken on cigarette butts left at the scene proved to be Brusca's undoing.

Down on the freeway, it was carnage. Falcone had been a marked man for some time and therefore never travelled alone. On this occasion, he was in a convoy of three vehicles. The explosion obliterated the front car, killing three bodyguards instantly. Those in the last car escaped with minor injuries. In the middle, Falcone and his wife, Francesca Morvillo, received horrific wounds. Both died that evening in hospital.

Paolo Borsellino was there to see his friend and co-worker draw his final breath. In the aftermath, Borsellino is said to have worked even more tirelessly against the Cosa Nostra. Many believe he knew his number was up. 'I am fighting against time,' he apparently told a colleague.

It didn't take the Mafia long to confirm his suspicions. On a Sunday afternoon two months later, Borsellino went to visit his mother in central Palermo. When he reached her gate and pushed the intercom button, a car bomb exploded. The blast obliterated a dozen or so vehicles in the street and damaged every apartment in the vicinity. Needless to say, Borsellino died instantly – along with five bodyguards with machine guns who'd travelled with him to ensure his safety. Survivors equated the scene with the aftermath of an earthquake.

The monument slips by and our train passes Palermo's Falcone–Borsellino Airport. Next it turns sharply away from the scraggly beaches and sapphire water of Golfo di Castellammare and heads south into the interior. Wine country. Out my window, tight rows of grapevines occupy gentle rolling hills. Sicily's northwest is famous for Rapitalà, a mild white wine, and Bianco di Alcamo, a dry and fruity drop made mostly from Catarratto grapes – perfect accompaniments for fresh seafood, *babbaluci* and possibly spleen.

We pass through the town of Àlcamo, where I watch swallows darting in and out of mud nests in the roof of the railway station. The platform is empty but for two overweight station employees cracking jokes in a torrent of hand gestures and shoulder shrugs. 'Three *carabinieri* walk into a bar . . .'

Next is Gibellina Nuova, a modest town of five thousand people in the Sicilian interior. It's called 'Nuova' because the old town was entirely wiped out by an earthquake in 1968. The new Gibellina was built ten kilometres to the west. In the aftermath of the disaster, an architect named Alberto Burri transformed the destroyed town into a ghostly monument to the deceased, known as Il Cretto (The Crevice), by covering it in a white stone slab, twelve hectares in size – a giant 'ground zero'. Channels have been cut through the slab to mimic the original streets of Gibellina. Walking along these silent grooves is said to be one of the more eerie experiences in Sicily.

Mazara del Vallo

Eerie, too, is the wiry fellow with thin grey hair and dark shades who accosts me from a park bench along the waterfront of Mazara del Vallo an hour later. He's sitting beside what looks like a forgotten pile of bricks at a worksite. In fact, they're the paltry remains of a Norman castle built in 1073 by Roger I.

'Where you from?' the fellow says in slurred Italian.

'Australia.'

No reaction to this. It's like he's getting the question out of the way so he can get to the meat of the matter.

'Married?'

'Yes.'

'Kids?'

'Not yet.'

He barks, 'Kids are trouble!'

'I'm sure.'

'I have twins,' the man continues. 'Two boys.'

'Congratulations.'

'They still live at home.'

Judging from the age of my new acquaintance – who, I now realise, is alarmingly drunk for eleven am on a hot morning in May – his 'boys' must be thirty, at least.

'Really?'

Just as I'm beginning to wonder where this is going, out comes the denouement. '*And they're both fucking the same woman!*' He makes a hole with his forefinger and thumb then pokes the gap a few times – in case we'd not grasped the concept of 'fucking' in Australia.

'Incredible,' I reply politely. It's hard to tell if the man is furious or elated about the antics of his progeny. I won't be sticking around to find out.

As I follow a bone-coloured street lined with stumpy palms, a bead of sweat rolls across my temple and onto the lens of my sunglasses. I stop again so my face can harvest a breeze from the green-jelly sea.

Africa is so close. From Mazara, it's a measly hundred and forty kilometres away across a body of water known as the Canale di Sicilia. I'm nearer to Tunisia than Catania. The Italian mainland seems worlds away; Rome, a different country. No surprise that it was at this spot in AD 827 that the first boatload of Saracens, an invading army of Arabs, Berbers and Spanish Muslims, walked ashore.

No surprise either that Mazara del Vallo has Italy's highest percentage of immigrants, most of them from the

Maghreb – the Arab states of North Africa. Five thousand alone are thought to come from Tunisia, though illegal migration across the ocean renders the figure untrustworthy. The town has an elementary school run by the Tunisian government where kids learn Arabic and French. On the flipside, most local Italian schools offer Arabic language courses.

With this in mind, I'm hoping to hunt down a Tunisian restaurant to sample some *mloukhia, guenaoia, chakchouka* and *mhalbya*. (Would it be rude to submit that the names of Tunisian dishes evoke the sound of a chewing camel?) I'll finish with a plate of plump dates and an apple-flavoured hookah.

In fact, I have difficulty finding *anything* to eat. Mazara del Vallo doesn't seem to pride itself on fine dining, or dining full stop, save for what people cook at home. There are a few establishments along the *lungomare*, but they're all recommended in *Lonely Planet*. Every traveller knows the cardinal rule about never eating in one of those.

So, despite the town's Tunisian-ness, I end up with a quintessentially Italian snack for my lunch – a takeaway *panino* lined with strips of rosy red pancetta from a place called Bar Normanno. It was Mother's Day at the beginning of the month and on top of the receipt for my food is a little cartoon of a mother cradling a child, and a message of good wishes to all the mums: '*Auguri a tutte le mamme!*'

Mazara's eleventh-century Cattedrale del San Salvatore is grander than I expect, topped by a trio of green, majolica-tiled domes like half-watermelons. A carved stone relief on the façade shows a rider on horseback (Roger again) clutching a dagger and leaping with menace towards the prostrate form of a Saracen soldier. The Saracen is in danger of being smote first by the dagger and second by the horse's not insubstantial set of bollocks. Churchgoers walk beneath this image and inside to pray for peace and good will among men.

Outside in the square I'm pleased to find a Baroque statue of Vitus, the patron saint of Mazara del Varro. The town also has a church and festival in his honour. Vitus was a Sicilian who died a martyr in AD 303 during the Roman persecution of Christians. In the Middle Ages, a custom developed of marking the saint's feast day by performing a manic dance in front of his image – the 'Saint Vitus Dance'. Later, the name attached to rheumatic chorea, a nervous disorder that causes dance-like movements of the hands and feet.

If Vitus is the patron saint of involuntary spasms, I'm guessing he's also the patron saint of leg jiggling. I could leg jiggle for Australia. It's a habit that drives Gill mad: whenever I start bouncing one knee up and down, she angrily invokes the name of the saint: 'Quit it with the Vitus!'

As I stand before the statue in Mazara del Varro reflecting on this, I suddenly think I detect the faintest trace of a jiggle in one of the statue's own legs. The tiniest movement, then nothing. I wait and stare. Is this a visitation in the same vein as the weeping statue of Mary in Syracuse? Have I been 'chosen'? Maybe I'll develop the power to cure the lame simply by touching them with a jiggling foot. Maybe I'll become famous and enjoy a personal audience with the Pope. Oprah, even!

Or maybe, just maybe, the heat is getting to me.

The Mazaro River puts its modest puncture in the coastline here, spilling emerald waters into the ocean. The narrow harbour is lined on both sides by hulking fishing boats. At the time of my visit, Mazara del Vallo comprises Italy's largest fishing fleet. But it's on the decline: young people are choosing to stay ashore.

A group of middle-aged fishermen are hunched on the ground in front of their boat, repairing piles of orange netting. They're fat from wine and pasta but strong as oxen, with Popeye forearms and fists that could knock a shark unconscious. As I pass, one of the men whispers a comment, eliciting chuckles from his companions. I'm guessing he said, 'Check out this guy. Look at his soft hands. You think he's ever done a day's work?' I think about yelling out a retort: 'I've been on a Sicilian fishing boat, too, I'll have you know!' But I'm worried they'll press me for details, and then I'll have to admit I held my wife's handbag while she drove.

The men's levity may be short-lived. During these very minutes, a story is brewing that will fill tomorrow's newspapers. Another group of fishermen from the town has just made a gruesome discovery off the coast – a net filled with four fish-pecked human bodies. On reading this story, I think to myself, 'Mafia'. Surely it's a quartet of local businessmen who haven't paid their *pizzo* (extortion money) and are now sleeping with the fishes.

I'm wrong. They're illegal immigrants. Thousands of desperate souls attempt each year to cross from North Africa into Europe aboard flimsy, ill-equipped boats. Many of them fail, fatally.

The situation doesn't appear to be improving. In 2007, seven Tunisian fishermen were charged in Sicily with rescuing forty-four immigrants from the waters of the Canale di Sicilia. The men argued that the immigrants would otherwise have died – and from the facts of the case, this seems patently true. The seven were eventually released, but the message from the Italian authorities in charging the fishermen in the first place seemed clear: don't help these boatpeople – we don't want them here.

Back in 1998, another group of Mazara fishermen hauled a happier catch aboard their vessel: the rusted remains of a seven-foot bronze sculpture more than twenty centuries old. The Dancing Satyr (Satiro Danzante), as it's now known, has become the symbol of Mazara del Vallo. Pick up any tourist brochure and you'll see the statue's cheeky mug on the cover. A fifteenth-century church has been converted into a museum to house the artwork. It's even appeared in the Louvre and at an expo in Japan.

Satyrs were goat-like fellows from Greek and Roman mythology, usually portrayed cavorting with the god of wine, Dionysus (Bacchus to the Romans). The Mazara satyr has its head and feet thrown backwards in what commentators call an 'orgiastic frenzy'. The description is reasonable – satyrs were randy little beasts, often portrayed with irrepressible erections. (The Dancing Satyr, for the record, has been short-changed in this department.)

Since the sculpture has been such a boon for the town, the hunt is on to find another one. Petroleum industries are using dredging probes off the coast of Mazara to help locate any Greek or Roman goodies that might have tumbled out of a wrecked ship a few millennia ago. I'm sure this is a fool-proof method. To me, though, the headline 'Dredging probe pinpoints artefacts' lacks appeal. Give me a bobbing boat-load of gruff Mazara fishermen any day, perspiring in the first light of dawn as they heave a mysterious ancient object aboard in a hand-repaired net full of flapping mackerel.

I think about staying in Mazara del Varro for a night. I like its ramshackle feel – especially the old Arab quarter called the Casbah – and the hint of the Maghreb on the breeze. Money's a bit tight, so I won't be able to afford the wonderfully beery-sounding Hopps Hotel at the eastern end of town. But in Piazza Santa Veneranda there's a monastery with dorm beds for twenty euros. And I could hang out with my friend, the park-bench drunkard with the depraved sons.

Then I come to my senses. A monastery is the last thing I want. It will mean an early curfew, abstemious facilities, lots of tiptoeing about and, in all likelihood, answering to a nun as daunting as our first landlord in Catania.

So, it's on to Marsala.

Marsala

I've read somewhere that Marsala has Sicily's most progressive council. That's not necessarily saying a lot. However, when we hiss to a stop, I do see flower boxes on the platform, freshly painted wrought-iron seats, a lovely bar with that rarest of Sicilian commodities, a smiling barista, and a neat line of billboards promoting healthy living.

Not bad for a place that's famous for its booze.

Locals were already making sweet Marsala wine when Englishman John Woodhouse arrived in the late 1700s. Woodhouse was familiar with the sherry industry from his time in the Spanish town of Jerez, which lends its name to the beverage. In particular, he realised the exportability of Marsala wine – all it needed was fortification with ethanol or brandy.

By the middle of the next century, Marsala was a star on the global wine stage, and Woodhouse (presumably) a wealthy man. That's if he didn't drink all the profits – stories emerged of the Englishman running drunkenly through his Marsala vineyards, stark naked.

Prohibition in America did nothing to harm the popularity of Marsala. Sicilians apparently got around the problem by labelling bottles bound for the US as 'hospital tonic'.

Later, though, the status of Marsala wine began to slip. It became more common for use in cooking than drinking. I can vouch for this: in my family's library is a thirty-year-old *Women's Weekly Italian Family Cookbook*, dog-eared at the page for Chicken Marsala. I think my dad even put a splash of Marsala in his saucepan of Red Death kidneys.

There's not a lot to distract me in Marsala's *centro*. Instead, I walk out of the town and towards the coastline, a few hundred metres across an empty paddock. One of my brochures mentions the purity of the ocean here, for which the town has received a prize called the Bandiera Blu (Blue Flag).

The water seems nice enough, though it doesn't put me in any hurry to visit the place that came second. A bunch of seedy teenagers are standing there, two of them pissing into the sea. And the rocky shelf down to the water is liberally strewn with Parmalat milk containers and rusted La Gina tomato tins.

This award-winning spot is where Giuseppe Garibaldi's 'Red Shirts' landed on 11 May 1860, having sailed from Genoa with the mission of overthrowing the Bourbon government and liberating the Kingdom of the Two Sicilies. A fortnight later, Garibaldi's Mille (one thousand men) took Palermo. By the time they reached Messina after a successful march across the island their numbers had swollen to twenty thousand and a unified Italy was a reality.

Centuries earlier, other boats plied these waters. It was here in 241 BC that Rome and Carthage fought the Battle of the Egadi Islands – the decisive conflict in the First Punic War. In 1969, the timber remains of a *liburna* (Punic warship) were found in the sand. Archaeologists subsequently retrieved human bones from the boat, indicating that the crew of sixty-eight oarsmen probably perished in the battle. Other discoveries included food remains, knives, lengths of rope, and a bird-bone needle used for sewing nets. Most interesting of all was the bundle of cannabis stalks, possibly kept on board for the crew to chew on. Presumably their stash of methamphetamines dissolved in the ocean when they sank.

Speaking of white powders, my train to Trapani an hour later passes directly by the famous salt-producing region of the island's western edge. Here, Sicily turns into Holland, with dead-flat scenery and windmills galore. The latter are mostly abandoned (salt production peaked a hundred years ago), but a few are still used for pumping water into the pans. When the water evaporates in the blazing Sicilian sun, a bed of salt crystals remains. These are piled into enormous mounds several metres high and covered in a protective crust of terracotta tiles. From the train window, they look like little houses.

'*Di lu mari nasci lu sali e di la fimmina ogni mali,*' goes the Sicilian proverb ('From the sea comes salt, and from the woman comes every bad thing'), which seems a fraction unreasonable but better than this one, at least: '*Fimmina trintina, jèttala a la marina*' ('A woman in her thirties, throw her in the sea').

Trapani

It's seven pm when the train pulls into Trapani. The sun is low in the sky but it will be another sticky hour before nightfall.

Trapani is a very large town by Sicilian standards – seventy thousand people – and everything is crammed onto a slender peninsula surrounded by water. I track down some cheap accommodation and knock on the front door, only for it to creak open of its own accord, like in a horror film. A frumpy woman appears at the top of a short staircase and leads me inside. This isn't really a hotel, more like a family home – a family eager to save money on electricity. It's ghoulishly dark.

The first thing I opt for is a shower. There's only a communal bathroom. It's right next to the television in the living room. The concertina door doesn't shut properly, leaving a wide gap. The family members sit on a mottled couch watching TV, and every now and then when I look through the crack I can see them glancing in my direction.

Turning the taps off, I realise there's no towel. I'm forced to open the crack a bit wider and ask for one. Then I realise I don't remember the Italian word for towel. (It's tricky: *asciugamano*.) None of the family speaks English. Being naked, I can hardly open the doors and perform the action of drying myself. Instead, I'm forced to use a bit of linguistic chicanery.

'Excuse me,' I say in Italian. 'I am wet. Can I have the thing to use for drying?'

Despite these inconveniences, my room is extremely neat, in a starchy, militaristic fashion. The walls are of the starkest white, drawing attention to a wooden crucifix hanging a metre above the bed. In the corner of the room stands a small sink, just begging to be pissed in – especially in view of the awkward location of the shared bathroom. And a pair of shutters opens out to a rusty and precipitously narrow balcony with views of the street. In short, pretty good value for fifteen euros.

Outside again, I'm stopped in my tracks by the sight of the evening sky – intense gradations of colour beginning with deep plum above, through to a final leaching of dusty pink on the horizon. A passing plane has left a thin white scar of vapour trail, like someone's fingernail scratch on a crayon canvas.

Restaurant-wise, there isn't much open. Eventually I stumble upon the Trattoria da Salvatore, a family-run eatery in the middle of town. Salvatore himself meets me at the door. I'm dying for a bowl of the local specialty, *cuscus con pesce*. It sounds like a remarkable dish: fillets of sea bass or bream are poached in a light tomato, garlic and chilli broth, added to steamed mussels and prawns, then poured over handmade couscous that has been folded through with gently fried onions, various aromatics and some slivers of toasted almond. But Salvatore delivers devastating news: no *cuscus* tonight. I almost never recover. In the end, I push the menu aside and ask him to serve whatever fresh seafood is available, done in whatever style he chooses. He dashes off to the kitchen, where I soon hear the sizzle of white wine in a hot pan.

Thankfully, the *cuscus* replacements are simple and superb. First, a classic *spaghetti alle vongole* – spaghetti with clams. Next, two fillets of *triglie* – red mullet, grilled and doused in a light sauce. Side salad. Crusty bread. *Vino della casa*.

Afterwards, I walk to a waterfront bar and order a Heineken.

'Good timing,' says the barman. 'The game's starting soon.'

I'm guessing he's talking about football. Juventus is taking on Real Madrid in the semi-finals of the Champions League. The most popular football club in Italy, Turin-based 'Juve' is especially revered in Sicily, where the team opts to play the occasional 'home' game.

I thank the fellow for the tip. He pauses in the middle of cleaning a glass and eyes me with interest. 'Are you Spanish?'

'Australian.'

'Why are you interested in the Champions League?'

'I used to play football myself.'

If not an outright lie, this is at least misleading. I played for a handful of years from the age of about six. My parents have video footage of me from a game: I'm out on the wing, not even watching the other players but skipping around in circles and stopping to examine insects in the grass. No Francesco Totti, then.

A large crew of middle-aged men gathers at the bar for kick-off. By day a bunch of taciturn dockhands and ferry drivers, the men look transformed in the glow of the screen: football, their fountain of youth. Juve races to a 2–0 lead and they holler with excitement. By way of contrast, a couple of teenagers sit in a side room, sullenly feeding coins into an electronic poker machine.

When a third goal seals the result, the old fellows begin a spontaneous jig, right there at the bar. Everyone joins in. Even I get swept into the fray.

A few beers later, I retire to my modest and monastic room, cover the crucified Christ with a t-shirt while I relieve myself in the corner sink (hey, Bill Bryson does it!), then tuck myself under a threadbare sheet and sleep unexpectedly well.

I'm up by five thirty am and out of the 'hotel' in fifteen minutes. Later when I tell Gill about my early start she looks physically repulsed. My wife's not a morning person. If she'd been with me in Trapani, we'd have left at an entirely different time. Put it this way: when we stay in hotels together, I'm the one who enquires what time breakfast *begins*; she's the one who asks what time it *ends*.

The streets are quiet, exacerbating the cries of circling gulls. I hang over a wall and stare at the stony black sea.

Inland I can see the medieval mountain town of Erice, which we visited with our friends in late December.

The port, meanwhile, is frenetic: docks, wharves, shipping containers, factories, and every variety of ferry. Boats leave from here for the Egadi Islands, for Pantelleria (Sicily's most distant island, a hundred and ten kilometres away) and for Tunisia. Signs are in Italian, Arabic and occasionally English. By the time I find a timetable, I'm left with only four minutes to buy a ticket and board the seven am boat to my destination, Favignana. But the hydrofoil dock I need is all the way at the other end of the port. Bugger.

I make it – *just*. There's nothing like the threat of missing an important travel connection in an overseas country to make you run like a startled whippet.

The Egadi Islands

Ten minutes into the hydrofoil trip to Favignana, I'm seasick. I was already bilious after the enforced sprint back at the port, so an unsteady boat's no help. The salt-streaked windows in the cabin won't open and it's too bumpy to go onto the deck for fresh air. There's nothing to do but sit tight, within arm's reach of the vomit bag in the seat pouch.

Finally we lurch into the sheltered harbour of Favignana. As I step onto the pier I notice a line of tiny schoolchildren, all holding hands, oversized schoolbags on their backs; they're waiting to board the hydrofoil to take them to school in Trapani. It's among the most delightful sights of the whole day – that they're leaving just as I've arrived.

Favignana is shaped like a butterfly – hence its nick-name, *la farfalla*. Most of the island's two thousand residents live on the northern end of the butterfly's 'body', where a town of jumbled white cubes crowds around an azure bay. The wings, meanwhile, are made up of sparse farms of long-haired sheep, a series of *tufa* quarries, and a succession of tiny coves where electric-blue waters lap against perfect sand or shelves of pale rock. A single barren hill, the three-hundred-metre Santa Caterina, supervises the scene.

At the port, dozens of small blue-and-white boats are sardined together, spilling over with fishermen. The catch of the day arrived hours ago and has already been shipped to various corners of the Sicilian mainland. Now the locals are cleaning the decks and mending their nets. They wear thick black gumboots and orange overalls of heavy-duty rub-ber held up by braces. I've seen a few images of Favignanan fishermen before now, in coffee-table books and on souvenir postcards – middle-aged men baked in the Sicilian forge, all with massive shoulders and barrel chests, a few allowing their hair to run wild into sun-bleached curls. That's exactly how they look in the flesh, too. Each one is the kind of fellow who, after losing a finger in an accident at sea, would hang his bleeding hand over the side of the boat to improve the burley.

The men yank nets from the back of their boats, checking for imperfections and for crustaceans inadvertently snared in the morning's trawl. Tiny critters are plucked free and tossed into the sun-splashed sea, its sparkle muted by floating fish scales and a thin rainbow film of fuel.

A handful of older male residents – former fishermen, I assume – join me in watching the action. They wear vests over flannelette shirts, and weathered caps. I imagine many of them are missing fingers.

There's nothing especially newsworthy to report from my half-day excursion. It's simply five hours of bucolic bliss. To get around, I rent a bicycle rather than a scooter (still spooked from the incident on the Aeolian Islands) and explore Favignana's deserted nooks and crannies. Highlights of the ride: the herd of cows chewing and snorting over clumps of seaweed on a windswept beach; the swim at Cala Azzurra, a perfect turquoise bay with water as clear as a freshly vacuumed pool; and the celebratory lemon gelato back in the main town once I've finished circumnavigating the island.

While waiting for the return ferry to Trapani (I'm due back in Catania tonight), I look across the harbour to a factory-style collection of brick buildings on the far side of town. This is the *tonnara*, full of boats, nets, gaffes, weights and other fishing paraphernalia.

Favignana is famous for a ritual cull of bluefin tuna called the *mattanza* (from '*matar*', the old Spanish word meaning 'to kill'). It must be starting soon – the season generally runs from the second half of May to mid-June. The first *mattanza* is announced by the ringing of a bell in the *camparia*, the central building of the tuna station.

I call to a trio of old locals sitting on a bench seat, 'Excuse me, when's the *mattanza* this year?'

If I'd known my question would lead to some kind of tribal warfare, I wouldn't have asked. Two of the men turn

to each other and break into a five-minute blur of gesticula-
tion and argument in the local dialect. Finally, with their lips
flecked white, they seem to reach a truce. One of them turns
to me and says, 'It will be late.'

It's interesting to see locals still passionate about the *mattanza*, because the truth is that this age-old fishing ritual has
been dying its own bloody death for decades. Tuna numbers worldwide have plummeted since the introduction of
sophisticated new fishing methods. These days, floating factories owned by international conglomerates scoop up whole
schools from the open sea, guided by helicopter spotters
and sonar. The best of the bluefins are snap-frozen, flown to
Japan, and, within a day, sold at Tokyo's Tsukiji Market to
high-end sushi restaurants.

The *mattanza* has been reduced to little more than a tourist novelty. Once it was a legitimate business for the island,
with as many as ten thousand bluefin tuna pulled in over a
month-long season. Now the fishermen are lucky to haul in
a few hundred, most of them much smaller than in previous
decades. When Favignana's tuna cannery closed in the early
1980s, a thousand people lost their jobs.

But I can see why tourists still find the *mattanza* mes-
merising. The ritual is carried out by a small group of local
fishermen who set up a complex series of netted chambers in
the waters off Favignana, designed to guide tuna from one
chamber to the next. The fish are eventually corralled into
la camera della morte (the chamber of death). This final section has a bottom net which can be hauled up with ropes,
bringing the bluefin slowly to the surface. There, in an area

one hundred metres by twenty metres, the fishermen wait with ten-foot sharpened gaffes to bludgeon the giant creatures and haul them from the water. It can take as many as eight men to lift the bigger fish – tuna can reach forty years of age and half a ton in weight. Over the course of a few hours, the chamber of death becomes a square of thrashing pink foam and flailing silver.

Atlantic bluefin tuna have been trapped in various ways around the Mediterranean for centuries – the Phoenicians minted coins with an image of a bluefin, Aristotle wrote about the fish, and the Romans described similar fishing methods while revelling in the healthy properties of the tuna's flesh. Favignana's *tonnara* dates to the ninth century AD. It was established by the Arabs – the specific songs (called *scialome*) that the fishermen still sing today during the various stages of the *mattanza* have Arabic roots. The group is still led by a *rais* ('boss' – from the Arab word for 'head').

However bloody it might be, there is a depth of tradition, ritual and superstition attached to the *mattanza* that is clinically absent from modern commercial fishing. Each year, Favignana's fishermen play a delicate waiting game. The question around town becomes: when will the *rais* ring the bell? The reaction of the old locals suggests it's still an integral part of Favignana's culture.

Modern fishing companies increasingly take a different approach. They say: why wait for a bell? And so Atlantic bluefin tuna numbers have dropped ninety per cent in four decades. It's entirely feasible the fish will become extinct in the not too distant future.

With those sobering thoughts, I bounce back to Trapani on the ferry, my mouth filling with its own miniature ocean of saltwater as I once again try very hard not to regurgitate.

After the ferry, it's a six-hour bus trip back to Catania. By the time the driver pulls into the terminus at Piazza Borsellino, it's dark. Thankfully I know the fifteen-minute walk back to the apartment like the back of my hand.

First I pass through Giardino Pacini, a small but historic park known locally as Villa dei Varagghi ('villa of yawns') because of the countless elderly men who sit on its benches during the day and fall asleep.

Next I come to the Pescheria, closed at night and more than a little creepy, with locked storefronts, angular stacks of empty wooden pallets, and a smudge of moonlight reflecting in the fish scales caught between cobblestone cracks.

Now I'm on Via Garibaldi, dimly lit by streetlamps. I nod hello to one of the neighbourhood characters, a cross-dressing street vendor who sells second-hand Mills & Boon–style books from a trolley on our street each day. 'Cross-dressing' might be overplaying it: he's just a shabby homeless man in a wig of blonde curls. He never acknowledges Gill whenever we pass, only me: 'So handsome!' he growls with what's left of his voice.

I stop at the only open café to buy a tray of *crispelle* – fingers of donut, dipped in honey and showered with icing sugar. They're for Gill, either to thank her for allowing me this time away (the two nights are the only ones we've spent apart in Sicily), or to placate her if she's angry that I didn't get back a bit sooner.

Now I'm right near home. As usual, a few ne'er-do-wells are loitering outside the Eliseo cinema. I spy a 'Coming Soon' poster out of the corner of my eye. It reads: '*Vacanze di due donne affamate di sesso!*' (The travels of two sex-starved women!)

My last stop is the *tabaccheria* diagonally across from our apartment. While I'm there grabbing a couple of essentials, a cute six-year-old girl with Coke-bottle glasses walks in. She reaches up and fumbles some euros onto the counter, reciting an order for two packets of Camel cigarettes.

'For your papa?' asks the shop owner. He's a gentle fellow who Gill and I uncharitably refer to as 'Jaws' in private conversation, because, well, his teeth aren't the best. The girl nods.

I cross the road to our *palazzo* and buzz the intercom. The gate clicks open. I walk across the courtyard, past Jesus Christ who is lit up in the niche outside our front door, and into our tiny living room.

'Hello, stranger,' says Gill with a smile. I can smell garlic cooking in the kitchen. She's been to the *enoteca* to get wine, too.

I've seen plenty of places I'd rather live than Catania on my trip to western Sicily, but tonight it actually feels good to be back.

20. Leaving

> 'Do you think you still belong to this world?' I shouted.
> 'To this land here? To Sicily?'
> – Elio Vittorini, *Conversations in Sicily* (1941)

Here's a catalogue of the detritus I spotted on Catania's beach, La Playa, when Gill and I visited on a crisp, quiet day back in January:

- plastic fork
- mousepad
- tin cans (2)
- cigarette butts (11)
- fishing paraphernalia
- cotton buds (1 packet)
- roll-on deodorant
- unidentifiable piece of rusted metal
- orange plastic covering of car tail-light
- sodden newspaper
- glass bottles (2)
- syringe
- chocolate bar wrapper
- stainless-steel pot-scourer

- jacket
- dog shit (2 dried coils, 1 fresh)
- bus tickets (2)
- paracetamol (1 strip)
- blue pens (2)
- rusted lighters (3)

'That's more stuff than we actually own,' said Gill when I showed her my list. Then she spent the next half hour watching me with an eagle eye, making sure I didn't hoard the filthy flotsam to save money on our next visit to the chemist.

Every time we've been to Catania's beach, we've found the five-kilometre strip of mushroom-coloured sand strewn liberally with litter. There's never a bin to be seen, either, or a single noticeboard or sign promoting an environmental message.

The whole of La Playa is a bit depressing, to be honest. Catania's international airport being right nearby doesn't help. The main landing strip, as I noticed on our arrival the previous year, literally begins in the dunes. Beach sessions are interrupted by the high-pitched scream of engines as passenger jets pass a hundred metres overhead. The water feels coated by aviation fuel – or maybe that's a slick from Catania's port, a kilometre north of here, or even from Sicily's petrochemical heartland fifty kilometres away to the south. Keep your mouth shut when you swim, that's my advice.

Our friend Massi, the guitarist, once walked onto the beach, took one look at the state of it, then stood on the sand yelling an open rebuke to his fellow citizens: 'No, no, NO! Why, Catanese, why?!'

Sicily's reputation with rubbish isn't good. Read a few online travel forums and you'll find complaints like this: 'The litter in Sicily is horrendous. It totally ruined our holiday. We will *never* return there and we would advise anyone travelling to prepare themselves for the filth. It's appalling. Sicily is the toilet of Europe.'

Hysterical? Yes. Complete nonsense? No. People world-wide are prone to littering, but in Sicily it seems to be carried out with conviction rather than stealth. Once Gill berated a boy for dropping an empty can at his feet, and rather than appearing guilty at being caught in the act, the boy looked baffled – what on earth was this foreign woman banging on about?

Education, then, is an issue. So is recycling: the rates of recycling in Sicily aren't even a tenth of some other parts of Europe. The problem as it applies to the beach, though, is really one of neglect. Outside the strictly defined sum-mer, Sicilians give beaches a wide berth. There's never a soul on them – certainly nobody who might remove rubbish. Coastal resorts in October look eerily abandoned, like those empty boats found in the Bermuda Triangle with dinner still on the table. Not for Sicilians, then, an autumn stroll along the ocean's edge, feeling a salty breeze heralding the shift of seasons.

Subsequently, it's nearly impossible to catch a bus to the beach outside summer. Services are generally suspended. For Gill and me to get to La Playa at any time outside of the hottest months, it's a long walk through some of the city's worst suburbs. ('Dispiriting' is how the ever-quotable Lawrence Durrell described Catania's suburbs – 'cavernous and dirty and overgrown'.) Once you're clear of those, you have to cross the airport expressway, then scramble through a fence, before passing an outlet pipe oozing espresso-coloured liquid into the dunes, and a concrete wall tagged with a huge swastika and the message '*COMMUNISTI BASTARDI!*'

One morning in late May we try to get to Noto Marina, one of Sicily's more popular beaches. We know there's a bus service from Catania, but it runs 'according to demand'. Already the island is beginning to swelter. It was a month ago that I nearly died of heatstroke walking to the Roman ruins at Morgantina. It hasn't rained for weeks and the fields are tinged with brown. The weather is literally *begging* people to swim in the ocean.

'No service to Noto Marina,' says the guy at the bus depot.

'Why not?' I ask.

'*Non è la stagione!*' It's not the season.

A few days later, though, it finally *is* the season. An announcement is made in *La Sicilia*: 'This year's official bathing season will run for exactly 102 days, from 5 June to 21 September – a seven-day increase on last year.'

Official bathing season? Seven-day increase? Gill and I are mystified. We catch an official-bathing-season bus down to La Playa to explore.

A metamorphosis has taken place. The once grubby beach has been combed by a grader and covered by rows of militantly aligned deckchairs for hire. Wooden boards form walkways in every direction – can't have people walking on *sand* after all. There's a whole town's worth of temporary cabins. The latter, we discover from a sign, can be rented out for the entire summer, for fifteen hundred euros and a pound of bureaucratic flesh. ('Six nominated people per cabin must provide a passport-sized photo and documents to be allowed ingress.')

Virtually deserted just a week ago, the beach now swarms. Africans wander the shoreline spruiking their carved wooden giraffes, charter boats bob up and down off the shoreline, couples play paddleball, volleyball and Frisbee, or have dancing lessons, or do water aerobics, or use toning machines, or stand under coin-operated showers, or buy postcards from stands, or dump their children at the 'Mini Club *per bambini*'. I see a baptism taking place: four men enter the water fully clad in white robes, three of them with their hands on the other's shoulders. Then someone mumbles a few words and they dunk the fourth fellow into the airporty brine. I'm so used to the notion of going to the beach for vast tracts of time to do absolutely nothing, all this activity comes as a shock.

Some sections of the beach are even sponsored: 'Lido Azzurro, Summer' reads one newly erected banner, with a long list of 'official partners' below. Extraordinary. The whole of La Playa, in fact, has been given a new epithet: Tourist Village on the Sand.

'Oh, I've heard about this,' says Gill, before recounting a discussion she had with a student earlier in the week.

Gill: 'What are your plans for the summer?'
Student: 'I'm working as a waiter at a tourist village.'

Gill: 'What's a tourist village?'

Student (laughing at Gill's ignorance): 'You know, a *tourist village*. Where everyone goes in the summer!'

Gill: 'No, I don't know. In Australia, we don't all go to one particular place in the summer; we go anywhere we want.'

Student: 'Well. In *Italy* we go to tourist villages.'

It's noteworthy to see Italians, responsible for so much unique expression in fashion, design and other walks of life, suddenly conforming so determinedly to the rules of summer by the sea.

But Gill and I are after something a little different.

'You must try the Black Beach,' say a few locals whose judgement we've come to trust.

The Black Beach (official name, San Giovanni Li Cuti) is an almost-hidden bay beside some busy roads in Catania's northeast corner. It tends to get discussed as though it's the city's best-kept secret.

When we see it, we realise why people would want to keep it a secret – in the same way they would a venereal disease or a fetish for tasting their own ear wax. It's *ugly*.

Consider the colour of the sand. A black beach is fine for somewhere frigid and atmospheric: Finland or Alaska, or the set of *The Piano*. In scorching, hectic Catania, though, it's like lying on bitumen. Sunbathers cram together on the patch of hot dark sand or on makeshift timber platforms that lead down from the road. Few people swim – it's too hard to negotiate the outcrops of volcanic rock on the shore, and the water is uninviting in any case. Perverts lean over the railing behind the beach to stare down at women in bikinis. (A friend of ours reports getting followed home two times after morning sessions on the Black Beach. Admittedly she's an attractive blonde who was sunbathing topless at the time.)

Topless blondes are sadly absent during our visit. Instead, when I lean over the railing to see who's on the beach, I cop an eyeful of a middle-aged Italian man wearing tight red Speedos, a matching midriff top, and – inexplicably – shiny black shoes and black socks.

This in the country that brought us Giorgio Armani.

With the city's beaches proving a disappointment, Gill and I look further afield for our sun-and-sand fix. The Giga school is into its end-of-term exam period now, giving Gill plenty of extra time for making the most of the Mediterranean. I scour the map for chunks of attractive coastline outside of Catania. South towards Syracuse is heavy industry, so we head north instead.

First, Letojanni. The day of our visit coincides with a local festival – one of Sicily's more mundane festivals: no jousting or ricotta-making, just a laboured procession of the town's guilds and religious bodies through the streets. Areas are cordoned off, and even walking the few hundred metres from railway station to ocean proves onerous.

Next, Giardini Naxos. The weather turns grim so we bail from the beach and walk through a wet but admittedly lovely lemon grove instead. There's the occasional chunk of ancient rock in the grass – no less than the remains of the first Greek colony in Sicily, dating to the eighth century BC. A nearby *trattoria* offers an English-language menu of considerable mystery: 'Beaf', 'Veal Salute in Butler', 'Massels and the Clamps'.

A third beach town: Santa Teresa di Riva. The pebbled shoreline here is pleasant enough, but I quickly get distracted and drag Gill on a one-hour hike up to the comatose village of Savoca, overlooking the coastline from a ridge of almond trees. Savoca sprang briefly into life in the early 1970s when Francis Ford Coppola used it as a location for *The Godfather*. You won't suddenly run into Marlon Brando (well, not *now* you won't), but if you want to sit in the seat where Michael Corleone sat while asking the local barman for his daughter's hand in marriage, you can. And that's exactly what I do when we arrive at Bar Vitelli, flushed and sweaty from the walk up the hill.

'I'll never wash this arse again!' I say, a little too loudly, when finally I get up from the famous chair.

After more trial and error, Gill and I find our perfect seaside retreat: the Archies. That's our name for Aci Trezza and Aci Castello, a pair of neighbouring coastal villages thirty minutes north of Catania.

Aci Trezza boasts a handful of sea stacks of black volcanic rock rising like sharks' fins two hundred metres from shore. These are the famous Faraglioni del Ciclope, the boulders that the Cyclops Polyphemus hurled at the escaping Odysseus after the hero blinded him in his cave.

From ancient mythology to modern realism: Aci Trezza's other claim to fame is its use as the setting for a masterpiece of Italian literature, Giovanni Verga's *The House by the Medlar Tree* (*I Malavoglia*, 1881). In this story, Verga – whose legacy we first discovered on our daytrip to Vizzini – tells of the relentless hardship faced by a family of fishermen; I can't help but think of our neighbours.

The main square – named Piazza G. Verga, of course – is renowned for its seafood restaurants. We have an expensive lunch there one day, for a treat. Waiters in waistcoats work in pairs to fillet a whole roasted fish on a tray beside our table, dispensing the flesh onto our plates using a pincer of spoons.

There's no place to swim in Aci Trezza – it's too rocky. For that we go to Aci Castello, a ten-minute walk away. It takes its name from a (reputedly haunted) castle perched on a low promontory bulging out into the sea. Below the castle, perfectly flat shelves of rock just made for sunbathing drop away to pristine water.

Trust our luck. No sooner do we locate this mellow patch of Mediterranean coastline than someone has to self-ishly ruin everything by carrying out a deadly massacre. Just two days after one of our swimming sessions at Aci Castello, a thirty-two-year-old local man marches into the town hall and guns down four people. His work in the hall done, he passes an elderly gentleman sitting on a park bench and shoots him in the head. Then he hijacks a car and forces the driver at gunpoint to take him to a nearby town, where he walks into a church and kills himself. According to reports, the man failed to secure full-time employment as a driver for Aci Castello's mayor and therefore became 'disgruntled'. The story grips Sicily for weeks and wipes the gloss from the thought of more mornings in the sun with a view of Polyphemus' boulders.

Still seeking the perfect beach, we do something drastic and leave Sicily altogether. For half a day.

Setting out early, we take a two-hour train from Catania to Messina in Sicily's northeast corner, then a half-hour passenger ferry across the strait to Villa San Giovanni in Calabria, the province that constitutes the toe of the Italian boot.

Messina is a famous city. Not necessarily in a good way. The misfortune this place has faced over the past two hundred and fifty years is barely believable. After its heyday in antiquity and then as a setting for scenes in several of Shakespeare's plays (*Much Ado about Nothing, Antony and Cleopatra*), Messina hit upon a horrid run of calamities. I don't want to trivialise the deaths of almost a quarter of a million people, but here are those calamities laid out in a handy table:

Year	Event	Outcome
1743	bubonic plague	48,000 deaths
1783	earthquake	50,000 deaths in the region
1848	war	Revolt against the Bourbon monarchs; Messina bombarded for three days (total deaths unknown)
1854	cholera	20,000 deaths
1908	earthquake	85,000 deaths; the deadliest quake in modern European history
1943	war	4500 deaths; the most heavily bombed Italian city in World War II

All of this happened to *one city*.

Our ferry from stricken Messina nudges against the pier at Villa San Giovanni and we jump down onto the ramp with Neil Armstrong-like gravitas. This is our first moment on non-Sicilian soil for almost a year.

Next, it's a twenty-minute local train to Scilla, a sleepy coastal town with a renowned beach. This place was a big deal in antiquity. Its modern name derives from one half of the dastardly duo of monsters, Scylla and Charybdis, described in vivid detail in Homer's *Odyssey*. Scylla – pronounced *SILL-ah*, same as my surname – was a 'savage, extreme, rude, cruel and invincible' dragon-like beast with three rows of teeth in each of her six heads. (Nothing like me, by the way, except occasionally when I wake up from an afternoon sleep.) Her partner in crime, Charybdis, was a lethal sucking whirlpool capable of turning ships into splinters. The two occupied either side of a narrow strait of ocean – traditionally associated with the waterway between Sicily and Calabria – rendering safe passage of the strait almost impossible. The hero Odysseus lost six crewmembers to the creatures.

There's little to report from our chunk of time in Scilla. No savage monsters appear. The closest we find is a fluffy puppy with a pink tummy, asleep on a pillow, beneath a menacing 'beware of the dog' sign: '*ATTENTI AL CANE! SI PREGA DI NON TOCCARLO!*'

Other than that, there's a charming beach (albeit one with more disturbing signs of 'tourist village' treatment), majestic views from a castle on the headland, and a bowl of toasted-almond *granita* so good it could cultivate a new religion.

The day is ruined only when we step back on Sicilian soil. There, we endure a succession of breakdowns on trains and buses, resulting in a five-hour trip to Catania – longer than we spent in Calabria itself. The small mercy is that we're alive: one year earlier, a train derailed near Messina and hit a bridge, killing eight people.

Still, it's not good enough for the portly man in the seat behind me on one of the legs of the arduous trip. He's clearly from the Italian mainland. 'Sicily!' he snaps to nobody in particular. 'It's the *fucking Third World*.'

For Gill and me, getting out of Sicily for the day ends up being a dry run for the real thing. We've decided to leave and go back to Australia; not because Sicily is the *fucking Third World*; not because people are getting murdered in nearby beach resorts; and not because the espressos give me heart palpitations. The equation is simple: we don't have a dime, and I need a job.

A job doing *what*, though? I came to Sicily expecting the island's rich Greek and Roman heritage to reinvigorate my flagging interest in ancient history. Clearly it hasn't. Take our last full day in Catania, for example. As Gill and I sit among open suitcases and half-packed piles of clothes in our apartment, I suddenly say, 'Do you know, I've never even visited the amphitheatre in Piazza Stesicoro?'

Here you have Catania's most prominent Roman ruin – indeed, one of the largest amphitheatres in antiquity, its leftovers sprawled in a sunken hole in the middle of the city's main roundabout – and I haven't once thought to buy a ticket and check it out.

'Off you go then,' says Gill.

I sprint down to the *centro*. It takes me fifteen minutes to whip around the site. I'm back in front of my suitcase in under an hour.

'How was it?'

'*Boh.*'

Once the decision to leave Sicily is made, it's a weight off our shoulders. Suddenly everything seems fun. We feel transient again, like proper tourists. We embrace the summer. And we hit the town.

Our nights usually start with a drink at the Agorà Hostel. It's a dingy backpacker joint (as I said, we don't have a dime), but one with some atmosphere. It's around the corner from the Pescheria, for one thing, and next to the remains of a Roman bath. And Catania's mysterious underground river, the Amenano, cuts directly through the basement of the hostel. A grotto-cum-wine-bar operates there, right next to a channel of flowing water.

Next port of call is a nightspot, Nievski, with its Cuban revolutionary theme and hordes of indie-looking locals milling about on the wide staircase outside.

Then it's on to live-music venue Lo Zo, down past the train station, or Scenario Pubblico, where DJs spin lounge tracks over video installations, or L'Insonnia, where our friend Massi plays guitar in his band Drift'n Blues ('BLUES FOR YOOOUUU!').

It's not all clubs and bars. In our final week, Gill and I watch a classical quartet in candlelit Chiesa di Santa Maria dell'Aiuto, an exquisite church ribbed by pink-marble columns. The church is in our part of town – the dodgy part – and it's fun to notice a few concertgoers, presumably from Catania's more affluent north, glancing askance at the surrounding neighbourhood: a snarling dog on a leash out the front of a mechanic's garage, overflowing garbage bins down a dark back alley, and impossibly thin men lurking beside a grubby Baroque fountain.

We also make a point of finally crossing off some left-over items on our Catania 'to do' list. There's our visit to the birthplace-turned-museum of composer Vincenzo Bellini (1801–35), the city's favourite son. It's charming. The tiny flat is cluttered with old pianos and harpsichords with yellowing keys, photos of Catania from the nineteenth century, vintage opera posters, Bellini's letters, and even his ashes. French windows are flung open to the street and the space swells with morning sun and arias from *Norma*.

We eat lunch at La Paglia, one of a handful of atmospheric restaurants in the heart of the Pescheria. After the waiter takes our order, instead of walking into the kitchen, he strides out into the bustling market to buy the fresh ingredients required. Who cares about the bare brown walls of the dining room, or the dowdy tablecloth? My *zuppa di pesce* is an oversized bowl of zingy tomato broth clumped high with calamari, clams, prawns and bream, straight out of the chafed hands of a fisherman. Extraordinary.

In a flash, our final night is upon us. We organise a party in the courtyard of our *palazzo*. Gill's colleagues from her school come along, plus our Italian friends and, of course, our next-door neighbours. Desi's fiancé Gaetano offers his DJing skills for the night. There's something about his penchant for wearing denim that has me expecting Italian soft rock. Instead, he surprises everyone – especially the spinsterish occupants of the upstairs apartments – by playing mostly hardcore gangster rap. It's very loud, too. At one point, as Eminem screams about drugs, bitches and chainsaws, a plate-sized piece of stucco breaks away from the wall and clatters onto the courtyard.

Surprisingly, the police don't come. They're probably too busy on nearby Via Plebiscito.

Gaetano at last segues into more family-friendly music, and the party takes a new direction. Desi and her brother Davide clear a space in the courtyard and start busting their Latin dance moves. There has been plenty of *acqua* under the *ponte* since they were teenagers winning prestigious dance competitions held in Rome, but Desi and Davide burn up the black cobbled courtyard with salsa and samba and more.

Following their lead, we all pile onto the dance floor, champagnes in hand, to show off our signature styles. Mine is the *tarantella*, a southern Italian specialty which is said to mimic the confusion of a person bitten by a tarantula.

Around midnight, when most people have left and Gaetano is drawing on his stocks of mellow ballads, we have a final chat with Angela. Erminia is fast asleep on her lap, having danced her seven-year-old feet to a standstill.

'She'll miss you,' says Angela, glancing down at Erminia.

I feel that Angela is leaving something unsaid: namely, that she herself will miss Gill. The two have bonded over work, weather, washing, not to mention the inexplicable antics and annoyances of their husbands. When we assure Angela that we'll be back sometime down the track to catch up with everyone again, she glances over at Carmelo – who has a cigarette in hand as usual – and rolls her eyes as if to say, 'You'll be lucky to see *him* again.' Angela is concerned about how hard her husband works – and how hard he smokes. It's a genuine fear for his mortality. She deals with it by employing typical Sicilian stoicism and humour.

Although Carmelo and Angela are not the type for overt displays of affection, they have their moments. Once during siesta, when everyone in the neighbourhood was asleep, I opened our door a fraction to let a breeze through, and out in the courtyard I could see Angela and Carmelo in two chairs. He was leaning back in her arms, while she cradled his head and cut his hair, gently snipping at his few thin and greying locks. This wasn't a functional cut, but a slow, tender, we-haven't-done-this-for-a-long-time cut.

When I told Gill about this later, she got misty-eyed and started blabbing about some hair-washing scene between Meryl Streep and Robert Redford in *Out of Africa*, which she was appalled to learn I couldn't recall and, in fact, hadn't even seen.

We have a seven am flight from Catania to Rome the next morning. The party doesn't wind up until three am, yet at five thirty Gaetano is knocking dutifully on our door to pick us up and drive us to the airport.

I'm a wreck. I've slept for forty-five minutes. I think I'm still drunk. And I'm definitely still packing, having left everything to the last minute as usual. There's a mad scramble and then we're away, without even the chance to stand on the stoop of the door and bid the apartment *arrivederci*.

In my haste, I forget to leave the door keys in the letterbox as requested by Signor Pull-the-Rent-in. Instead, they stay in my jeans pocket all the way from Catania to Rome to Kuala Lumpur to Brisbane. I guess it means if we ever want to go back there, we've got an open door.

But would we *want* to go back? Yes, in a heartbeat. Why? Because there's so much we'll miss.

The food, for one thing: *la cucina Siciliana*. I knew I was going to eat well in Sicily when I saw a plate of pasta on the street that someone had cooked for a family of stray cats and I wished I had the recipe.

My standout dish? There are many contenders but the title goes to the *casarecce al nero di seppia* (homemade pasta with squid ink) that I ordered at a modest *trattoria* run by the Catanese mother-in-law of our Irish friend Patrick. This is not a pretty dish, believe me. You'd be forgiven for thinking the chef had dredged the meal from the kitchen's exhaust hood – it's a sticky black mess in the middle of a plate – but the flavours and textures are sublime. There's something about this meal that encapsulates Sicily for me: it's simultaneously weird and wonderful, messy and minimal, brutish and beautiful.

This schizophrenia applies to Catania itself. I'll never forget one late afternoon in the middle of winter when Gill and I found ourselves sheltering from the wind and shivering beneath the awning of a typical black-stone *palazzo*, stamping our feet on a path strewn with ash to stay warm, and wondering if there was a worse place in the world. Suddenly, off to the west, the sun appeared below a bank of storm clouds on its trajectory towards the horizon. Low, intense rays washed the side of a nearby church in vivid honey and peach and illuminated the building's tiled *cupola* against a swell of dark dusk in the eastern sky. A photographer's dream.

It must have been a moment like this that inspired Sicilian poet Renzino Barbera to reinterpret the Bible's creation myth:

. . . On the sixth day,
God accomplished His work
And, pleased with all the beauty
He had created,
He took the Earth in His hands,
And kissed it.
There, where He put His lips,
That's Sicily.

Not everything we did and saw in Sicily felt kissed by God's lips. There were low moments. A few of these I've mentioned; others will stay in the pages of my diary. By and large, though, they never amounted to more than some scrapes and bruises, a bit of sleep deprivation, and the occasional theft. It wasn't upheaval or tragedy (plenty of people go overseas and get shot dead, after all) so much as inconvenience.

Indeed, sometimes we felt like the personal playthings of the God of Trivial Inconveniences: the water heater in the bathroom went on the blink; Gill burnt her hand on our corroded excuse for a stove; I got drenched in a flash storm while buying a newspaper to look for rental apartments and the paper turned to mush; I dropped a one-euro coin at the Pescheria and it rolled under a butcher's counter into a drain full of pig's blood; I attempted my first risotto for dinner only for a thirty-minute blackout to strike at the critical moment. At the end of each day, though, we were still sitting together at a table, sharing thoughts and experiences, and sipping wine. It was all good. (Except when we discovered that our plastic bottle from the *enoteca* was empty; then we really *did* have upheaval and tragedy on our hands.)

More difficult, perhaps, than the occasional mishap and hassle, was the task of forging relationships with the local people, or of being accepted in general. It's a stereotype that Sicilians are a closed book, and I'd hate to perpetuate the notion. Yet to describe the average Catanese as approachable would be difficult.

Take Pippo, for instance. Pippo ran a roast chicken business a few doors down from our apartment. He timeshared a shop with Turi, our neighbourhood pizza guy – the one who got covered head to toe in foam during Carnevale. Pippo sold chickens during the day; Turi used the same wood-fired oven to make pizzas at night.

Pippo's dealings with me bring to mind the famous Mafia code, *omertà* – which in a specific sense amounts to a refusal to cooperate with authorities on any matter, but more generally can refer to a code of silence. I bought my first bird from Pippo in November. I subsequently bought a chicken a week from the man. And his first spoken word to me was at 12.40 pm on Pasquetta (Easter Monday). The word was '*Ciao*', grumbled in my direction as I left with my lunch.

So, five full months after we moved into an apartment fifty metres away from his shop and became regular customers of his plump chooks (the best I've ever tasted, by the way: roasted to a caramel-brown on a rotisserie and stuffed with herbs, olives, onions and sausage), Pippo deigned to talk to me.

Granted, it's an extreme case, but in the tale of Pippo is the kernel of a day-to-day reality.

Gill had her own problematic encounters with locals. Some of her dealings with Sicilian men, truth be told, weren't very pleasant. For all the sweet and gracious fellows we met – epitomised by Carmelo, who would often insist on accompanying Gill to the greengrocer to ensure that the vendor selected only the best produce for her and sold it at the best price – there were a dozen who whistled, honked, propositioned and ogled. The cheeky teenagers who approached her during the evening *passeggiata* to flirt (usually by asking to borrow a cigarette lighter: '*Hai un accendino?*') were, of course, harmless. Others were less palatable. An eighty-year-old man drove by in a rusted Beetle, wound down his window, and flapped his tongue at her. A younger passerby hissed aggressively in her direction. And one day she turned the corner into a backstreet to find a fellow facing a wall, pants pulled down around his thighs, determinedly having one off the wrist. On seeing Gill, he simply tugged harder.

All of this generally happened when she was alone. Only on one occasion did I witness any lechery first-hand. We were on a train, and Gill was being eyeballed by a middle-aged man on the seat opposite us. He was all tracksuit and jewellery and cologne. Our train plunged into a pitch-black tunnel, and when we popped out the other end into day-light, I almost expected to find Gill's blouse open and hair tousled, a stunned look on her face, while the fellow lit a post-coital cigarillo.

He was lucky he didn't try. Not because of what *I* might have done, but because of what *Gill* might have done. When it comes to dealing with sleazy men, Gill tends to get – how to put it? – *combative*. Already I could see her scanning the carriage for some means by which, should the man choose to rest a hand on her knee, she might sever the offending body part from its limb. That's if she was merciful enough to settle for removing his *hand*.

I was almost tempted to warn the fellow that if he wanted to keep his genitals intact, he'd be well advised to look out the window instead of at my wife's breasts.

Castration isn't a bad analogy on which to end. At the very least, it brings things full circle from Gill and me and our lives in modern-day Sicily back to the island's mythical beginnings.

When the Olympian gods roamed this part of the world, Uranus was married to Gaia. It was an unhappy alliance. The latter forged an immense sickle with a blade made from flint, and asked her sons to castrate their father. Cronus, the youngest, agreed to the deed. He ambushed Uranus, sliced off his genitals and cast them into the sea. (This is why I've always wanted daughters rather than sons.)

From the spilt blood, life was forged, and from the testicles came the goddess Aphrodite. The bloodied sickle, meanwhile, was buried near Messina, formerly called Zancle – 'sickle' in Greek. Or perhaps it was tossed into the sea near Trapani, formerly called Drepanum – 'sickle' in Latin. So many sickles! It may even be that the word 'Sicily' itself has some etymological connection with 'sickle', though that's disputed.

As I ponder the castration myth, I can't help but devise an appropriate new slogan for the island: *SICILY. YOU'LL NEVER COME AGAIN!*

It's a bit unfair. As I've already established, the place can be majestic on a good day. And the funny thing is, now that Gill and I have left, whenever we reflect on the time we spent in Sicily, *all* the days seem like good ones.

'But you still owe me a *proper* honeymoon,' Gill will add, adept as my gorgeous new wife is at getting the final word.